Lives in Context

We are mindful of the paths we have taken to get to this place in our lives. To those who have helped us find this place we dedicate this book.

•

Many new and emerging researchers (past graduate students and others) have contributed to our thinking about researching lives in context. Many participants in our studies also have extended our understandings of what it means to be a life history researcher. To those scholars and participants we also dedicate this book. This text, after all, also represents elements of our lives in context.

Lives in Context

The Art of Life History Research

Ardra L. Cole
J. Gary Knowles

ALTAMIRA
PRESS

A Division of
ROWMAN & LITTLEFIELD PUBLISHERS, INC.
Lanham • New York • Toronto • Oxford

ALTAMIRA PRESS
A division of Rowman & Littlefield Publishers, Inc.
4501 Forbes Boulevard, Suite 200
Lanham, MD 20706

PO Box 317
Oxford
OX2 9RU, UK

British Library Cataloguing-in-Publication Information Available

Library of Congress Cataloging-in-Publication Data

Cole, Ardra L.
   Lives in context : the art of life history research / Ardra L. Cole [and] J. Gary Knowles
      p. cm.
   Includes bibliographical references and index.
   ISBN 0-7591-0143-4 (alk. paper)—ISBN 0-7591-0144-2 (pbk. : alk. paper)
      1. Sociology—Biographical methods. 2. Biography—Research—Methodology. 3.
Interviewing. I. Knowles, J. Gary, 1947–

HM511 .C657 2001
301'01—dc21
                                                          2001016066
Printed in the United States of America

♾™ The paper used in this publication meets the minimum requirements of American
National Standard for Information Sciences—Permanence of Paper for Printed Library
Materials, ANSI/NISO Z39.48–1992.

Contents

✛
Preface

Introductions are crucial steps in life history research. They are the beginning points that often make or break the power of a researching relationship to bring forth illuminating understandings of the life and phenomenon being explored. When two or more lives come together in readiness for research conversations, the onus of responsibility for developing the relationship rests on the researcher or researchers. More often than not, "the researched"—the person who has agreed to be the focus of a life history exploration—comes to the first moment of involvement with particular expectations and is mindful of or curious about the purpose of the spotlight's focus. He or she is anxious to know of the extent, direction, and tone of the inquiry work, anxious to know what is expected. To know the direction of conversations, or interviews as some might call them, is to relax a little and not be caught unaware. After all, it is his or her life that is about to be scrutinized.

We want to make known the way we plan to proceed, the way in which the book unfolds. The tone of our writing and the heart of our epistemological orientation will become clear as you read, as will the structure and form. Understanding the basic structure at this point, though, may be helpful.

The book is in two parts, each representing a different kind of text. The two parts can stand alone almost as separate "texts," although our intention is that they be read as complements to one another. Part 1 contains our words and ideas supplemented by voices of other scholars.

We present, discuss, and illustrate a perspective on life history research that is based on principles of reflexivity, relationality, and artistry. Here we make known theoretical elements of our orientation, the basis of our practice. Throughout we point readers to connections with elements of chapters in part 2.

Part 2 contains chapters by a variety of life history researchers. Our intention is to present perspectives and ideas about life history research that have application in a wide variety of inquiry contexts and academic disciplines. To aid us in this we solicited the help of others who have recently done life history work. Intentionally, most of these researchers are relatively new to life history work. Their accounts of researching, with attention placed mostly on issues of process, make up the second part of the book. They are stories of researching that illuminate the theoretical, practical, professional, and personal qualities of doing sound life history research. They are intended to provide points of resonance for a wide variety of readers. Our goal is to provide a number of views into the process of life history inquiry so that newcomers and more experienced researchers alike may gain from reading about issues and processes that were crucial to the work of these various researchers. Read together, our texts are intended to be reciprocal and responsive, collaborative and complementary, focusing on the central elements and purposes of life history work.

Researching lives is always a delicate affair, often highly intrusive. Life history researchers step into lives only to retreat after a time; yet, those examined lives live on both within and without the researcher's experience. The business of doing life history work is complex and consuming, exhilarating and elusive, demanding and defining, even tiring and tedious, but with understanding the lives of others comes the possibility of understanding oneself and one's location in the world.

To illustrate some of the complexities of life history research and to provide an overview of the kinds of issues and processes we will illustrate and discuss, we begin the book with an excerpt from an unpublished, book-length manuscript written by Gary. It is from a larger account of the experiences of a professor, Thomas, within the academy. The excerpt has been edited for this purpose and does not contain all of the nuances of form that appear in the original; nevertheless, it sets a tone for this book on researching lives in context.

ACKNOWLEDGMENTS

Over the past sixteen or so years, we have had the privilege of working with many research participants who have taught us much. Our intentions have always been to work with them in ways that honor the spirit, tone, and tenor of their lives. This is never an easy task. The challenge has been for us to be creative while remaining true to who we are as persons within communities and families *and* as members of the academy.

There are several groups of people who have made this book possible: the contributors to this volume, graduate students and experienced researchers, and research participants.

We acknowledge the substantial contribution made to the book by the researcher contributors. Their accounts of researching, and reflections on it, serve only to illuminate the process of working sensitively and fully with others. Their work both expands and mirrors elements of our own and we are mindful about how they have taught us. We are humbled by their efforts: Jacquie Aston, Lori Ebbesen, Kathleen Gates, Ilze Arielle Matiss, Maura McIntyre, James A. Muchmore, Jeff Orr, Avi Rose, Elizabeth Oates Schuster, Suzanne Thomas, and Renee Sarchuk Will.

The graduate students whom we have taught have left indelible fingerprints on our teaching of qualitative and reflexive inquiry courses (of various stripes and colors conducted in different institutions)—they have both responded to and challenged us in our teaching, and our individual and collective pedagogy have been well served. They, along with the many doctoral dissertation and thesis researchers we have worked with since the late 1980s, have helped shape our perspectives on researching lives in context. Having to guide new researchers brings both intellectual and procedural challenges to the fore and serves to heighten one's awareness of the value of seeking to walk the talk and practice what we preach. We are thankful, also, for the contributing work of Hugo Bastidas, who labored diligently to help forge perfect citations and an accurate reference list. He also helped out with library searches and critiqued early versions of the manuscript. A special thanks is in order for members of Ardra's 1999–2000 Qualitative Research in Education course who, by merely using and discussing early versions of the first chapters, provided helpful critique. Rose Barg and Renee Sarchuk Will provided useful comments on early drafts of several chapters. Mary Sharpe and Dave Stewart took their sharpened pencils and editorial eyes to the manuscript draft. Dave Stewart's assistance with developing the index is much appreciated (a life history researcher himself, his questions about process and form are made clear in the index's emphasis).

Without research participants nothing that is documented or represented in this book would have been possible. We remember the first participants with whom we worked, individuals who were willing to give us a chance—budding researchers that we were back then. Gary stumbled upon the life history method amid a sea of positivism and had no opportunities for being mentored into the means and the methods of the approach. Ardra was fortunate to have been introduced to life history research by Ivor Goodson, a colleague and renowned scholar in the area. Separately at first, and then together, we learned about life history researching mainly through engagement with research participants. The main thing that helped us learn and develop confidence in those first explorations of lives was the energy that we put into forming relationships with those very first research participants. They taught us the importance of being ourselves, of remaining true to that for which we stood, and of not creating researcher-researched hierarchies. In the interim, and in this book, we have honed our research skills and have articulated, so as for readers to see, exactly what it is we stand for. Financial support and recognition from funding agencies has made much of our life history research possible. We acknowledge the generous support of the Social Sciences and Humanities Research Council of Canada for its support of Ardra's life history research in teacher education.

We also thank those reviewers of the manuscript, invited by the publisher, who offered useful suggestions for strengthening the book. We are indebted to Mitch Allen, publisher at AltaMira Press, for his encouragement in recent years to develop the book and his patience with our good intentions to meet deadlines.

Beginnings

Researching
the Professor: Thomas

J. Gary Knowles

A s is the case with many pivotal life experiences I came to an exploration of Thomas's life by accident. At the time of our first meeting I
was enjoying a well-earned reprieve from teaching and other university
work on the very same island on which Thomas eventually was to live for
three years. I had rented an artist's studio in an attempt to stimulate the
flow of my creativity. The remoteness of the island and the studio, and its
relative isolation from services and cultural "distractions," were ideal for
my two-month-long summer respite. I eventually completed some of what
I thought then was my most creative writing and left feeling restored. The
context also seemed to aid Thomas on his own road to restoration.

I met Thomas on the government ferry on his first trip to the island,
just a couple of weeks before I was due to leave. As usual, we "come-
from-aways" stood out from the locals. Thrust together by circumstance we struck up a conversation and, gradually over the course of
his ten-day stay, some elements of his life story emerged.

That we were both situated in the academy helped to set the context for
his story's gradual unfolding. His life had been torn apart by colleagues' decisions and actions. Many elements in those first conversations rang true for
my own experiences. These similarities simultaneously overwhelmed and
energized me. From these first conversations, which took place in the studio,

---

This passage is drawn from an unpublished manuscript that represents a life history study
of Thomas, an environmental studies professor. It is edited for the purposes of this book.
Here, the process of the work is the focus.

while we were hiking the island, on the ferry, or on the front deck of the small bed and breakfast establishment at which Thomas stayed (well out of earshot of his chatty host), we decided to collaborate in a process of life history inquiry. Each of us saw the possibilities as mutually beneficial. For each of us, agreement to the process was very intuitive. We had little idea where it would take us. As for me, I already had some personal insight into the kind of experiences Thomas had initially described. I had been burned by a similar academic decision and felt that I could listen attentively, respond appropriately, record faithfully, analyze insightfully, and represent, meaningfully and respectfully, elements of his life as uncovered through a life history research process. His story, interwoven with elements of my own, budded, blossomed, and flourished within the context of our relationship.

At the time he was still smarting from the power that the particular academic institution had wielded over his professorial and personal life, and was in the midst of planning his future. Years earlier I had a forced leave from the university. With that experience and a two-month respite behind me, it was an opportune moment for both of us. He was at a crossroads. I had the time.

Over the course of our intentional life history conversations, we told many stories, all in the spirit of collaborative inquiry. So it is that, in some strange way, the revelation of Thomas's life is a representation of my own as well. But such a self-revelation is very subtle indeed. Like any good qualitative researcher, I acknowledge that the lenses of analysis and representation are almost exclusively mine. To be sure, Thomas assisted in the processes of inquiry beyond our conversations, but only as one who verified or challenged the veracity of my points of description, categorization, analysis, or textual representation. This was one element of our collaboration. In the end, he sanctioned my views; even so, I must take full responsibility since the story is not a mutually constructed text. I am the sole author of the written account; he is the sole author of the life stories as told. My account of his life cannot do justice to the complexities of his life as lived. Written text about a life is limited by the peculiar intersection of readers' and the author's perspectives (perhaps their individual and collective lives) and the possibilities of coconstructed meanings about the life lived. As a mode of representation it offers insight for those who are adroit with the subtleties and nuances of language.

The stories told by Thomas revealed epiphanic events—critical incidents, turning points, or milestones—within his life that brought to him profound realizations about the meaning of experiences he had had and possible courses of subsequent actions. These are the elements of his life that aided me in developing a structure to tell his story. They are the warp of the long, woven blanket. My goal was to uncover Thomas's particular stories of experience within the academy and the meanings attributed to that experience. His life history as told and analyzed is but a series of multiframed glimpses into some of the key experiences of his life as it was, and remains, connected to the academy and to his professional self.

My account of Thomas is about a life in context, a life situated within the complexities of family and community, institution, and the professoriat at large. It is about a life profoundly influenced by social, economic, historical, religious, and educational circumstances. It is about a life shaped by influences of family and cultures; by existence within communities and within natural and cultural landscapes; by personal beliefs and independent actions. It is about a life guided by gentle and not-so-gentle resistance to the status quo. It is about a life of decisions and their consequences. My theories about the relationship of his life to broader circumstances are expressed throughout. All of these qualities make it a life history account.

The story I've told in the completed manuscript is about the paths a life has taken amid sets of competing personal and professional agenda. It is about a life beset with a need to cope with professional adversity. It is about a life dreamed, a life hoped for. It is about a life alternately enriched and depleted by the gains and losses of personal and professional interactions and investments. It is about the personal as it influences the professional.

To tell his story I sought to connect with and understand the complexities of Thomas's life. I collected a range of information from Thomas in a variety of forms. Like the traditional field-based ethnographer, I sought "data" from three main sources: interviews (or, given the manner of their occurrence, tone, pace, and temporal nature, "conversations"); observations of elements of Thomas's life; and artifactual evidence, primarily biographical information, personal and professional documentary texts (letters and journals, curricular, programmatic, and scholarly materials, and copies of institutional correspondence and tenure and promotion case materials, for instance), and family and institutional photographs. I also drew heavily on my own knowledge of the academy as a context of professorial life.

Our conversations, initially spontaneous and energetic, were directed by common interests and points of experiential resonance. From and during these early inquiries I took no field notes. Rather, I wrote reflexively about our experiences in conversation. I wrote of my intellectual and emotional responses to Thomas and his stories. I recorded later conversations. These were then transcribed and given to Thomas for review purposes. On most occasions he returned the transcriptions with corrections of various kinds—usually additional statements of clarification and minor revisions of grammar and punctuation. We had agreed to edit his spoken text for the purposes of print media so that it was consistent in grammar, tense, and flow. For example, he did not want staccato and repetitive patterns of speech to appear in the text, even though he knew they would add a degree of authenticity. He was used to articulating his thoughts in text in a coherent fashion. This was his choice and one of the few conditions of his collaboration with me.

We both used the transcripts to help set the direction and tone of subsequent conversations. Often they were the starting points for our subsequent discussions as I sought clarification of questions that arose from earlier initial analyses. At every point I urged him to contextualize his experience in terms of the historical, political, religious, educational, social, and economic influences of the time and place. I wanted him to reflect on what had happened around him at the time of his earlier experiences. In addition, I accessed various reference texts, such as historical and contemporary debates about tenure and the conditions of the professoriat, to help me understand the institutional, contextual influences.

My observations of Thomas in various contexts were limited, restricted to the time frames of my visits to the island and, later, to his new Canadian institution. After our initial meeting I returned to the island nine times to work with him. Each time I spent several days. I made the first visit in the fall of 1995 and subsequent ones at opportune times until he left the small island community. My last face-to-face conversation with him for the purposes of this project was immediately before the winter break of the 1998–1999 university year. Subsequently, we communicated by electronic and surface mail. We remain good friends.

One of my major dilemmas was how to craft a representation of his life, given that the collaborative analyses of the various research texts (interview transcripts, personal and institutional documents of various sorts, professional and personal photographs, and so on) and their transformation into important life themes and critical incidents came fairly easily. I eventually elected to follow a chronology of sorts although I have used particular pivotal stories of experience as metaphors to illustrate aspects of the more recent, major events and circumstances of his life. There are many other possible textual arrangements and structures that I could have used to convey the essentials of Thomas's life history. Within the account of his life most of the lines are mine but we both agree that the story itself is his and his alone. My own story, one containing some similar elements, is not told but, nevertheless, in the crafting of his story I acknowledge the power, beauty, and potential of two professional lives intersecting by chance. I have made meaning of his experience through the lenses of my own life experiences and perspectives.

Given the richness and emotion of his stories, I wanted to honor them by capturing close details of their elements. At first Thomas was hesitant about the wisdom of doing this but, in the end, he agreed that, by not portraying his intense emotions, significant elements of his experience would be lost. I also have told of his romantic, lovely vision of life with another. Initially, this part of his story was also a point of insecurity for Thomas. Together, we disguised elements of his story and made changes that increased his level of comfort. It was essential that he feel safe with the story told.

Thomas Albert is not his real name. He chose to use a pseudonym. We both worked diligently to conceal our collaboration within the academic context in which he is now situated and I have changed many of the circumstances and locations of his life and work so as to protect his identity. Elements of his story are fictionalized but remain faithful to his experience as a whole. As researchers concerned with creating and maintaining high standards of ethical practice within researching processes, we are both satisfied with the means we have used to conceal his identity and the identity of others. Despite these changes we both agree that the essential elements of the story convey the heart of the meanings that he has attributed to experience. This is his life history, after all.

1

EXPLORING METHOD

1

What Is
Life History Research?

- *Broad purposes*
- *Philosophical/theoretical roots in various disciplines*
- *Clarification of terms*
- *The role of context*

Ask a roomful of life history researchers what life history research is about and you are likely to get a roomful of diverse responses, all loosely connected to a central epistemological construct illuminating the intersection of human experience and social context. Our intention in this book is not to debate the various interpretations or to advocate a particular kind of life history research. Rather, we want to explore, in a more general way, what a life history orientation to research might mean, and how such an orientation might play out in researching practice within the human sciences (the social sciences or, as we prefer to call these diverse explorations into the human condition, studies of human lives). We are concerned with and about the *process* of researching and the centrality of relationships to the researching endeavor. We are especially interested in the relationship

- of researcher to the topic or focus of study;
- of researcher to research participants;
- of researcher to the research representation;
- of reader to the research representation;

- of research topic or focus to pertinent literature; and
- of participants' lives to the contexts within which they are situated.

For us, the term "life history" acknowledges not only that personal, social, temporal, and contextual influences facilitate understanding of lives and phenomena being explored, but also that, from conceptualization through to representation and eventual communication of new understandings to others, any research project is an expression of elements of a researcher's life history. In saying this we forthrightly challenge any claims of researcher "objectivity" in the study of human lives. As in other forms of qualitative research, the life history researcher serves as the central "instrument," the prime viewing lens. Put another way, the researcher is a person and that person—along with her or his own complex personal history—is a guiding influence in all aspects of a study. Put simply, in social science research, people are studying other people, and all research is in some way autobiographical. After all, it is an endeavor where the perspectives of two or more individuals converge and intersect. As sociologist Schwalbe (1995, 331) surmises, "It could be that all my studies of other people are partly a roundabout way to know myself better." The autobiographical and the relational, then, are two qualities central to our life history research orientation.

Another central construct that distinguishes our particular approach to life history is the explicit attention to the aesthetic, both throughout the process of researching and in the form of representation. In recent years social sciences research, and particularly educational research, has given rise to a new genre of investigation commonly referred to as arts-based or, as we prefer to call it, arts-informed research. This kind of inquiry is a challenge to the rigid, linear, and formulaic qualities of conventional scientific inquiry—"the scientific method"—as it is applied in the social sciences. Arts-informed research brings together the systematic and rigorous qualities of scientific inquiry with the artistic and imaginative qualities of the arts. In so doing the process of researching becomes creative and responsive and the representational form for communication embodies elements of various art forms—poetry, fiction, drama, two- and three-dimensional visual art, including photography, film and video, dance, music, and multimedia installation. Our approach to life history research, then, is arts-informed. Such inquiry processes are organic and fluid and the representation of the work reflects qualities of multidimensional lives through multiple media forms.

Life history inquiry is not, centrally, about developing reductionist notions of lived experience in order to convey a particular meaning or "truth" (be it truth or Truth). Rather, it is a representation of human experience that draws in viewers or readers to the interpretive process and invites them to make meaning and form judgments based on their own reading of the "text" as it is viewed through the lenses of their own realities. When a photographer who seeks to portray the human condition by taking uncontrived portraits of human life, makes a public presentation of her work she presents both an interpretation that is guided by her own theoretical constructs and positioning, and invites viewers to also engage in an act of interpretation informed by their own theoretical positions and experience-based understandings. The potential that life history research has for understanding lives, be they individual or collective, rests not only in the intentions of individual researchers but also on the fundamental purposes and processes of life history inquiry methods, and on the audience or readers as interpreters of the life history text.

BROAD PURPOSES

In as much as it is humanly possible, life history inquiry is about gaining insights into the broader human condition by coming to know and understand the experiences of other humans. It is about understanding a situation, profession, condition, or institution through coming to know how individuals walk, talk, live, and work within that particular context. It is about understanding the relationship, the complex interaction, between life and context, self and place. It is about comprehending the complexities of a person's day-to-day decision making and the ultimate consequences that play out in that life so that insights into the broader, collective experience may be achieved. Always, lives are understood within their respective and collective contexts and it is this understanding that is theorized. Clusters of individual lives make up communities, societies, and cultures. To understand some of the complexities, complications, and confusions within the life of just one member of a community is to gain insights into the collective. In saying this we are not invoking an essentialist claim that to understand (however partially) *one* is to understand *all*. Rather, we are suggesting that every in-depth exploration of an individual life-in-context brings us that much closer to understanding the complexities of lives in communities.

PHILOSOPHICAL/THEORETICAL ROOTS
IN VARIOUS DISCIPLINES

Researchers' definitions of life history research are influenced by their epistemological orientations and by their professional or scholarly autobiographies, that is, the school, discipline, or profession within which they are situated. For example, a life history study by a psychologist looks quite different from one conducted by a sociologist or anthropologist.

Regardless of discipline, researchers who pioneered life history research in their respective fields each recognized the individual as a window into broader social and societal conditions. The conditions with which the researchers were concerned and that defined the purposes of inquiry varied with each discipline. For example, in psychology, pioneers of the life history method such as Allport (1942), Kluckhohn, Murray, and Schneider (1955), Murray (1938), and White (1952, 1963) saw individuals and their stories as windows into their psychological conditions and personality development. Taken together with other psychological data, individuals informed the "construction" of their own case histories. In clinical psychology, of course, Freud's (1909, 1911) accounts of his cases have become classic life history texts. Dollard (1935) is noted for his work that casts life history as a way to understand cultural and social phenomena rather than understand only individual lives and personalities. Sociologists, particularly those from the Chicago School who hold a social constructionist orientation (Bertaux 1981; Denzin 1989a, 1989b; Plummer 1983; Shaw 1930)—later known as symbolic interactionism (Blumer 1969)—viewed individuals and their stories as living illustrations of social conditions. Sociologist Clifford Shaw (1930) solicited individuals' life stories and supplemented that data with demographic and other sociologically relevant information to create case or life histories. The celebrated studies of Polish peasant lives by Thomas and Znaniecki (1920) evidence a historical turning point for both the disciplines of sociology and anthropology and the profession of field-based social science researching. The life history account of Polish peasants represented an intricate interweaving of personal lives and sociological theorizing that the authors claimed could rival any scientifically derived generalization. Anthropologists such as Langness (1965) and Watson and Watson-Franke (1985) treated individuals as informants of their culture. Their collection of individual life stories through oral accounts, when taken together as a database, became a life history. Perhaps the largest number of classic life history works came out of the field of anthropology (see Langness and Frank 1981, for a historical overview).

More recently, life history research has found its way into other disciplines, such as:

- Aging and gerontology (Achenbaum 1999; Lewis 1998; Myerhoff 1982; Ray 1998; Steir 1978; Wrye and Churilla 1979);
- Education (Ball and Goodson 1985; Casey 1993; Cole 1991; Cole and Knowles 1995; Goodson 1981, 1988, 1991, 1992; Goodson and Cole

1994; Knowles 1992, 1993; Measor and Sikes 1992; Middleton 1992, 1993, 1998; Smith et al. 1988; Woods 1987)
- Family studies (Detzner 1992; SmithBattle and Leonard 1998)
- Health sciences and health promotion (Burke and Kern 1996; Ebbesen 1999; Larson and Fanchiang 1996; Saillant 1990; Walsh and Crepeau 1998)
- Music and music education (Schmidt 1994; Schmidt and Knowles 1994, 1995)
- Nursing (Bramwell 1984; King 1989; Leininger 1985)
- Psychiatry and clinical practice (Hall 1998; Miller 1994)
- Social work (Gilgun 1999)
- Sociocultural studies (Hones and Cha 1999)
- Women's studies (Vozzola 1998).

While in each discipline and through the eyes of each researcher the life history method is individually and contextually shaped and appears slightly different, life history research across disciplines is based on the fundamental assumption about the relationship of the general to the particular, and that the general can best be understood through analysis of the particular. According to Goodson (1995, 98), life history research represents "stories of action within theories of context." The Personal Narrative Group (1989, 6) cites life history accounts as "particularly rich sources because, attentively interpreted, they illuminate both the logic of individual courses of action and the effects of system-level constraints within which those courses evolve."

Contemporary life history research methods, growing out of the early works, have changed through time and by influence of researchers. In the early years of its inception, life history research, though somewhat radical in its valuing of the individual as knowledge source, was still quite strongly influenced by positivist traditions. A perusal of Dollard's (1935) criteria for life history evidences this point, as does Thomas and Znaniecki's (1920) claim of their theory's scientific generalization based on a study of Polish peasants.

A conventional life history research project typically involves a small number of participants (traditionally referred to as "subjects" or "informants") whom the researcher studies in considerable depth. Data are gathered, usually over an extended period of time, using standard anthropology fieldwork techniques such as interviewing, participant observation, and document or artifact collection. These data are then thematically interpreted and considered in relation to relevant discipline-based theories, and represented in the form of detailed and rich life history accounts. These accounts represent both the researcher's interpretation of the research participants' lives, and the researcher's theorizing about those lives in relation to broader contextual situations and issues.

While at a surface level the methodological design and procedure of life history research has remained relatively intact over the years, at a deeper level much has changed. No longer are life history researchers (among others) content to distance themselves from research questions, participants, interpretation, and even representation. To the contrary, a fundamental shift has pushed researchers away from dichotomies of self-other, subject-object, and subjectivity-objectivity to an acknowledgment of an intersubjective realm of being and meaning that places them squarely in the research frame. As Behar (1996, 174) puts it,

> In current anthropological and feminist writing [and we would include contemporary life history research here] . . . we are seeing efforts to map an intermediate space we can't quite define yet, a borderland between passion and intellect, analysis and subjectivity, ethnography and autobiography, art and life.

Anthropologist Myerhoff (1974, 1979) was one of the first life history researchers to challenge the conventional researcher-subject relationship by infusing her work with her own reflexive presence and attributing interpretive authority to the relationship she developed with her participants. In contemporary life history research, this kind of reflexive stance is expected. The researcher self is visible in the research text and the researcher is every bit as vulnerable, as present, as those who participate in the research. The reflexive presence of the researcher in contemporary texts has given rise in research literature to new debates and assertions about the role (or existence) of objectivity in research. Indeed, some suggest that researchers have become so preoccupied with their own situational influences on researching activities that they have overtaken the research stage. Patai (1994), for one, identifies this as "nouveau solipsism." Such criticism, however, gives short shrift to the significance of the researcher's presence; it undervalues the role of the medium in delivering a message. Who a researcher is, and the vantage point from which she operates, is important information for the reader of a research account.

CLARIFICATION OF TERMS

The recent rise in personal experience methods for understanding elements of the human condition is clearly reflected in social science literature. There is a preponderance of research accounts and publications focused on methodological procedures and issues that suggest that, collectively, researchers are in a process of sorting out and thinking through this phase in the development of the research genre. It is also apparent that researchers choose diverse ways to describe research that involves studies of people's lives. A quick inventory of two such publications reveals the following list of terms: autobiography, autoethnography, biography, case history, case study, ethnography, interpretive biography, life history, life narrative, life story, narrative, narrative account, oral history, oral narrative, personal experience story, personal history, and story (Denzin 1989a; Hatch and Wisniewski 1995b). As these authors point out, while it is difficult to make absolute distinctions between and among the various personal experience methods—and indeed some, such as Ayers (1995, cited in Hatch and Wisniewski 1995b, 114), suggest that such an exercise has questionable merit—we think it is important to delineate different research approaches.

We offer the following list of terms to aid in this delineation. Our purpose is not to get caught up in the terminology, or debates about it, or to pretend that the lines among the various approaches are clearly drawn. Rather, we want to point out that language is important. Words used to describe different research methods are codes that reflect, among other things, features of epistemology, purpose, and process. We are not purporting to offer definitions of the various methods; we are merely laying out a code to help make clear how we understand life history research and how we talk about it throughout this book. The examples we cite reflect how we characterize the various texts. Others, including some of the authors of the texts, might differently describe their work.

Autobiography: This is a structured account of a life written by and about oneself. Howarth (1980, 364), using an artist analogy, describes autobiography as a self-portrait:

> The artist-model must alternately pose and paint . . . work[ing] from memory as well as sight, in two levels of time, on two planes of space, while reaching for those other dimensions, depth and the future. The process is alternately reductive and expansive; it imparts to a single picture the force of universal implications.

Some examples of autobiographies include: *Curriculum Vitae: Autobiography* (Spark 1993); *Teacher* and *I Passed This Way* (Ashton-Warner 1963, 1979, respectively); *Neill! Neill! Orange Peel* (Neill 1972); *The Road from Coorain* (Conway 1989); and *Written by Herself, Autobiographies of American Women: An Anthology* (Conway 1992).

There is an implied finality, a completeness, to autobiography that is not present in a similar genre of self-writing or memoir. Hampl (1996, 209) points out the fragmented and in-progress quality of memoir and its role in self-understanding:

> Memoir is the intersection of narration and reflection, of storytelling and essay writing. It can present its story *and* reflect and consider the meaning of the story. It is a peculiarly open form, inviting broken and incomplete images, half-collected fragments—all the mass (and mess) of detail. It offers to shape this confusion—and in shaping, of course it necessarily creates a work of art.

Among the many recent feminist writings in the genre of memoir are *French Lessons: A Memoir* (Kaplan 1993); *Bone Black: Memories of Girlhood* (hooks 1996); *A Life in School: What the Teacher Learned* (Tompkins 1996); and *Runaway: Diary of a Street Kid* (Lau 1989).

Autoethnography: As the name suggests, an autoethnography places the self within a sociocultural context. Unlike autobiography, which is focused on oneself for purposes of self-representation and/or self-understanding, autoethnography uses the self as a starting or vantage point from which to explore broader sociocultural elements, issues, or constructs. *First Field Work: The Misadventures of an Anthropologist* (Anderson 1990) and *At Home in the World* (Jackson 1995) are examples of autoethnographies. Examples of edited collections, in which individual personal accounts are used collectively to interrogate a broad theme or social issue, include: *Ordinary Lessons: Girlhoods of the 1950s* (Franzosa 1999); *This Fine Place So Far from Home: Voices of Academics from the Working Class* (Dews and Law 1995); and *Inside Separate Worlds: Life Stories of Young Blacks, Jews, and Latinos* (Schoem 1991). We spend considerable time working with teachers, encouraging them to create personal histories (see below) of their experiences of teaching, learning, and schooling. These personal accounts serve as a basis for interrogating constructs of schooling and education. These self-based, reflexive explorations of teaching and schooling (Cole and Knowles 2000; Knowles and Cole with Presswood 1994) also are autoethnographies.

Biography: This is a structured account of a life written by another, usually according to literary conventions. Denzin (1989a, 17) lists the following as characteristic assumptions of biography: the existence of others; the influence and importance of gender and class; family beginnings; starting points; known and knowing authors and observers; objective life markers; real persons with real lives; turning-point experiences; and truthful statements distinguished from fictions.

On the latter point, Wagner-Martin (1994, 8–9) reminds us that the story told by biography is, in some respects, as much fiction as the narrative created by the fiction writer, and yet the reading public persists in believing that biography is an art dependent on fact. The author is referring here to the point that every story of another's life also reflects elements of the life of the author.

Biographies are prevalent in both classic and contemporary literature and in what bookstores typically call "popular nonfiction" (although, clearly, the appropriateness of the term "nonfiction" is open to debate). Within the context of social science research, biography is also increasingly prevalent as a method and form for understanding and representing people's lives. Social science biographers combine literary devices and conventions with relevant theoretical frameworks and contexts to produce theorized literary accounts of individual lives. Examples include: *Sylvia!* (Hood 1988) (also, *Who Is Sylvia?: The Diary of a Biography* [Hood, 1990], which is the author's account of researching and writing a biography); *John Burroughs: An American Naturalist* (Renehan 1992); and *Escalante: The Best Teacher in America* (Mathews 1988).

Case history: This term is sometimes used synonymously with case study, however, case history differs because of its association with and use in social and health services. Case histories are typically compiled on a person, group, or institution as part of a case study or to serve a client need. It is not a research term.

Case study: We think of case study more as a design than a method, in that it can be accommodated within a range of research paradigms and disciplines. Its defining feature is its focus on what can be described as a case—a program, condition, event, person, process, institution, or cultural/ethnic or similarly defined group. Merriam (1988) provides a comprehensive explanation of qualitative case study research in her book *Case Study Research in Education*.

Ethnography: The broad purpose of ethnography is to gain an understanding of the symbolic meanings attached to the patterns of social interactions of individuals within a particular cultural group. The term "ethnography" is used to describe both the way of studying human life—systematic investigation through a process of intensive and extensive participant observation, participation, and interviewing within a designated cultural group—and the product of researching—a rich and detailed interpretive description of life within the context of the research setting. Examples of ethnographies are prevalent in social science research, especially within anthropology and sociology. Some of the more well-known ethnographies are *The Girls in the Gang* (Campbell 1984); *Keeping Them Out of the Hands of Satan: Evangelical Schooling in America* (Rose, 1988); *Coming* *of Age in New Jersey: College and American Culture* (Moffatt 1989); and *An Academic Village: The Ethnography of an Anthropology Department* (Williams 1993). Educational ethnographies include *The Man in the Principal's Office: An Ethnography* (Wolcott 1973); *The Color of Strangers, the Color of Friends: The Play of Ethnicity in School and Community* (Peshkin 1991); and *Jocks and Burnouts: Social Categories and Identity in the High School* (Eckert 1989).

Recently conventional ethnography has come under criticism for its focus on description and for what some might call a passive stance. Critics also cite the lack of participant involvement in the research, except as "informant" of the cultural group, as an inappropriate expression of research hierarchy. Such criticism has given rise to a variation of ethnography called "critical ethnography," which essentially is conventional ethnography with a political purpose. Instead of studying a group for purposes of interpretive description, critical ethnographers study a group with the intention of invoking social change. Inherent in the agenda of critical ethnographers are intentions of empowerment and emancipation for members of the group being studied. Examples of critical ethnography are *Schooling As a Ritual Performance* (McLaren 1986); *Street Wise: Race, Class and Change in an Urban Community* (Anderson 1990); and *Lives on the Edge: Single Mothers and Their Children in the Other America* (Polakow 1993).

Even more recently there has developed a form of contemporary ethnography that focuses on alternative forms of representation and that challenges issues related to the researcher-researched relationship. Contemporary ethnographers experimenting with alternative approaches employ a variety of representational forms, such as fiction, poetry, and drama, to communicate the research "text." For examples of alternative ethnographies see *Opportunity House: Ethnographic Stories of Mental Retardation* (Angrosino 1998); *Composing Ethnography* (Ellis and Bochner 1996); and *Kaleidoscope Notes: Writing Women's Music and Organizational Culture* (Jones 1998); "Ethical Issues in an Ethnographic Performance Text" (Saldaña 1998).

Interpretive biography: Denzin, in his book *Interpretive Biography* (1989a, 11), uses this term to describe the process or method of doing biography— "creating literary, narrative, accounts and representations of lived experiences. Telling and inscribing stories."

Life narrative or life story: A life narrative or story is a written or oral account of a life or segment of a life as told by an individual. These terms, along with others such as personal history and personal narrative, are often subsumed under the rubric of narrative or biographical method. In the introduction to their book *Storied Lives*, Rosenwald and Ochberg (1992, 1, 8) demonstrate this interchanging of terms:

> How individuals recount their histories . . . shapes what individuals can claim of their lives. Personal stories are not merely a way of telling someone (or oneself) about one's life; they are means by which identities may be fashioned. . . .
>
>   A life story is more than a recital of events. It is an organization of experience. In relating the elements of experience to each other and to the present telling, the teller asserts their meanings.

Elsewhere in their description they use the terms "narrative," "narrative accounts," "personal stories," "personal narrative," and "personal accounts." This is a good example of how attempts to make minute distinctions can become a semantic exercise. Sorting out subtle semantic differences is not as important as making clarifications based on epistemology, purpose, and process.

Narrative accounts: The terms "narrative" and "narrative account" are frequently used to describe a form of information or data display, such as, "The text appears in narrative form" or "The following narrative account. . . ." It is important, however, to distinguish this use of "narrative" from "narrative" that is epistemologically rooted. Not all research texts that use narrative forms are grounded in assumptions that reflect a narrative view of the world.

Narrative: Like life history research, narrative method is variously defined, influenced by a researcher's orientation and discipline. (See Polkinghorne 1995, for a helpful discussion of the multiple uses of narrative in qualitative research.) Generally speaking, narrative method in research is based on the assumption that human experience is episodically ordered and best understood through a reconstruction of the natural narrative order in which it is lived. Significance is given to the personal, temporal, and contextual quality of connections and relationships that honor the complexities of a life as lived as a unified whole. The focus of narrative research is on the individual, and the fact that life might be understood through a recounting and reconstruction of the life story. Epistemologically, narrative method in research draws on both the field of linguistics and hermeneutic philosophy (Dilthey 1987; Ricoueur 1984, 1991). Within education, Connelly and Clandinin are among the most well known for their extensive writings on and examples of narrative method (see, for example, Clandinin and Connelly 1994 2000; Connelly and Clandinin 1990). From a psychological perspective, numerous examples and discussions of narrative method can be found in a series titled *The Narrative Study of Lives* (Josselson 1996; Josselson and Lieblich, 1993, 1995, 1999; Lieblich and Josselson, 1994, 1997).

Life history: Both narrative and life history research rely on and depict the storied nature of lives; both are concerned with honoring the individuality and complexity of individuals' experiences. The two methods part company, however, with respect to broad purpose and analysis. We think of life history research as taking narrative one step further; that is, life history research goes beyond the individual or the personal and places narrative accounts and interpretations within a broader context. Lives are lived within the influence of contexts as far ranging as cultural, political, familial, educational, and religious spheres just to mention a few. (More important, such divisions of influence are arbitrary in their delineation. Lives are far too complex but these categories remind life history researchers of the kinds of questions that may help yield rich information about a life lived.) Whereas narrative research focuses on making meaning of individuals' experiences, life history research draws on individuals' experiences to make broader contextual meaning. Another way to think of life history research is as it relates to the way in which history is defined.

History is a documentation of stories told and recorded about the past through the identification of significant people, places, moments, events, and movements located in time and context. Exploring the issues of "the times" and their place in the complex scheme of things is central to historical analysis. To be a student of history is to interrogate the meaning and significance of the past as it influences the present and the future (keeping in mind that such study and the articulation of historical meanings are clearly made within the domain of the scholar's cultural and situational perspectives). The significant historical elements, when connected, help give meaning to the present. So it is with an individual life, yet the layers of influence are many and rich.

Examples of life history research include *I've Known Rivers: Lives of Loss and Liberation* (Lawrence-Lightfoot 1994); *Translated Woman: Crossing the Border with Esperanza's Story* (Behar 1993); *Educating Feminists: Life Histories and Pedagogy* (Middleton 1993); *I Answer with My Life: Life Histories of Women Teachers Working for Social Change* (Casey 1993); *Teachers' Lives and Careers* (Ball and Goodson 1985); and *Studying Teachers' Lives* (Goodson 1992).

Oral history and oral narrative: These terms are often used synonymously. Like personal narratives, personal histories, and life stories, oral history is a method focused on the reconstruction of a life. In oral history, however, the narrator has a more predominant role in the representation of the life as told. Etter-Lewis (1993, xii) explains:

Oral narrative, sometimes referred to as oral history . . . preserves an individual's own words and perspectives in a particularly authentic way. It is a collaborative transaction that reconstructs a life once lived; and it is a text that makes relevant to the present metaphors of a narrator's past. . . . The spontaneity of oral narrative reveals a virtually unedited and sometimes unprocessed view of personal meaning and judgment that is not altered by the usual limitations of written language.

My Soul Is My Own: Oral Narratives of African-American Women in the Professions (Etter-Lewis 1993) is a good example of oral history research.

Personal experience story: An anecdote or story told or written by a person about his or her experience is called a personal experience story. Such stories do not necessarily represent epiphanic or pivotal moments in one's life, nor are they contextualized or theorized. Personal experience stories often are part of information gathered in a study of a life.

Personal history: Similar to autoethnography, a personal history is an account of one's life or segments of one's life written or told for purposes of understanding oneself in relation to a broader context—familial, institutional, and societal, for instance. Personal history inquiry is like life history research with its focus on life in context; unlike life history, however, personal history inquiry is usually self-conducted and more focused. Its purpose is to illuminate the meanings of past experiences as they influence future actions. For a more extensive exploration of personal history research within the context of teacher education, for example, see Carter (1993), Carter and Doyle (1996), Cole and Knowles (2000), Knowles (1994), Knowles and Holt-Reynolds (1991, 1994a, 1994b), and Knowles and Cole with Presswood (1994).

Story: Polkinghorne (1995, 7) describes "story" as "a special type of discourse production . . . that combine[s] a succession of incidents into a unified episode." Commonly used by researchers of lives and personal experiences, story—both fictional and "real"—is "the linguistic form that preserves the complexity of human action within its interrelationship of temporal sequence, human motivation, chance happenings, and changing interpersonal and environmental contexts," Polkinghorne (1995, 7) writes. Similarly, Scholes (1981, 206) describes a story as "a narrative with a certain very specific syntactic shape (beginning-middle-end or situation-transformation-situation) and with a subject matter that allows for or encourages the projection of human values upon the material."

ROLE OF CONTEXT

The slogan "Context is everything" could well be the hallmark of life history inquiry. As we have noted, the distinction between biographical research methods, or narrative inquiry, and life history research rests in the degree to which understandings of context play out in the search for understandings of individual or collective lives. Lives are never lived in vacuums. Lives are never lived in complete isolation from social contexts. Even those who choose to live as hermits or recluses do so for reasons that are bound to be context-related. Actions that place an individual beyond the borders of society or social order are likely to be connected to experiences of family and community or to understandings of society and of the human and natural environments. Such actions are likely to be a result of very particular interpretations of context. To be a human being is to have connections with others and the collective societal influences and institutions, be they historical, political, economic, educational, religious, or even environmental (as in physical landscape and climate, for example). To be human is to experience "the relational," no matter how it is defined, and, at the same time, to be shaped by "the institutional," the structural expressions of community and society. To be human is to be molded by context.

In their book *The Art and Science of Portraiture,* Lawrence-Lightfoot and Hoffmann-Davis (1997) describe the important role that context plays in researching lives. Although they do not name their work as arts-informed life history research, the assumptions and qualities defining their method of "portraiture" are consistent with the perspectives we represent in this book. Lawrence-Lightfoot, in *The Art and Science of Portraiture* (1997, 41), describes the role of context this way:

> By context, I mean the setting—physical, geographic, temporal, historical, cultural, aesthetic—within which the action takes place. Context becomes the framework, the reference point, the map, the ecological sphere; it is used to place people and action in time and space and as a resource for understanding what they do.

Think about how often, in daily life, we comment on the role that context plays in aiding our understanding. "Oh, I didn't recognize you out of context," we might say to someone with whom we have interacted perhaps several times in a particular setting, only to pass her by on the street, in a restaurant, or at a bookstore. Or, "That quote is taken completely out of context. That's not at all what he meant," we might exclaim in disgust upon reading a line in a newspaper or magazine article taken from a favorite piece of poetry or prose or familiar piece of published nonfiction, or perhaps a political address. Or, "He's like a fish out of water," we might observe of someone seemingly "out of place" in a particular setting. How could we pretend to "know" any of these people or the meanings they attach to their words without knowing their respective contexts? How much can we ever really know, anyway, is also a valid question.

As researchers we can only ever "come close" to understanding the experiences or life of another and we can only go so far in unraveling the complexities of the broader social condition. As life history researchers, we sense that we can more fully know and understand these uniquenesses and complexities, because of our commitment to understanding lives in context.

In a recent study of teacher education professors (Cole 2000b; Cole et al. 1999a, 1999b, 1999c) our attention was poignantly and repeatedly drawn to the many obstacles faced by those who, in subtle and more overt ways, attempt to challenge the status quo of and within their academic institutions. Their various experiences, taken separately, paint a picture of individuals struggling to make a difference through the work they do as teacher educators. The stories alone are compelling and provide insights into individual aspirations and commitments. Placed within the context of the academy as a societal institution, however, the stories and struggles they portray become even more potent. The image of the lone faculty member fighting the odds is brought into sharper focus with a better understanding of the odds she is fighting. Institutional forces are powerful.

For example, each of the women in the study received subtle and not-so-subtle reminders of her "proper" place in the male-defined hierarchy of her institution (Cole 2000b; Cole et al. 1999c). One woman faculty member was invited to join a committee and was then given the responsibility to make and serve coffee. Another, who chaired a labor-intensive committee and was left to carry out all the very time-consuming clerical work, was succeeded the next term by a male faculty member, who was provided full clerical support. Another discovered well into her employment term that it was the women on faculty who were assigned to teach courses with the highest enrollments. And yet another talked about not having access to vital information typically communicated in all-male venues such as the locker room, bathroom or urinal, beer parlor, or golf course. These examples of experience gather force and momentum when the context of the academy—its history as a male bastion of power built on norms and values of rugged individualism, competition, and hierarchy—is also made clear. The academy is an adverse arena for many women faculty members. Context is all-powerful.

In Gary's research account about Thomas, the professor, we are reminded of the fact that, similarly, the institutional context and the many nuances of meaning it evoked for Thomas and others, was the one element of his experience that was misread. This was particularly so with respect to the extent that it would eventually play out on how Thomas lived his academic life. From a researching point of view and given the "after-the-fact" inquiry process, to understand the complexities of that context would have been beyond the realms of possibility given the political and ideological issues at stake in gaining full entry into it. The best that was possible was to move around the perimeter of the context and take "snapshots" that might illuminate the central issues.

2

Principles Guiding Life History Researching

- *Relationality*
- *Mutuality*
- *Empathy (reflexivity, being the "other")*
- *Care, sensitivity, and respect*

We view researching as an activity that is an extension of who we are as individuals (a position that is reiterated numerous times throughout this book). Even in cases where we collaborate with other researchers, say, on a research team for the purposes of achieving common goals so that we act together as a collective or group, each of us still maintains our individuality and individual perspectives. Within a group effort, as we work with participants or as we develop analyses or express support for particular courses of researching action, we express who we are as persons. We act in person—in concert with our intellectual understandings of the researching enterprise. This is our take.

Under these fundamental assumptions there is nothing mysterious about the principles appropriate for guiding life history work. These principles are, we hope, the very same ones we apply to our everyday lives. If we act in ethically and morally responsive ways, in the broadest sense possible, with those who live and work around us, then the chances are we will do the same with those people with whom we research. That is another of our assumptions.

Being schooled in researching protocol does not magically induce an infusion of ethical principles into our actions—although we imagine that if the "ethical review" or "human subjects review" process, completed in preparation for fieldwork, is conceptualized as "Big Brother looking over a shoulder," then some individuals would be prompted to be vigilant about their behaviors contrary to their normal patterns of action. Such inauthentic behavior is bound to be cast aside when complex relational difficulties arise or, perhaps, when the guard is momentarily dropped.

Assuming that we each acknowledge the place of principled actions in the researching process, to engage in authentic researching behavior is to be oneself. To focus on developing the personal and professional qualities of relationality, mutuality, and empathy, as well as care, sensitivity, and respect is, for us, both emblematic of and crucial to life history researching. These are the principles and conditions we strive to exemplify and create. Such conditions invariably will yield rich information and insights. These are the conditions that elevate the representations of the researching process and analyses into richly evocative, experience textured, relationally authentic, and meaningful "texts." This is true for research texts in the form of academic prose (in the manner of, say, traditional ethnographies or life histories) or postmodern layered articulations of meaning; or for texts that include or are predominately alternative in representational form and are arts-informed renderings (such as having poetic, literary, kinesthetic, dramatic, or musical qualities, or combinations of them); or for texts that attract viewers because of a visual richness achieved through the use of graphics or two- or three-dimensional artworks or other media, such film, video, or computer disk. Authentic and mutually satisfying relationships that define researching activities will inevitably show up in the "official" and "unofficial" stories of researching told to others.

RELATIONALITY

When we think about the relationship between researcher and participants we think about two (or more) people coming together for purposes of inquiry into an area of mutual interest. We think about the formation of a relationship like any other genuine personal or professional relationship—one that demands attention and needs care, thought, sensitivity, respect, and trust in order to develop. We think about qualities that honor each person in the relationship and that strive toward an egalitarian ideal. By this we do not mean to deny the power differential inherent in a relationship between a researcher and participant by virtue of their roles. We do not mean to suggest that researchers and participants deny elements of difference between them by virtue of race, gender, class, ethnicity, circumstance, or position. We mean that researchers (because usually they initiate such relationships) must do all they can to challenge the hierarchical principles and practices that traditionally define the relationship between researchers and those whom they research.

In chapter 1 we identified the notion of relationship as central to the research endeavor. In this chapter we describe principles to guide a research process in a way that honors this notion of relationship. Our perspective on research relationships is at odds with conventional views that promote distance, formality, and adherence to clearly defined role boundaries; views that consider any deviance from these characteristics as a threat to the quality of the research—"contamination," as some might say. From this mainly pragmatic stance the research relationship is analogous to a business deal with carefully articulated terms of agreement.

In sharp contrast, we consider the research relationship from a more humanistic standpoint—complex, fluid, and ever changing with boundaries that blur in kaleidoscopic fashion. Like Lawrence-Lightfoot and Hoffmann-Davis (1997, 138), we see research relationships as "central to the empirical, ethical, and humanistic dimensions of research design, as evolving and changing processes of human encounter." For us, intimacy and authenticity in relationship are foundational to research quality and to knowledge production, which is what research is about.

Intimacy in research is described by Busier et al. (1997) as including qualities of mutual care and friendship; revelation of respect for personal vulnerabilities; and attention to issues of relational reflexivity, relational ethics, power-in-relation, and the temporary nature of understandings, especially as influenced by the evolution of the research relationship. In writing about the role of intimacy in research relationships, Ardra and Maura McIntyre, reflecting on their research relationship, assert that the more blurred the boundaries between the personal and professional became, the closer they were able to get to "knowledge producing." The knowledge gained through their research together had a "depth and resonance reflective of the relationship in which it is embedded" (Cole and McIntyre 2001). Similarly, Lawrence-Lightfoot and Hoffmann-Davis (1997) consider intimacy—depth of connection, interpersonal resonance—as integral to knowledge development. Drawing on Oakley (1981), they state, "Authentic findings will only emerge from authentic relationships" (138).

In part 2 of this book, several authors use examples from some of their research projects to explore the relational quality of research. Gary Knowles, in chapter 8, writes about authenticity in research relationships and a researcher's responsibility to maintain a commitment to research participants. Jacquie Aston, in chapter 9, explores the influences of shared gender on a research relationship and on the insights gained through researching. And in chapter 10, drawing on her research with women social activists, Kathy

Gates discusses the ethical dimensions of a research relationship through the concept of fidelity—a way of ethically being-in-relation.

MUTUALITY

Figuring Out the Researching Process

Challenging conventional notions of the research relationship requires us also to think differently about how the roles and responsibilities of researchers and participants are determined. For researchers operating from a traditional perspective, this part of the process is straightforward: research "subjects" assume a passive role, giving consent to participate and providing data to the researcher; responsibilities for decision making about how the research will proceed are assumed solely by the researcher.

Even in more contemporary forms of qualitative researching, where researchers claim to denounce their exclusive authority over the process and where participants assume a more active role in decision making throughout, there is an implicit expression of hierarchy. Often this expression is implied through language. For example: Hammersley (1979) talks about striking a "research bargain"; Goodson and Fliesser (1994), a "fair trade"; Bogdan and Biklen (1998) refer to "gaining access"; Marshall and Rossman (1989), to "gaining entry"; and Seidman (1991) talks about "making contact" and "getting stories."

In earlier attempts to find more appropriate ways to talk about the research relationship we favored the term "negotiation" (see Cole 1989; Cole and Knowles 1993; Knowles and Cole 1995) to describe the process of what we called "partnership research." We wanted language that would communicate the notion of mutuality in purpose, process, and result; words that would reflect the kind of equitable and authentically collaborative relationship that we strive for. But now that term has connotations for us that reflect badly on the kind of relationship we advocate. "Negotiation" is reminiscent of a business deal, a process of barter, collective bargaining, or a contractual agreement. It reminds us of political and financial negotiating that often involves elements of coercion, corruption, and deception. It no longer seems an appropriate term.

As before, we admit that we do not want to get bogged down in semantics; however, we are aware of how language acts as metaphor and how, as is brilliantly illustrated by Lakoff and Johnson (1980), we unknowingly come to live by or enact those metaphors. So how *do* we describe the decision-making process and agreements made between researchers and participants about their roles and responsibilities? While we take this part of the research endeavor very seriously, we prefer to think of it as a natural part of relationship formation—as part of the "conversation-in-relation" (McIntyre and Cole 2001)—rather than as a formally defined set of negotiations that mark the boundaries between researcher and participant. For example, Hammersley (1979) recommends establishing rules about behavioral boundaries and developing clauses to clearly set out expectations. Similarly, Yow (1994) suggests that failure to adhere to clearly defined boundaries can lead to faulty expectations. Seidman (1991) cautions researchers against developing friendships or becoming too familiar with participants so as not to lose control of the distance required in a research relationship. He recommends presenting a detailed written statement of rights and responsibilities of the researcher and participants.

We take an opposite stance. If two (or more) people come together for purposes of researching an area of mutual interest (a central assumption about the research enterprise that we make explicit throughout the book), then surely those two people can figure out how that work should proceed. Again, this is not to deny that research participants may have initial fears or preconceived ideas about what might be required of them as research "subjects" (which is how most people, initially, will think of themselves). We assert, however, that given appropriate attention to such research histories and time for exploration of what the research might entail, researcher and participants can settle into a collaborative stance and, jointly, figure out elements of the researching process. For example, technical and procedural issues of time and place, as well as ideas and issues related to the documentation and security of information gathered, can be mutually agreed on. Concerns about confidentiality and risk can be openly explored. Individual needs and preferences with respect to participation and representation can be identified and addressed at the outset or as they arise. We are suggesting here that researchers work toward the cocreation of a conversational space where issues of researching can be openly and thoughtfully considered as they occur in the natural rhythm of the researching process. (Of course, we are assuming that researchers are working with a small number of participants in any one project.) Having said this, we acknowledge that institutions that sponsor research usually require strict adherence to a set ethical protocol that includes formal statements about the research and conditions of informed consent. We believe that it is possible to follow these required procedures without jeopardizing the development of a more informal, natural, and mutually satisfying relationship.

Developing Empathy through Reflexivity

Do you still keep in touch with your mother?
My mother passed away a couple of weeks ago. We were close friends. . . .
What about your brother?

He died a few years ago under mysterious circumstances. . . .
So all you have left is your sister?
She passed away when she was eight. I have no family.

I'd like to know what type of child you were.
Well, I was the youngest in the family. I have two siblings, both brothers—
one six years older and one eight. I am the baby of the family.
What did that mean to you?
It meant a lot of things. . . .
What type of things did you do as a family?
Our family was kind of dysfunctional you might say. . . .

These excerpts are typical of the kind of exchanges that take place in life
history interviews. The questions are personal, intrusive, and may
evoke memories of difficult experiences and events in a participant's
life. As life history researchers we ask these kinds of questions all the
time—but not because we want to invade privacy or evoke pain (or
pleasure). Usually, such questions are intended to elicit information that
will assist in developing a contextualized understanding of human phenomena and experience. The first of the above introductory excerpts is
from a conversation Ardra had in a life history study of beginning community college teachers (Goodson and Cole 1994). The questions asked
(and the responses they elicited) helped her to uncover threads of the interwoven fabric of the teachers' professional and personal lives; similarly with the second example, which came from a life history study of
university faculty members who were teacher educators (Cole and
Knowles 1995; Trapedo-Dworsky and Cole 1999). To the extent that both
studies aim to understand life history influences on professional practice, they are similar. They differ, however, in one important respect. In
the first, Ardra was the researcher; in the second, one of the researched.
In the first, she directed the conversation; in the second, another researcher guided her responses.
   Research looks distinctively different from either side of the microphone. As researchers, it is important to understand that fact—experien-
tially as well as theoretically. Reflexivity in research is essential for the development of empathetic research practice. Reflexivity in research is tied
to issues of (inter)subjectivity and the importance of acknowledging one's
stance or position as researcher. It is also about developing and operating
from an ethic of care for research participants and relationships established as part of a research endeavor. Being reflexive in research leads to
heightened awareness of self, other, and the self-other dialectic. Understanding in the experiential sense—from the perspective of a research participant, what it means to be engaged in "researching the personal"—is
critical for the development of sensitive and responsive researchers.

Ardra was a participant in a life history study of her practice as a teacher educator (as part of an ongoing self-study research program and as part of a larger study of teacher educators she was coconducting). She did this partly to complement her ongoing self-study agenda but mainly to explore the question: What does it mean to be "the researched"? She worked with another researcher, Madeleine, whose agenda was to learn more about conducting life history research. Madeleine engaged Ardra in a series of life history interviews, or conversations, and observed her teaching and working with graduate students in different contexts. Field notes from those observations formed the basis for more focused conversations about her practice.

A substantial part of each conversation was devoted to joint reflection on the research process. They talked about how they experienced their respective roles of "the researcher" and "the researched," and discussed a whole range of technical, procedural, conceptual, political, ethical, and relational issues from their respective positions. Ardra used the experience of being the researched as a basis for reflection on and analysis of some of her theoretical and practical understandings about life history research. She engaged, both on paper and in her mind, in a kind of dialogue with different forms of her knowing of and about life history research. What follows are some excerpts from her writing about that experience. Because most of her experience-based responses were imbued with affect of strong intensity, she focuses mostly on how she *felt* about various elements of the research process, rather than about "methodological correctness." Ardra's theoretical "voice" echoes from some of her other published writings on methods and issues in life history research. The dialogue between voices illustrates the tension between the two ways of understanding life history research. Excerpts from the published writing reveal an emphasis on theoretical knowledge about research methodology and a lack of adequate attention to the emotional preparation or empathetic understanding about what it means for someone to be the researched.

ARDRA'S REFLEXIVE ACCOUNT

Anxious Beginnings and Intrusions into Daily Life

> First meetings . . . set the tone for subsequent encounters. The purpose is to engage the interest and commitment of the participant and to initiate a collegial relationship. . . . The conditions of the research need to be negotiated and agreed upon in advance of any investigative work. (Cole 1991, 192–193)

Madeleine and I met prior to the formal beginning of our research to talk about how we wanted to work together and what we hoped to achieve, and to work out the details of our collaboration. We had the advantage of knowing one another prior to this research commitment and we already had a collegial working relationship built on mutual trust and respect. There was no question about my being interested in and committed to our research project. After all, we were researching a life and it was mine! And, since I also had another agenda centered on "researching the process," one might say my interest was doubly vested. So, in theory, after our initial meeting, we were ready to proceed. I was not prepared, however, for the anxiety I experienced after that meeting and prior to our first interview.

The day before our first "formal" interview Madeleine called to confirm our plans. Hanging up the phone, after communicating my excitement about our project and my eagerness to begin, a wave of self-doubt overcame me and my head began to spin with questions. Will I be able to respond to the kinds of questions she is likely to ask? If so, how? What will I "look like" on tape and in print? What parts of me and my life will I and we reconstruct? Will I portray myself and be portrayed honestly? . . . Accurately? What does that mean anyway? All the rest of that day and night, thoughts and feelings about our upcoming interview did laps in my mind.

As a research participant, who also was a researcher, I felt that I had a definite advantage over other research participants. I thought I knew what to expect; however, my theoretical knowledge about life history and other forms of personal research provided little insight into the actual experience of preparing for the research. In addition, although the time we spent negotiating our research relationship at the outset and the mutual trust we had already established were invaluable, I was still not prepared for the multiple ways in which engaging in the research invaded my life. Preparing for the research entailed much more than negotiating some procedural and relational issues up front.

With this experience in mind, I think back to the numerous times I have initiated research relationships with participants. Did they experience the same kind of uncertainty and anxiety as I now did as a participant? Were my words of explanation and assurance adequate? Did I do all that I could to try to help them understand and prepare for the researching process? How did they feel about our relationship? Were they intimidated? What were their early concerns? Did they have concerns about the way in which they would be represented? To what extent did they have opportunities to express their concerns or anxieties?

Incompleteness of a Retold Life

Perhaps because of the personal nature of our inquiry, and perhaps because of its intense and continuing nature, the research became an intrusion into my day-to-day life. It was always there—sometimes at the forefront of my thinking, other times tucked away in a corner of my mind. I wondered and worried over my level of coherence in the interviews (perhaps as only an academic might do), about the "relevance" of my responses, about what exactly I had said and its "accuracy"—all matters that, really, seemed relatively "trite" from the other side of the microphone. I found little comfort in my theoretical knowledge and in echoes of my own words of reassurance to those whose lives I had researched. I shared some of these concerns with Madeleine as part of our reflection on the research process.

Between the time we talked and the time I saw [the first transcript] in print . . . (a period of two to three days) I was very, very aware of being the one researched. . . . [I experienced] a little bit of anxiety . . . and a lot of uncertainty. That uncertainty was played out very explicitly when I finally got the transcript. I, almost literally, rushed in [to my office] and closed the door. I was on my way to do something [else] and I could not help but stop [to look at the transcript]. I had spent a lot of time wondering what I would look like in print. I have had enough experience with interviewing and with analyzing transcribed tapes, et cetera, not to worry about how inarticulate people tend to appear because that just happens [in oral speech]. I can look past that to some extent, but I was very aware and concerned about how what I said might come across, whether I was able to accurately articulate what I wanted to.

The incompleteness of the picture of my life that we were reconstructing through the interview process plagued me. Numerous times in our conversations I, in retrospect, belabored certain points in an effort to preclude an "inaccurate" or incomplete representation. Knowing in theory, and being repeatedly assured by Madeleine, that we were "retelling parts of my life, not reliving it" were not enough to assuage my concerns.

Upon reading the transcripts I was reminded of the unidimensional, oversimplified nature of a retold life. I said:

As I read the interview transcript, [I experienced] a high level of awareness about how simplistically lives are presented [in the retelling]. That comes across again and again and again. It is important to always remind ourselves that, as [Madeleine] said earlier, [the retold story] is a sketch . . . a frame. . . . Sometimes the whole picture becomes distorted. [For example], the [account] about my goals and achievements; as I read it, as I rendered it here, [that part of my life] seems so simplistic and not at all how [things really happened].

> In a matter of only a few minutes of conversation, which translated into a couple of pages of transcribed text, I presented a synoptic account of the academic and career goals I had set throughout my life and how I had worked toward their achievement. In print, my career path—which in reality was circuitous and serendipitous, characterized more by uncertainty and spontaneity than by calculated planning—appeared as a carefully mapped and direct route. My account of some of the critical incidents in my life appeared as a series of events, void of emotion, circumstance, and context—void of life. The life I lived and the story I told to represent elements of that life were quite disparate.
>
> In partial response to the incompleteness of a retold life, we repeatedly acknowledged the importance of having sufficient time to reconstruct the life I was telling:

That scenario I was playing out seemed, in the retelling, to be absolutely simplistic. By retelling it, I completely removed any of the richness and emotion that were lived. . . . In part this is a recognition that life is so complicated and it takes a long time to recapture other than bare, essential qualities.

> The following excerpt from a dialogue reveals more of my frustration and examples of Madeleine's reassurances about the incompleteness of my rendition.

Ardra: I think that the picture [in my account] of the person I once was is incomplete in some significant ways and so, perhaps, the portrait [I am rendering] is quite distorted.

Madeleine: If we use the image of a portrait, [your story of your life] is [being] sketched in. It is very rough [at first] and details are added in layers and layers. You can change the portrait by the addition or elimination of certain areas.

Ardra: That's a nice image. It does kind of capture what it is we are doing.

Madeleine: [The image] changes. . . . When you start, there is not a [clear] conception of how it is going to end and, even in the creation, it changes.

Ardra: Knowing that there is not the pressure to complete the portrait today, or to render a very finely detailed watercolor, really frees me up as a participant.

> Life history inquiries usually involve a series of interviews that each, typically, lasts from about one to two hours. During that time

participants are asked what we researchers call "open-ended" questions intended to elicit, in a free-flowing conversational style, recollections and reconstructions of elements of the participant's life. The spontaneous, responsive nature of these kinds of interviews can be at once enabling and inhibiting for participants. From a participant's perspective it is much easier, in many ways, to respond to a surveylike, "closed-ended," or bounded question than to the kinds of open-ended, limitless questions characteristic of life history interviews. For example, consider a question such as, Can you take me back to your hometown and tell me what it was like to grow up there? While such a question is likely to engender rich, contextual information, it can also be overwhelming in its scope. Questions like this always left me thinking and wondering about my responses for days after the actual interview. I was acutely aware of how selective I was in my responses, and of how incoherent and incomplete they were despite my attempts to be thorough and accurate within the constraints of time and situation.

My own experience of being "the researched" made me wonder about those I have interviewed. I recall being repeatedly overwhelmed by the richness and eventfulness of the stories people told about their lives and, yet, I wonder now how satisfied they were with the life they orally reconstructed. Did they, too, worry over the representation of their stories in print? Beyond the inevitable self-criticism of the sometimes incoherent or unpolished nature of running speech when it appears in print, I cannot recall any research participant outwardly responding to their accounts the way I did. Why was that? Did they not feel sufficiently comfortable to do so? Did I not encourage them enough? Were they intimidated by the process? Did I not take sufficient time or care to help them feel like a research partner?

Acknowledging Authority over the Story Line

In the spirit of life history research epistemology we assumed that, in the reconstruction of a life, everything is relevant. We were guided in our work by our belief in the authority of the research participant in matters of disclosure and identification of story lines to pursue. While I valued my authority in these matters, believed that everything was indeed relevant, and that I was the editor of my own text, the open-ended nature of the life history interviews and my having control over my telling were points of tension for me. In spite of what

I knew at a theoretical level, I worried about the relevance of my responses and their seemingly digressive nature. I shared my concern with Madeleine:

[During the interview] I thought, "I am going off on a tangent here. What does this have to do with anything?" even when I know that it does. . . . The nature of this research is such that the participant—the researched—can get so lost or caught up in her own story that, if left on her own, she could go on forever and ever and ever. Because it is so self-absorbing, I think it is very easy to lose the focus of the research. I was getting caught up in [telling] my own story and with making sense of it.

There is a tension between [allowing the conversation] to go off in a direction that, as you say, is important to go off in because there is a reason for the digression, and [identifying] the link between the digression and the purpose of the research. I wonder whether . . . the person being interviewed needs some reassurance that, indeed, this all does fit together and this all is related to the research topic.

As a researcher, I had earlier written:

The extent to which the researcher can know what information is essential and what lines of inquiry to pursue is debatable. . . . The informant must be given a certain degree of authority to determine the events to identify for discussion or further exploration. (Cole 1991, 201–205)

From the perspective of the research participant, however, I was less comfortable with the decision-making role. At the same time, I valued feeling in control of my telling. In conversing with Madeleine I stated:

I was very aware that you did not have a script or . . . a series of questions to cover, or that [the interview] wasn't just an oral survey kind of a thing. I think that told me a few things. One of the things it told me was that I was more in control of what was being said here and [that] it was my story that I was telling. I was not just responding [to a set of questions].

I vacillated in my response to being placed in control over the direction our conversations took. Although it was important for me to feel that I had a role in determining the line of inquiry, I was concerned about the relevance of what I was saying in relation to the purpose of the research. I think back to the times when, as a researcher, I provided the same kind of encouragement to participants as Madeleine did to me. I wonder whether, in the process of telling their stories, the participants in those studies worried over the relevance of what they were saying in spite of my reassurances and (hopefully) obvious interest. Often, they punctuated their responses with uncertainties such as, "Are you sure this is what you want?" or "I'm not sure if this is the kind of answer you're looking for but . . ." Then, I interpreted those kinds of queries as participants' attempts to please me, the researcher, and I typically tried to reassure them about there not being a "right" answer. Now, based on my own experience as a research participant, I wonder whether their questions of me were indications of a level of discomfort with the decision-making role that I was encouraging them to assume.

Given the traditionally passive nature of participants' roles in research, how do we help them to feel comfortable assuming more active roles in the design and conduct of inquiry? How do we communicate the value of their input? How do we help participants to be more willing to contribute to the interpretation and representation of their lives?

Self-Disclosure and Exposure

As a researcher I place ethical issues at the forefront of my research agenda, and I encourage other researchers to do the same. In a recent article I commented on the importance of attention to ethical issues in personal research:

Ethical issues infuse [life history] research projects at every point of their implementation. . . . With the advent of more intrusive research methods and the requirements of personal investment in research, consideration of ethical issues takes on a new prominence. . . . [Researchers need to attend to issues such as:] confidentiality . . . consent . . . access to data during and after study . . . negotiation of control . . . and equity of influence. (Cole and Knowles 1993, 489–490)

My experience as a research participant gave me pause to reflect anew on some of these issues. While the more formal elements of "ethical requirements" (such as confidentiality and consent and so on) for the treatment of "human subjects," to use the objective language of the academy, are obvious in their often articulated simplicity, in reality there are profound implications that arise from them.

At a couple of points in our interviews I made brief references to matters that I did not wish to further pursue in our discussions, because they were too painful, because I felt that I could not adequately explain them in the context of the research, or because I simply did not want to go public with the information. As always, I was reminded of my authority over the text and that I was the editor of my own public story. These instances gave me pause to reflect both from the perspective of the researched and the researcher.

As a researcher, one needs to stand or sit back, assess the situation, and make some decisions . . . about how far to push [the participant to provide] the kind of information that is really going to inform the research. . . . There is, on the one hand, the need to respect the individual and to be sensitive to the individual's behavior in relation to self-disclosure. And [there is the need to] allow time [for the] relationship to [form] and trust [to develop] so that, over time, perhaps more self-disclosure will take place. But [on the other hand], the researcher has to ask the questions, "If that [self-disclosure] is not going to happen to my satisfaction as a researcher, how do I respond?" and, "Am I really getting information that is going to help me address the research question or area of focus sufficiently well?"

There is no easy resolution to this dilemma; however, my experience of being the researched has led me to underscore the importance of sensitivity and respect in matters of self-disclosure. It was important for me to be reminded of my authority over the text, that I held the power to decide what I would disclose. I was made to feel comfortable with that power and with the decisions I made. Now, more than ever, I am convinced that researchers must maintain high levels of ethical and moral responsibility toward those they engage in personal research. Although I believe that we are all editors of our own text, and that we do make choices about self-disclosure, I wonder how research participants feel about the choices they make. How do they resolve any dissonance possibly experienced in the process of making decisions about what they reveal of themselves? How do we, as researchers, participate in that resolution process?

Because of the personal nature of the research and the content of the interviews, I was mindful of potential political implications of my involvement in the research. I, therefore, took particular care with the audiotapes and their transcripts to protect my anonymity and confidentiality in my own workplace. Although I had complete trust in Madeleine, she was unable to transcribe our interviews so, unlike most research participants, I was able to make arrangements for the transcribing to be done. I was satisfied that the personal data from our interviews was safe with the person with whom I had entrusted them until, somehow, one of the audiotapes and a hard copy of a tape transcript went missing from her desk. Hours of searching and retracing actions proved fruitless. I was (and am, still) left to wonder what had happened and why. Subsequently, I wondered aloud to Madeleine about how careful researchers really are about protecting the confidentiality of their participants when engaging the services of others. Aside from assigning pseudonyms to the data, what efforts are typically taken when entrusting personal information to others? Beyond any information given on institutionally required "human subject" or "ethical practices" consent forms, how much do participants know about what happens to the data during and after the study? I also wonder how comfortable participants typically feel about asking researchers for details about the security and use of the data.

Accepting Authority over the Text

Participant access to interview transcripts throughout a life history study is important for several methodological reasons:

The life history interview is the forum where much of the interpretation takes place. Here points are clarified, statements verified, and information from previous interviews and from supplementary sources validated. The participant, then, must have access to the information throughout the conduct of the inquiry (Cole 1991, 203).
The cyclical feeding back of interpretation in life history research enables the storyteller to give more thorough consideration to initial statements, impressions, comments, and reflections. (Cole 1991, 191)

The importance of my having access to the interview transcripts, and opportunities to elaborate points or clarify inaccuracies in interpretation, was repeatedly evidenced in our study. In some cases, after reading a transcript of an interview, I was dissatisfied with the way in which I had responded to a question or had portrayed a person or event. In those cases, it was important for me to be able to clarify and/or elaborate. For example, in one interview I described some of the values I thought I had learned as a child. In response, I spoke about some of what I perceive to be my mother's values and how I responded to them as a young person. The result, in the transcript, was a distorted image of my mother and an inaccurate representation of my formative values. In a subsequent interview I was able to correct the misrepresentations and more directly respond to the question.

In other cases, I was able to address inaccuracies in interpretation. For example, the following brief exchange set the scene for further clarifications at a later time.

Ardra: [During my summers living outside of the city] I spent most of my time on the beach, playing in the sand and walking on the rocks. One of my mother's friends there had a son who was in a wheelchair and he liked to play games, so I played games with him. . . .

Madeleine: So even when you were on holiday, you had this nurturing role, looking after someone.

Later, in one of our discussions after I had read the transcript, I picked up on this interchange.

Ardra: We talked about when I was a child, the summers we spent on the seashore, and you asked me what I did there, and so on. I mentioned my mother's friend['s son] who was in a wheelchair and your response was an interesting one.

Madeleine: I used the word "nurturing."

Ardra: Yes, you said, "So even when you are on holiday, you had this nurturing role, looking after someone." My response to that [upon reading the transcript] was "No, absolutely not. I never felt nurturing in any way." . . . The point of clarification, I think, is that this person [in the wheelchair] was an adult, not a little boy. . . . I did not explain that. It was not a nurturing kind of thing. . . . You mention [nurturing] later on, too, and I had the same response.

At another point in the same discussion I referred to another segment of the previous interview:

Madeleine: I get a strong sense of who you were as a child. It is very much the kind of person you are today. I don't know how you were in the midpart of [your life] but, as a child, duty was really ingrained into you—this feeling of responsibility and all of this nurturing—all of the characteristics of a good teacher. You are saying "I always wanted to be a teacher." It was self-fulfilling.

Ardra: Here is this nurturing business again.

Madeleine: I am confusing responsibility and nurturing.

Ardra: I think it is just a different use of words but . . . still, I don't characterize myself as a nurturing [person] . . . and I don't see teaching as a nurturing kind of profession, at least not in the mothering sense.

There were also several other instances where I had, and took advantage of, the opportunity to negotiate the interpretation of the life—mine—that we were reconstructing.

From a researcher's standpoint, I believe that sharing the responsibility for interpretation is important for the validity and integrity of the life history account. From the perspective of a participant, however, I was more concerned with my own peace of mind. After I read each transcript, it was essential for me to be able to respond to perceived inaccuracies and misrepresentations that became apparent.

And I did. I took seriously my authority over the text, striving to have aspects of my life represented as accurately as possible.

When I think back to the numerous times I provided research participants opportunities to clarify inaccuracies and misinterpretations I might have made during our conversations, I am puzzled by their general acceptance of the portrayals. Seldom do participants take issue with or attempt to clarify points or passages. Is this because they are completely satisfied with their representations or are they perhaps intimidated by the suggestion? Perhaps they are uncertain about how to proceed. In any case, the question remains: How do researchers appropriately encourage research participants to exercise their rightful authority over the [created] text?

Researching and Re-Searching

Life history (and other forms of personal) research demands that stories and chapters of a life be reopened, re-examined, and retold. In the process of reconstructing aspects of my life, in an attempt to make meaning of those experiences and their relation to my professional practice, I experienced moments of revelation, confusion, sorrow, and joy. Awarenesses and questions emerged, dilemmas and contradictions presented themselves, and unresolved issues reappeared. Consequently, the research activity extended the boundaries of our original research agreement and became personal in another way—it became part of my own quest for personal-professional understanding. The unanswered questions, the unresolved contradictions, and the dangling threads of conversation impelled me to know more, to broaden and deepen insights gained and meaning made through my work with Madeleine. Thus, despite the research with Madeleine being formally concluded, my personal journey continues. As I revisit those segments of my life that did not appear as public text, and strive to make stronger connections between who I was, am, and may be, I do so alone. The research is personal and private. How then, as a research participant and researcher of the self and the personal, do I respond to my own words written several years ago (1991, 193)?

In life history research, participants are encouraged to recall and [perhaps] confront past events, events that may not always be pleasing to remember. . . . Prior to engaging the participant, the researcher needs to consider the potential impact or consequences of the research on the participant and be prepared to see him or her through any unforeseen difficulties.

Because of the nature of our inquiry—life history—I knew, at the outset, that I would be replaying scenes from my distant and recent past as
well as adding script to both past and current actions and events. I was
aware of the critical incidents and influences in my life that I would be
revisiting, and I knew, more or less, what I was prepared to talk about
and what I was not. What kind of support, then, was reasonable to expect from Madeleine? She took the time and care, before we started, to
describe in detail what the research entailed, and she communicated
her sensitivity and responsiveness throughout the research process. I
felt supported while engaged in the research we undertook together. I
could not have expected any more. Her obligations to me do not extend
to any personal inquiry I choose to engage in as a spin-off from our
work.

My experience as a research participant leads me to ask: What is
the responsibility of the researcher? What are the expectations and
boundaries of the research relationship? While I abide by my moral
and ethical commitment to support research participants throughout
the research process, it may not always be possible to anticipate how,
by engaging in an inquiry, it might influence a participant. In some
cases, participants may not overtly express their responses to issues
and difficulties that may arise during the research. They may choose
instead to deal privately with any troubling or unresolved matters. In
cases like these (which I expect are fairly typical), the researcher may
be unaware of the participant's "private story." In such instances,
what kind of support is it reasonable to expect of a researcher?

There are cases in which the subject matter of the inquiry is particularly sensitive, thus increasing the likelihood of support needs
throughout the research and perhaps beyond. In studies where the
psychological, and perhaps physical risk, is obvious from the outset,
researchers must take special care to provide necessary support. For
the most part, though, perhaps the most important thing a researcher
can do to prepare participants for engaging in personal research is
provide sufficient information about the research process, at the outset and throughout the inquiry, that will enable participants to make
informed decisions about their participation. This, of course, assumes
that participants are engaged in the research as active associates, not
passive subjects, and that the research is undertaken as a collaborative enterprise.

Being reflexive in research means engaging in an ongoing process
of reflecting ideas and experiences back on oneself as an explicit acknowledgment of one's locatedness in the research. Being reflexive in
research also means heightening one's empathetic awareness. Re-

searchers engaged in personally intrusive forms of research have a special responsibility for sensitivity, care, and responsiveness. When researchers place themselves in the position of "the other" in a research endeavor, they can enhance their experiential understanding of what it means to be the researched. Such knowledge signifies the role of empathy in research practice.

CARE, SENSITIVITY, AND RESPECT

When we talk of care, sensitivity, and respect we are not talking about the theoretical; we are talking about the practical, the relational, and the very personal elements of a relationship between two human beings. We maintain that only theorizing about these or any element of the researching process has limited value. Rather, these are qualities that must be infused into the relationship.

Lawrence-Lightfoot, in her book *Respect: An Exploration* (1999, 9), focuses on "the way respect creates symmetry, empathy, and connection in all kinds of relationships." Through the stories of six individuals in different professional contexts, for whom respect is foundational to their way of being-in-relation, she explores the meaning of respect and what respect "looks like" in professional relationships. While the research-participant relationship is not explored in the book, it is exemplified. Between the lines of her stories of others is a story of the research relationship that made possible the passionate and rich renderings of the storytellers' lives. For Lawrence-Lightfoot, as for us, relationships imbued with "the life-enhancing glow of respect" (1999, 13) challenge conventional notions of power, knowledge, and control between participants and, when authentically developed, sustain and replicate themselves.

Researchers often talk about the importance of building rapport with participants in order to engage in the intrusive work of interviewing and/or observation. Seidman (1991), for example, maintains that the level of rapport needs to be carefully controlled so that the researcher and participant do not become too familiar, so that interviews do not become conversations, and so that meaning does not become distorted. According to Seidman, respect in a research relationship that is central to the research process amounts to expressions of common courtesies, such as holding doors and using appropriate salutations. Similarly, care and sensitivity are to be monitored. For example, he cautions researchers against allowing a research relationship to become so familiar that the participant might be moved to tears in the course of talking about a particularly troubling experience. If this happens, or if the researcher becomes upset, he suggests, "The best thing to do is nothing. Let the participant work out the distress without interfering or taking inappropriate responsibility for it" (1991, 82).

This is not what we mean when we talk about care, sensitivity, and respect. These qualities cannot be prescribed, strictly controlled, or intellectually applied; they must be authentically felt and lived. They emerge from engaging with self and other in mutually respectful ways. They reflect, perhaps always, the underlying self-applied principles that govern and guide a life. They are ethically imperative yet not ethically prescriptive. They are learned at a most fundamental level of human existence.

The principles discussed throughout this chapter are woven throughout many of the accounts in part 2. In addition to those already mentioned (chapters 8, 9, 10), Ardra Cole's (chapter 11) and Elizabeth Oates Schuster's (chapter 16) accounts also focus on issues of researchers' ethical and moral responsibility to research participants, particularly when participation in research may place participants at risk (in the case of Cole's research on the professoriat) or when participants are particularly vulnerable (as in Oates Schuster's research with nursing home residents).

3

Beginning a Life History Research Project

- *Beginning with yourself, understanding yourself as researcher*
- *Developing a life history project*
- *Role of literature*
- *Inviting participation*

Our views about being life history researchers rest on understandings about ourselves and others around us. One of our fundamental assumptions about researching—especially researching into the human condition and experience—is that such work must come from a deep professional and personal commitment. When such commitment is present the resulting scholarship will display a certain authority, with an obvious authenticity, and is likely to have moral, social, intellectual, and political roots that are grounded in personal and professional experiences. In effect we are claiming that all research of the kind we describe and advocate in this book—that is, work that is about the lived experiences of individual men and women, as well as children, understood in context—is work that both intersects with and emanates from our own experiences. In this way researching is an autobiographical act. To research is to reveal the autobiographical—the self or elements of the self.

As mature adults we all come to a formal inquiry project with a set of experiences, direct or vicarious, that have informed our actions about the focus, direction, tone, and emphasis of our work. Such influences are not subtle; they arise from a lifetime of "participant observation" and personal, formal, and informal learning. They arise from familial, educational, social, and work experiences. They arise, simply, from being human. There is nothing profound in this notion. We know it.

The theories that we individually hold are not happenstance. They develop from the meanings we have derived from ordered and casual experience and the theories of others that we hear and see articulated around the kitchen table; in school classrooms and hallways; through various media including newspapers, television, films, and radio; in university lecture halls and seminar rooms; through academic and literary books; in our everyday work experiences; and so on. Such theories as these that we come to hold as our own are, invariably, personal. We layer our theory building as we accumulate experience and knowledge. We have already argued against any notion of researching being an "objective" affair and, here, we iterate the position that it is an intensely personal endeavor. Try explaining how scholars can be motivated to pursue a line of inquiry over the course of a lifetime by omitting considerations of "the personal." We are yet to be convinced that there is one researcher out there who is not motivated by the personal. Even those scholars involved in topics of exploration that are, seemingly, divorced from the lives of people are propelled by the personal, be it in the financial rewards expected, the afforded status promised or imagined, the security given, the potential for power or political influence, or whatever.

In conventional forms of research personal motivations are often hidden behind cloaks or claims of objectivity or distance. Certainly, they are often camouflaged. Gary's experience of researching home education, for instance, which he has done since the early 1980s (when the practice of "home schooling" was still deemed grossly unpopular, even tarnished, by journalists and scholars alike), provides a number of examples of this. He has witnessed, for example, expressions of outright hostility toward parents and biases of ideology by so-called scholars whose claims were for objectivity and distance. These scholars simply held views that were in direct contrast to the parent-teachers whom they wanted to research; the researchers were out to prove a point. Some specific pronouncements about the home-school movement and its constituent members by scholars seeking researchable topics are indelibly imprinted in his mind. These scholars crafted questions that in the most blatant way contravened—even under the epistemological umbrella of the positivist orientation to which they were subscribing—accepted notions of scholarly distance and objectivity. If only these researchers, in their attempts to develop appropriate lines of inquiry, had simply acknowledged their biases and proceeded with the researching process, then appropriate judgments about the veracity of their work could have been made by readers and others, including the parents themselves, who were about to be researched. It is no wonder home-educating parents are now some of the most critical and reticent research participants. Too many of them have had negative experiences with researchers and, given their effective networking, many within the greater community of home educators are particularly savvy about the experiences of being "the researched" (see Kaseman and Kaseman 1990; Knowles 1992; Knowles and Muchmore 1995).

For us, as life history researchers, to claim objectivity, or to infer that we do not hold fast to particular personal theories about the human condition, is to act in bad faith with those whom we research. Such claims or inferences are neither morally responsible nor intellectually possible in work that delves into humans' lives. The professional is the personal. Researchers are first and foremost human. Does the obvious need stating?

To say that every person holds and expresses personal views about other human beings and the social order of things is also, perhaps, beyond the obvious. But we say it! We all hold personal, even intimate, perspectives and theories about the world around us and we play these out in our everyday actions. Why should the researching process be viewed any differently from typical, everyday encounters among people? A different standard of action is expected of researchers, especially university-based ones, by the public, a position that no doubt originates from the media-fed, natural science research model so commonly accepted as characterizing "good research." How can researchers as human beings put personal theories and their associated feelings behind, out of mind and action? They cannot. Besides, to claim "the professional is not the personal" (that is, assuming that research is a professional activity) is akin to insisting "the personal is not the political." Perhaps it is also like saying there is no connection between personal belief and political action. Or, by extension, it is like claims of research-based findings that there are no possibilities for political outcomes—be they intentional policy formation or substantial critique and discussion or abject rejection—when it comes to the work of researching human lives.

Research work can have profound social and political implications. As our moral responsibilities develop in our thinking, and as we progress in our careers, we find ourselves deeply expressing and considering, more than before, the moral dimensions and consequences of our work. In this regard, and because of the intimate relations typical of this work, life history researchers may be in a unique position to express morally bound action. Despite this possibility, however, for most human experience researchers their findings about the human condition are seldom and barely honored in the institutions of the state whose decision-making powers influence the well-being of society.

The influence of the bulk of scholarly research efforts rarely extends beyond the pages of arcane academic journals. We wish it were otherwise. A few reports make it to the media, fewer to legislative bodies; others make it to the shelves of bookstores; most wither and fade in academic libraries. Perhaps this state of affairs has come about because of the tendency in traditional scholarly work for researchers to disassociate from the messy dimensions of human life. As an example, when Ardra naively asked a researcher whether he was spending time observing in classrooms for his research on teacher effectiveness, he noted, in a somewhat patronizing tone, "Why would I introduce all that error variance? No, I'm running the 'Ss' here at the lab I've set up," meaning working with the teachers, not recording movements of rats in a box. It is also interesting to note that those who craft their researching activities for broad communication, and in widely accessible forms, are often thought of by their peers to have done suspect work.

To remove oneself from the messiness and complexities of lives is to become devoid of the erotica of life. We have puzzled about this. We want to shout from the rooftops encouragement for life history researchers to articulate clearly, within the definitions of their work, their humanness—the fundamental assumptions, experiences, and passions behind their inquiries—as an authentic way to engage in and represent the complexities of their findings. To do this is to honor oneself, those who are the focus of inquiries, and the journey or journeys taken. Such a position will not only engage readers (or viewers), but will also make clear the foundational underpinnings of the research.

In chapter 12 of part 2 in this book, Avi Rose presents an in-depth analysis of the role of the self in one's research. He articulates how he grappled with various dilemmas associated with researching a topic of an intensely personal nature (learning disabilities) and how such a personally relevant connection to the research enabled a level of access and understanding not otherwise possible.

BEGINNING WITH YOURSELF, UNDERSTANDING YOURSELF AS RESEARCHER

We research who we are in the same way that everything else we do is an expression of who we are. As researchers we need to acknowledge that in order to be authentic in the research that we do. The way we research is a reflection of how we orient ourselves to the world—our epistemological and ontological assumptions. We need to understand those assumptions before we begin, and we need to use that self-awareness as a guide throughout the research process. This is another significant way in which reflexivity is central to the research process.

The values, beliefs, experiences, perspectives, and physical, social, and contextual characteristics that shape who we are, as well as the passions, commitments, and motivations that drive us, are all very much present when we assume and carry out our role as researcher. When we embark on a research journey we take a lot with us. And even if we think we can "pack lightly" and leave a substantial part of ourselves behind at home or at the office—our biases, social location, hunches, and so on—we cannot. What we can do, however, is know the contents of the baggage we carry and how it is likely to accompany us on the research journey from beginning to end.

Personal History Research Accounts

One way to unpack our researcher baggage (to carry the metaphor a bit further) is to write what we call a personal history account in which we examine the path taken to a research project. Recall from our definition in chapter 1 that a personal history is an account of a segment of one's life written for purposes of understanding oneself in relation to a broader context. For purposes of understanding oneself as researcher, a personal history account might focus, for example, on segments of one's life that relate to informal and formal inquiry experiences inside or outside formal education settings, and experiences related to the origins of an interest in the topic or area chosen to research. The more detailed the account, the better it will help us gain insights into ourselves as researchers. On another level, the more time spent on writing a research (or intellectual) "history" the more comfortable we will become with writing in this way. This is important because, throughout the research process, a reflexivity journal, or accounting of the researching process, will keep self-awareness heightened.

In a chapter we wrote a few years ago, on the role of life history research in the self-study of teacher education practices (Cole and Knowles 1995), Gary illustrates the personal history research account with his own example. We reproduce excerpts from this writing to give a sense of what we mean by a personal history research account. Other such published accounts are *Knowing Her Place: Research Literacies and Feminist Occasions* (Neilsen 1998) and *From Positivism to Interpretivism and Beyond* (Heshusius and Ballard 1996).

Gary's Personal History Research Account

The journey to my present profession and location began in New Zealand where I grew up. As a young architecture professional I was asked to help design a new school. The project architect was content to follow the design brief as negotiated by the school's administrators. I was alone in noting the absence, in the design brief, of teachers' and students' voices and the inattention to the intimate connections between pedagogy and design. Against the recommendations of project colleagues I immersed myself in the life of a school; I tried to uncover the essence of teaching and the crucial ingredients of empowering school design representative of progressive pedagogies. Thus began an excursion into places of learning. I cautiously explored lives in context. Without being able to name what I was doing, and as undeveloped as my activities were, I now recognize my work in the school as participant observation and life history exploration. . . .

Several years later, disillusioned with the prospects of autonomy in the field of architecture, I determined to become an educator. After graduating from a baccalaureate degree teacher preparation program at an Australian postsecondary institution, I became a classroom teacher and principal in public, quasi-public, and private schools in Australia, Aotearoa New Zealand, Fiji, Papua New Guinea, and other South Pacific islands, before moving to the United States of America (USA). In these various multicultural educational settings—from a small, suburban community school, to large urban single-sex schools, to a rural, alternative, residential, self-supporting school—my teaching rested on principles of experiential learning and notions about the value of alternative education and pedagogies. The work of Goodman (1964), Illich (1970), and Holt (1969, 1976), for example, influenced my thinking because they too challenged the status quo in schools. More powerful for its lasting impact was the work of my compatriot, Sylvia Ashton-Warner. Her autobiographical account, *Teacher* (1963), presented her pedagogy in the context of her life and the lives of her students, experiences of teaching Maori children to read and write. Cognizant of the considerable inconsistencies and incongruities some observers have associated with Ashton-Warner's life and teaching (see Hood 1988, 1990) I, nevertheless, found a level of authenticity not often found in teaching texts. Yet, like many teachers, my practices were grounded in personal experiences and I lacked a philosophical framework to locate those practices. At this time, as a mentor to prospective teachers working in my classrooms and schools, I first thought of myself as a teacher educator. . . .

Early in my university work I became heavily involved as a preservice teacher educator and found that my pedagogical perspectives, while valued, were embedded in vastly different life experiences than those of my colleagues. My orientations, while compatible with some of the faculty, were nevertheless grounded quite differently. Looking to make sense of my pedagogical perspectives I came upon the notion that autobiographical writing might facilitate the exploration of my prior experiences in the context of present practices. . . .

While the interest in both my own pedagogy and the pedagogies of parent-educators was growing exponentially, I suffered from serious intellectual dissonance. Unable or unwilling—I am not quite sure—I did not reach into the recesses of prior experiences and revive the essence of the informal research activities in which I had participated—I regarded them as atheoretical. Nor did I question the foundations on which traditional educational research was grounded. In a sense I was paralyzed by the power of subtle and obvious suggestion, and socialization pressures, to accept and learn to understand and employ positivistic, statistical research methods. During this intense time my being cried out at the dissonance. My thinking was in disarray. I continued to deny that the dissonance and intellectual conflict were anything other than my failure to master the intricacies of mathematical and statistical frames of reference. And these feelings came despite achieving high grades in coursework. Only after six advanced courses in statistics and survey research, and ultimately not feeling that these approaches vaguely felt like mine to employ, did I seriously consider that there were other frames, other lenses, to view the world of teaching and classrooms.

The turning point in my thinking came from reading survey research associated with home education. Not only was most of the research poorly conceptualized, but there was also dissonance between the results and methods reported, and my own, much earlier, experiences in architecture and with anthropologists. Further, there was a level at which I found myself questioning the basis of the method and the value of the statistical devices. Perhaps it was simply because, for the first time, I read research reports that purported to examine something about which I could claim direct involvement and knowledge. All the other positivistic educational and sociological research I had read was beyond the realm of my experience and I was, at that time, intellectually unprepared to refute it.

Subsequent to my initial work with parent-teachers, I located my developing understandings about the place of exploring lives in context within the principles of symbolic interactionism (Blumer 1969). Life history theorists and researchers such as Plummer (1983), Bertaux (1981), and Denzin (1984) were influential because they philosophically and practically grounded the method. This newfound knowledge opened my eyes further to the possibilities of researching. Further, Goodson (1981, 1983) and Ball and Goodson

(1985) showed the utility of life history research for understanding teachers' lives within historical, political, institutional, and social milieu. (Cole and Knowles 1995, 132–135).

The more we understand ourselves as researchers, the better able we are to listen to and understand others. If we make explicit our own understandings, and know ourselves well enough, we are better able to understand what might be getting in the way of us listening to and understanding participants' experiences. Behar, in her book *Translated Woman: Crossing the Border with Esperanza's Story* (1993, 273), provides an illuminating example of the relationship between self-understanding and the understanding of another, and of the relationship between a researcher's history and locatedness and that of the "researched":

> Here, in this last section of reflections, I hold up a number of mirrors to my comadre's story, mirrors large and small, that are as revealing of me as they are of her. And at the end of the book, I emerge from the shadow of the biography to make a fuller connection back to my own life story from Esperanza's story, translating myself to dig down into the tangled roots of how I attained the authority to be the one inscribing my comadre's historia in this book.

Another role of the personal history research account is to gauge, perhaps increase, the power of our curiosities about an area of research interest. As researchers we have to be passionate about what we do; research questions have to come out of our own curiosities, our own passion to know; otherwise, we will not be sustained. We have to follow who we are and continually challenge ourselves. That is what keeps us coming back to our research. We all have to do that. We can be true only to the participants with whom we work and to the inquiries in which we engage if we are passionate about it, if our research is very much linked with our own interests, our own curiosities. And, when we are morally charged to do the work, that passion and commitment is likely to be infused in the written text and other representations of experience.

To conclude this subsection we offer a brief account written by Gary about the pathway he took to become involved in researching the lives of home-educating parents. (Other elements of the "story" are found in chapter 8. This is not intended as a repetition but, rather, a complementary account.) It extends his personal history account already offered. It illustrates the role of prior experience in a particular line of scholarship and how he followed his natural curiosities to find the topic. In a sense, the topic found him. It was a topic begging to be researched, given his background and a set of then-complex contemporary events. Gary recently wrote this account (a modification and extension of a 1992 article written for home-educating parents about the place and value of home education research; see Knowles 1992) as a way of introducing himself to some parent-teachers with whom he wanted to develop a research relationship.

Gary's Focus on Researching Lives of Home Educators

Since near the end of 1976 I have thought about home education from a variety of perspectives. Back then, I had just received an offer to be the principal of a remotely located, largely self-supporting, residential secondary school in the South Pacific. My skills in architecture and construction, along with my experience as a classroom teacher, would be holistically focused on this unique educative context. But there were no conveniently located schools for my two oldest children, then aged five and six, to attend. So, out of necessity, as we saw it then, we home-educated them. We believed then, as I still do, that the early years of a child's education were uniquely formative and that there were advantages to children lingering in a nurturing and richly educative home environment. So, the children were taught at home and experienced the full array of activities and learning environments possible in the unique community. Some time later I moved on from that school and the children were placed in formal schools, where they remained for the duration of their school years. During this time of having sole responsibility for the children's learning we were acutely aware of the paucity of literature that might have raised questions about the educative process and provided guidance to our thinking. But we were both teachers!

Several years later I moved to North America. Home education was far from my agenda. My interest in home education, however, was again piqued in the early 1980s by the prolonged court proceedings of the Singer family in Utah; the wife of the deceased John Singer fought the state of Utah to maintain the right to educate her children at home. (This was the same family that, years later, was involved in a barricaded standoff with police and federal officials.) Falsely, I first imagined that many families who operated home schools in Utah were doing so, as in the Singer case, from extremist positions. I cannot recollect now the exact reasons for my initial thoughts about home education in North America but I think that they had to be shaped and fostered by the media.

John Singer was a fundamentalist Mormon, a polygamist. A few years earlier he had taken a second wife—a woman who happened to be married. The second wife's legal husband, not unexpectedly,

opposed the idea. John Singer had built a one-room schoolhouse
on his property to home-educate his children, and the Summit
School District initiated legal proceedings. For many reasons, not
the least being the financial implications, the school district was
opposed to the idea of the Singers teaching their children at home.
After a bizarre set of circumstances, including a bombing of a Mormon church building, John Singer was shot by sheriff's deputies on
a cold, snowy winter's day when he trudged down the road to collect the mail. Several years later, and then in court, his wife was
challenging the justice system and the decisions of the school
board.

The controversial court case generated a huge amount of media attention, most of it highly biased and condemning of the home-
educating process. At the same time there were a hundred or so families in Utah teaching their children at home. Most of the media's stories, on television or in the newspaper, seemed inauthentic to me in
that they were substantiated by much speculation and hearsay and
personal opinion. I felt disgusted with the shallowness of the stories
and the unwillingness of the authors to question the fundamental assumptions that drove their and the public's almost unilateral support
for public schooling. (As an aside, contemporary Utah has one of the
highest rates of support for public schools in the United States.) In an
attempt to understand more fully I tried to locate literature on home
education. It was, at that time, virtually nonexistent. So, from as
much a point of curiosity as a sense of moral responsibility, I became
acquainted with several home-educating families within the greater
Salt Lake City region. Most of these parents were associated with the
Utah Home Education Association, a responsive and relatively wel-
coming organization, and it became apparent to me that these parents took considerably more moderate positions about their home-
educating endeavors than I first envisaged. Certainly, they were
unlike the Singers.

Clearly, some of the parents had religious, conservative, ideological reasons for operating home schools; others sought to develop and
emphasize the pedagogical benefits for their children. On the continuum, it was this dichotomy in the parents' perspectives, and the frequent joining of the two somewhat opposing rationales in many
home-educating families, that further fueled my interest in researching home education. My orientation had been pedagogical, yet borne
out of necessity. It seemed to me, almost intuitively now that I look
back, that to understand the method and the process was to understand the parents.

Since 1983, then, I have devoted much of my career as a researcher and professor to understanding the motivations, rationales, and practices of home-educating parents. Why do parents take upon themselves the awesome responsibility of educating their children at home? How do they do it? What do they do? And what does all of this have to do with lives or experiences had over time?

My interest in home schools or home education is parallel to my interest in public and private schools, although my teaching practices and beliefs about education tend to be at the less structured and informal end of a continuum, between formal traditional schools and informal "progressive" schools. As a result of this dualism I have often been criticized by colleagues in public schools for my interest in alternative forms of education. Often they felt my practices and theories were distant from their viewpoints and concerns. They were.

In early 1982 I began to read from the meager literature on home education; almost all of it was anecdotal and journalistic in nature. I started to develop a historical analysis of the home-education movement. I also developed a critique (or analysis) of home education as a method and gained the confidence of some parents and entered their homes with the purpose of understanding more about their processes and practices. I was purposeful, also, in that I sought families of differing perspectives for the purpose of regularly visiting with them and learning from them.

My preparation for researching at this time was largely as an educational ethnographer—as a researcher who becomes immersed in a "culture" (home schools) and rubs shoulders with the "natives" (parents and children) in efforts to understand their customs and practices. Using this approach I went about collecting information (mainly through field notes of observations and interviews) while being both an observer and a participant in the parents' and children's teaching and learning activities. When I did not understand what was going on, I asked questions. Often, when I had many unanswered questions, I informally interviewed the parent-teachers. I also collected other information in the form of documents produced by the home-educated students or parent-teachers.

By the beginning of 1987, I had extensive ethnographic information on the teaching and learning activities of parents and students in these various home schools. Based on my many conversations with parents, I felt that their reasons for taking on the awesome responsibility for educating their children were often more deep-seated than they at first suggested. Other researchers, such as Gustavsen (1981) in his groundbreaking yet highly traditional survey (it was the first published piece of home education dissertation research), failed to uncover these deep-seated rationales simply because they did not ask questions that might have revealed them. They did not, for instance, ask the kinds of questions important for understanding the influence of prior experiences.

In response to this line of thinking about home school rationales, I devised a series of "reflection topics" that parents could either write or talk to me about. The reflection topics were essentially questions about historical incidents in the lives of the parents; questions about being in families, about being in schools, and generally about growing up. This direction was sparked by my new-found understandings of life history research coupled with my own new, reflexive understandings of the relevance of my unique geographical and experiential understandings of learning and teaching to my own pedagogical practices. From the parents' responses, and from further conversations, I developed life history accounts (unfortunately not with the degree of sensitivity with which I might now complete this task), from which it became clear that many parents had painful childhood memories of family and school. These, indeed, were deep-seated reasons for home educating and preventing the replication of the same kinds of negative experiences in their children, powerful motivations for operating home schools. (I also asked similar questions of new public school teachers, hoping to find explanations as to why teacher education programs do not have the powerful effect on preservice teachers that teacher educators desire. Sure enough, beginning teachers had profound early experiences of schools and classrooms through which they viewed their introductions to formal theories of learning and of teaching in the university, and through which they subsequently assessed the worth of those theories for classroom practice.)

These were the formative experiences that, eventually, shaped a researching agenda that spanned into another decade and beyond. Gary followed his nose as it were, and allowed experiences and circumstances to shape a line of scholarship. Given that, as a large networking group, home-educating parents have been overresearched by survey researchers in particular, and have generally become very savvy about issues of researching, he used this account as a way to begin a relationship with families who did not know him. Home educators are mindful of the tendency of researchers to "steal" data and not return again. Over the course of working with them in a number of locations across North America, he heard many negative stories of researching work and its value for home educators, and it was from this perspective that he wanted to state his own orientation and intentions.

DEVELOPING A LIFE HISTORY PROJECT

The development of a sound life history research project is likely to arise from a combination of intentional, rational, and intuitive thinking and action coupled with unplanned, fortuitous experiences such as those that are serendipitous. Understanding the place of experience in relation to the research focus and articulating a personal connection with the topic are important beginnings in developing a life history research project.

The Role of Serendipity

Life is full of serendipitous moments and opportunities. So, too, is the life history researching enterprise.

To develop inquiry processes for life history studies we draw on the full range of our own experiences. To engage the life history method is not to rely on set, predetermined processes. Rather, each inquiry project is crafted in an organic manner given the full circumstance of the focus and challenge of the work. Such researching requires inspiration and ongoing responsiveness while still resting on the basic principle of connecting a life to its many contextual elements or conditions.

We take inspiration for our researching endeavors from wherever we find it. The world of artmaking and display is one such place. We often frequent galleries for that purpose. Several years ago Gary had a serendipitous moment that threw light on possible researching processes. It could even be described as an epiphany in his researching career. It occurred in an art gallery at Carleton University in Ottawa, Ontario, Canada, where he came across the photographic and installation work of Marlene Creates. Her photograph-based artistry has become a central inspiration to some of his inquiries (see Gary Knowles's and Suzanne Thomas's account, in chapter 17 of this volume, for an elaboration).

Stepping into the metered light and gauged climate of the gallery from the humid summer heat Gary found a life-historylike exhibit by the well-known Newfoundland and Canadian photographer. There, in her one-person, multi-installation, retrospective exhibit, titled *Marlene Creates: Landworks 1979–1991*, Gary was both intrigued and motivated by the resonance he felt with her art. Most of Creates's work portrays notions of space and place, and humans' impressions and responses. Two installations within the larger exhibit clearly expressed her method of artistic inquiry. One, about mapping memory ("The Distance between Two Points Is Measured in Memories"), explored "the relationship between human experience and the landscape and, in particular, the ways in which landscape is richly and profoundly differentiated into 'places'" (Creates, quoted in Garvey 1993, 20). She was primarily interested in how people remember place and she used black-and-white photography, personal narratives, and graphite map drawings on paper with artifacts/found objects to articulate her artistic findings about individuals' memories of the landscape.

The second, related installation within the show was called "Places of Presence: Newfoundland Kin and Ancestral Land, Newfoundland, 1989–1991." It was also multiframed and consisted of photographs, hand-written narratives, and graphic, hand-drawn memory maps, along with found objects as artifacts. It also represented, in Gary's gallery-going frame of mind, a unique articulation of the life history method. He recognized it instantly. Creates (in Garvey 1993, 30) describes her work:

> This series focuses on a set of hand-drawn memory maps and spoken texts in which my relatives in Newfoundland express memories about themselves and the land on which they were born. . . . The series concentrates on three precise bits of "landscape": the places where my grandmother, my grandfather, and my great-grandmother were born.
>
> These narratives and memory maps are accompanied by photographs of my relatives and of the landmarks I was directed to in their stories. I took the photographs of the places to rhyme with the memory maps they drew for me. The series also includes my own memory maps and stories of my experiences as a visitor to my ancestors' land. I also collected natural "souvenirs" there, including stones, leaves, and seaweed.

Several years earlier Gary had come to a point where he desired to express his artistic self within the dreary halls of the academy. Besides, and perhaps more important, he felt a need for "the artistic" in scholarly production (especially scholarly reports) and had been working toward infusing arts-informed perspectives into his researching endeavors (first expressed publicly in Finley and Knowles, 1995). While the parallels between academic researching and artistic inquiry were obvious to him, he had not made the personal connection in anything but superficial ways and had not applied the skills associated with his visual artistry to life history researching. He knew, however, that Creates-like processes and representational modes provided a multidimensional framework for life history work in a way that could infuse interest and give additional life to the outcomes of his university-based scholarly efforts.

Obviously Creates had family roots in the one-time remote island colony of Britain but subsequently had become disconnected from them. As an adult and emerging artist she had returned to Newfoundland from Ontario and Quebec and, almost immediately, began searching out elderly relatives, many of whom lived in remote, coastal communities. She visited them. There she captured, in stark black-and-white photographs, the raw feelings and persona of her distant relatives in their homes and of their "special" exterior places. She worked toward obtaining information, or data, about their individual sense-of-place. She created images of and stories from these elderly people and of the barren and bleak landscapes surrounding the places in which they lived. Encouraging them to use pen (or pencil) and paper, she "captured" their words and sketch maps that recounted their individual sense-of-place within their communities and the natural world. These narrative "data" were written accounts or narrated passages/stories. The drawings of "the place"—best described, perhaps, as crosses between cognitive memory maps, sketches, and geographical maps—were unique graphic depictions of place often completed in the trembling handwriting of these elderly relatives. Her photographs portray a moment of her relatives' lives within their dwelling places, and present images of their most treasured nearby place. Her installations often included found objects that typified some of her intuitive responses to the place and her relatives.

The complexities, yet also the simplicities, of Creates's life history-based, visual stories were obvious. She showed the personal strengths and attachments of her female and male relatives, men and women whose strengths were found in-place and in-community. And she revealed her own sense of their places—her responses to their contexts. Her work reinforced Gary's intuitive feelings about the limitations of traditional, oral, and text-based life history work. But Creates's work was far more than mere illustrations or representations; it offered insights into the creative artmaking inquiry process as well as challenges to traditional modes of representation.

Several questions and answers propelled his thinking about the value of Creates's work for his own. What had she told about these Newfoundlanders that a life history researcher going to the very same families and communities might *not* have told? Her relationships had an implied intimacy; after all, she was flesh and blood kin. Even so, she was unknown to these men and women. In most cases this was her first meeting with these relatives. Her method was so transparent. Why (or how) was her telling the same as her process? The qualities of emotive response by viewers of the art were, at least on the occasion of his visit to the gallery, visible to Gary. Viewers understood about the concept of place and attachment to it. They understood the passions of the elderly people. How did her work challenge the assumptions of viewers? What was it that imbued her authority on the subject matter into her work? How did viewers know that? In what way was her process analogous to life history research? Key components of life history inquiry were visibly present:

- Exploration of a life through recounting memories of experiences and the meanings attributed to them

- Evidence of substantial effort over time given to obtaining the stories of a life
- Contextualization of a life lived
- Representation of a life that honored the individual, celebrating life, yet raising to consciousness important understandings about the value of the life and its relation to larger questions of society

Serendipity: present in Gary's viewing of Creates's work and important in developing a life history inquiry.

We include this example to help make the point that the qualities of life history research that we have described so far carry over to the process of developing—conceptualizing and planning—a life history inquiry. The process is fluid and dynamic, heartfelt, principled, and intellectually driven. It is not an implementation of a set of predefined processes or an application of a "formula," nor is it a utilization of a template. Far more important than adherence to a particular convention is the authenticity of the work. In chapter 13 of part 2, Jim Muchmore writes about the role that serendipity played in his self-identification as a life history researcher.

By authenticity we mean qualities that are natural, genuine, and sincere. In other words, the project design needs to reflect our intellectual, creative, moral, and heartfelt passions and commitments, and it needs to do so in a way that makes sense (that is, naturally, genuinely, and sincerely). We need to strive for internal consistency and coherence, a kind of holism in which these variously rooted passions and commitments work together in synergy. If we operate on the principle of authenticity we cannot follow a recipe or prescription. In saying this we are not suggesting a laissez-faire approach to the conceptualizing and planning of a research project; on the contrary, what we are advocating requires a lot of effort, thought, imagination, self-awareness, and disciplinary knowledge.

In most books on qualitative research methodology the topic of research design is typically addressed through the component parts: defining a topic or focus; providing a rationale for the study; situating the proposed study in a literature context; defining a theoretical framework; and, explaining and describing the methodology, including how information will be gathered, analyzed, and reported upon. While we acknowledge that attention to each of these elements is important (although not necessarily in the order and level of detail usually suggested), more important for us is attention to the authenticity of the project "design" and how consistently and coherently it reflects a set of guiding values and assumptions that, in life history research, relate to understanding lives in context.

The what, why, how, who, where, and when questions that typically structure one's thinking about research design are significant; however, we maintain that it is the articulation of and adherence to a set of foundational principles, on which these questions can rest and be supported, that imbues the work with an authentic quality. Take away the supporting structure and the questions (and their answers) can easily tumble into a methodological abyss.

In short, developing a life history research project involves an authentic commitment to one's curiosities, the epistemological underpinnings and possibilities of life history methodology, the people and life contexts to be explored, and the professional communities and contexts within which one is situated.

THE ROLE OF LITERATURE

In conventional research models "the literature," as it is commonly and definitively called, has a well-defined role and place in the research process. The literature usually means published theories and research reports in a defined area of study—for example, in the area of social movements or emotional development or organizational culture or professional socialization and development. A thorough review and analysis of this very particular (and focused), pertinent literature is usually seen as the first step toward defining and framing a research project. The idea is to review (critique, examine, and compare) what has been done; find a flaw or hole in the knowledge base that needs to be filled (or locate an interesting dilemma or quirk in results/findings/processes described); generate an hypothesis or pose a research problem based on the discovered knowledge gap or weakness; and identify a theoretical or conceptual framework for the study based on the literature. Then the task is to proceed from the literature review to gather and analyze data showing, in the end, how this new research refutes or confirms existing theory or otherwise contributes to the literature. Not surprisingly, we are suggesting a more expansive and fluid role for the literature in researching and one that is infused throughout the research process.

We also have a more broadly defined characterization of the literature. We see literature that informs research as that scholarship that defines the general area or focus of our specific inquiry work. We liken the difference to a comparison between the terms "reference list" and "bibliography." In most conventions of scholarship a reference list cites sources that are explicitly used in a research text while a bibliography more generally lists writings that may have informed the work but that have not necessarily been cited verbatim or peripherally in the text itself. The former notes the exact sources, the latter acknowledges the more general influences. The bibliography is usually far more ranging in scope and traces, by its very nature, a kind of intellectual journey.

We also see the literature as that which more generally informs our perspectives and understanding of the contexts surrounding our work. It includes professional literature, perhaps pertaining to the area of study, perhaps that documenting the context-driven, experiential basis for our work. (Here we do not want to confuse such professional literature with artifacts or documents we may gather during the researching process. The former is likely associated with professional development or other professional issues while the latter may represent the day-to-day organizational decisions. For example, such organizational artifacts might include memos, policy statements, reports, and the like; these are "data.") When we are exploring a specific element of social workers' lives and work, for instance, one of the important kinds of literature to examine may be professional publications related to the field of social work practice and the particular aspect of the profession under study. This literature is likely to provide a different kind of information than more formal, academic scholarship based on research studies.

The perspectives brought forward in the various forms of mass media may also be important in the formation of a researching agenda and focus. Journalistic accounts of a phenomenon can be as much a part of the literature as formal scholarship. In the case of Gary's exploration of home education and the parents who engaged in it, and in the absence of anything but a very limited amount of questionable scholarship, the debates entered into by newspaper journalists, in particular, ended up being at the forefront of his decision making. Indeed, as these perspectives mirrored the understandings of a community and a society, they were essential. They helped frame the questions that drove his initial work.

Given the exponential increase in accessible knowledge—or in knowledge production and its publication or communication—the conventional view that a researcher must first complete an exhaustive search and examination of the literature is unnecessarily demanding. This may be especially so when there are very large bodies of literature to consider. Researchers are forced by circumstances to be selective. In a general sense, to set out to explore the sum total of scholarship done on any given topic is ludicrous. This is especially so if such an exhaustive review is expected before the researching process begins. There may indeed be specialized areas of study, ones ripe for researching, for which there is very little pertinent scholarship or intellectual texts that might inform a researching process and focus. On the other hand, the world is awash in published scholarship. In the field of education, for example, the number of conventional print and paperbound research and professional journals reaches well beyond the two thousand mark, and the Internet makes possible access to many more electronic publications. This is also true in the fields of social work and health care. In the social science disciplines the possibilities for publication and location of scholarship are numerous. There is, seemingly, no end to the sources and databases from which one can find scholarly literature.

Despite innovations in technology, there are practical limits to the size and direction of the net cast when accessing informed perspectives. The ways to judge the potential value and practicality of accessing a scholarship source are numerous, some resting in the practical and some in the theoretical. The following questions hint at some of the ways to respond to the tasks of accessing, reviewing, and incorporating literature into researching work. The potential variety of responses to these questions underscores the complexities of making decisions about the contribution of literature to the beginnings of inquiry work and, later, its more specific place within reports of researching.

- What are the epistemological assumptions of the researcher and how do they mesh with mine? How do they inform? How do they contradict?
- What is the relationship of the researcher to the participants and how are those relationships founded, communicated, and valued?
- What are the underlying (ideological, political, social) agendas of the researcher and the broader perspective articulated? Are the fundamental goals of the scholarship at cross-purposes with the potential work planned? How was the research funded, and by whom, and how does the research express or not express the perspectives of the funder? What are the affiliations of the author?
- How do the political and/or moral perspectives and goals of the researcher fit with the orientations of scholars whose work appears connected?
- What do the limitations of a researcher's resources of time, energy, and cost have on the scope and thoroughness of the literature that can be accessed and reviewed? How do library holdings or services (or similar) limitations fit into the scheme of things?
- Is there a scope of published literature (either very narrow or quite broad) that may not serve a researcher's need very well? Is a researcher being constrained in creativity or in understanding by the literature accessed? Is the literature accessed of an interdisciplinary nature or is it confined to a very narrow subject area (or areas)?

Thus far we have not said much about the role of literature that informs inquiry processes. The literature also includes sources pertaining to process—epistemology, framework, and method. Scholarship that documents researching processes, in this case life history work, is found in specific life history methods texts such as this one, more general texts on qualitative research, reports of life history research as in refereed articles and books, as well as more general popular press articles and trade books. Fuller articulations of method, often found in book-length reports, theses, and dissertations, are often helpful. We often find, however, that while the processes and topics of study in life history theses or dissertations may be helpful, their representations are quite conservative (such are, perhaps, the influences of "gate keeping" dissertation committee members and examiners), even though we know of many fine exceptions. Ultimately, however, notions about method and the concepts underlying life history processes are personally developed. The utility of "process scholarship" is that it opens many possibilities for researching. Such scholarship should not be sought so as to provide a research "template." It should merely inform.

If our work is intentionally cross-disciplinary, or seeks to challenge the status quo of knowledge production, or is intentionally multilayered in the representation of lives, literary or artistic literature may be important to access. Recall the role of serendipity we described earlier. Serendipity also has a place in figuring out literature. We never know when we might come across a piece of writing that, either in form or substance, might provide the intellectual or creative spark necessary to move research ideas forward. We need to be ever open to surprise and possibility from any direction or source, scholarly or not. (James Muchmore's contribution in chapter 13 provides another example of this notion.)

Scholarly and professional literature has an important role to play throughout the researching process, not only at the beginning, as is the case with most conventional research approaches. It is not uncommon for emerging researchers, before beginning any fieldwork, to conduct extensive literature reviews from which they delineate and critique previously published scholarship in very narrowly defined areas and lay out a theoretical framework for their study, only to discover that insights and learnings emerging from working with research participants do not "fit" or are only tangentially related to the areas of scholarship and theories previously defined.

Qualitative research approaches in general are based on a principle of emergent design. It is not possible to anticipate how the research process will unfold, because of the unpredictability and messiness of research into the human condition. Therefore, it is not possible to know in advance the kind of theorizing that will eventuate or the bodies of literature that will inform that theorizing, that is, if the researcher embraces the indeterminate nature of the research journey. Qualitative research is more like the flight of a butterfly than a bee: its path is meandering and indeterminate. It is not possible to predict at the outset where the inquiry process will lead as it seldom goes directly back to the places set out in an initial review of literature.

Much is possible when working within the life history perspective. The role of previously published scholarship has two main functions: to guide and to inform the focus of the work, and to provide support and inspiration for processes used. The latter purpose—and the resulting articulation of process—may be crucial when a researcher is working in a context where colleagues are unfamiliar with this kind of responsive and reciprocal researching or in one that is chilly to qualitative research in general. We do not advocate apologetic stances for the use of life history or qualitative researching approaches. We simply advocate moving forward with the best possible array of processes and conceptual understandings that will help resolve the issues or questions posed in the researching focus.

INVITING PARTICIPATION

As with every other element of the qualitative research process there is a range of perspectives on issues associated with participant selection, invitation, and involvement. Decisions in this regard are not haphazard; they are rooted in the principles and assumptions guiding the particular approach to researching. As life history researchers guided by principles of relationality, mutuality, empathy, care, sensitivity, respect, and authenticity, *how* we invite participation, *whom* we invite, and *how many*, will naturally reflect these principles. Similarly, if we accept the subjective and intersubjective nature of human experience and meaning-making, the dynamic, multidimensional, and contextual nature of knowledge, and the related unpredictability of the human condition, then concerns about "sample size" and representativeness, purity of "truths" told, and generalizability of research findings to populations of people become nonissues.

Our goal, then, is to locate a small number of individuals who will make a commitment to working with us over a period of at least several months for the purposes of gaining in-depth insights into an area of mutual interest. On occasion, participation might linger for far longer periods or be intentionally spread over several years, as Behar (1993) did when she worked with Esperanza in Mexico, and this requires a different quality of commitment. In our efforts to seek commitment from individuals it might mean inviting the participation of individuals who are well known to us; other times potential participants might be recommended to us by someone who understands the central elements of our project and perspective. In some cases we might happen upon individuals who, in the course of conversation, learn about and express an interest in our research (there's that serendipity again!), and, in other cases we might start from scratch to locate potential participants who are completely unknown to us. Starting from scratch may mean following a well-thought-out plan or it may mean relying on our intuitions, or something incorporating both processes.

The topic of participant selection is controversial. Many qualitative researchers would strongly disagree with most of what we have just said about ways of identifying potential participants or, at least, they would describe the process in more formal ways. For example, Patton (1990) and Goetz and LeCompte (1984) have developed extensive typologies of "sampling strategies" for qualitative research based on what they, respectively, call "purposeful sampling" and "criterion-based sampling." Basically, the idea behind these selection procedures is to locate individuals or sites from whom or which researchers are likely to learn most about their topic of inquiry. While we do not disagree with this commonsensical notion, we object to how this premise gets translated and the assumptions upon which such translations are based.

Take the word "sampling," for instance. The term is a holdover from positivism and statistically based studies that draw on random, representative samples of populations to draw generalizable conclusions—purposes and assumptions that are antithetical to qualitative research. Now, consider some of the terms used to describe the various selection procedures: "extreme- or deviant-case sampling"; "typical-case sampling"; "maximum variation sampling"; "snowball, chain, or network sampling"; "convenience sampling" (Patton 1990); "unique-case sampling"; "reputational-case sampling"; "ideal-typical-bellwether-case sampling"; and "comparable-case sampling" (Goetz and LeCompte 1984). Why are these highly technical and scientific labels used?

Let us look more closely at how a few of these strategies are described. Unique-case sampling is based on, not unexpectedly, the identification of "unique or rare attributes inherent in a population" (Goetz and LeCompte 1984, 82). In ideal-typical-bellwether-case sampling, "the researcher develops a profile of an instance that would be the best, most efficient, most effective, or most desirable of some population, and then finds a real-world case that most closely matches the profile." In network, chain, or snowball sampling, "each successive participant is named by a preceding group or individual" (Goetz and LeCompte, 79). Why, we wonder, is it necessary to dress up commonsense ideas in scientific garb? Is it because of a reluctance to let go of positivist ideals? Is it a reflection of a need for academics to elevate their work above the everyday—what Schön (1987), in his critique of the technical rationality paradigm that drives the world of academe, would call staying on the "high ground of theory" and out of the "swamp" of practice? We do not wish to perpetuate the scientization of research into the human condition. We urge the production of sound scholarship that is accessible above all else. Given that language is such a powerful conveyor of tradition, it is important to make thoughtful choices of research language.

Finally, it is also interesting to note that Patton (1990) considers "snowball, chain, or network sampling" and "convenience sampling" as the least preferable strategies—a kind of last resort. He describes convenience sampling as having "low credibility" and "inappropriate for anything other than 'practice.'" We now return to our suggestions for inviting participation where generalizations of findings to populations is not our goal, notions of population samples and sampling are not in our vocabulary, and commonsense prevails.

Given the research focus, what kind of consideration needs to be given to participant characteristics? To what extent is it important to take into account socioeconomic, sociopolitical, or demographic factors? How important is it to aim for diversity among participants? (How is "diversity" defined?) Then there are related considerations born out of the focus of our work and our own situation. How many participants is enough or optimum or manageable? Are there constraints of time and other resources? Is there a constraining time frame based on external conditions such as a window of opportunity or a particular life, family, community, or societal event? These are some of the questions to consider when making decisions about participant involvement. There are no pat answers to any of these questions. Like every other part of the research process, decisions about participant selection are more meaningfully informed by common sense, good judgment, and intuition, not to mention reflexivity, than by predetermined rules. Remember, in life history research we are opting for depth over breadth, and the aim in participant selection is not population representativeness. It is good to keep this in mind when making commitments to oneself and to others about who and how many participants to involve. It is much more important to work thoroughly, meaningfully, and authentically with one participant than to end up with very partial and sketchy understandings based on work with several or many. As the old saying goes, "a half-done job is not worth doing."

There are many ways to invite participation in a researching endeavor. Finding these participants, or the "right" ones (according to our essential considerations or characteristics), though, may be difficult. The personal historylike account written by Gary, who was seeking entry to the home-education community, illustrates one way we have used to locate participants. Writing popular press articles of relevance to a desired group of people is another possibility for initiating interest from potential participants. (Our work as life history researchers, also, ought to be written for audiences other than just academics. This may be especially so if our researching is driven by moral concerns.) Personal contacts offer satisfying means of extending the researching partnership.

Another approach Gary used to invite participants to engage in further in-depth exploration was through what he called reflection topics (Knowles, 1991b, 1992). Some parent-teachers he had met previously were keen to be involved in further research and to examine their lives reflexively. He invited them to consider these topics and to write about them on their own. There were several categories of questions or issues to write about. Under the heading of, for example, "past experiences and events," with a subheading of "school and childhood experiences," he asked parents to "[D]escribe memories, both good, bad, and otherwise, that you have of . . . school experiences." Under the heading of "present practices" he requested, "Explain your philosophy of education. In other words, what are some of your important beliefs: about education . . . teaching . . . how children learn . . . what your home school can provide. . . ." The issues raised in the reflection topics were extensive and the space here does not allow for their scope to be presented through examples. The topics ranged from those pertaining to past experiences to those grounded in the present. They touched on parents' experiences, beliefs, philosophies, and practices. The decision to use the reflection topics was in part made because of limited opportunities for face-to-face conversations—budget allocations were minuscule—and as a way to gauge participants' commitment while at the same time uncover compelling issues and experiences worthy of intense exploration. In a sense, it was part of the process for selecting parents for guided conversations. The reflection topics provided guidance for their writing and were, after the initial analysis, the basis for some of the later guided conversations.

Here we have mentioned many considerations and potential actions but, in the end, when we have developed a list of potential participants we have to make a start in the selection and invitation. We prefer to approach individuals directly (although we know that some will seek us out because they have heard about our work). We prefer not to be formal in this regard—relying on correspondence or research assistants who will not engage in the information gathering to make initial contact is not preferred. A phone call may initiate a face-to-face meeting or revive or rekindle a relationship from previous work or other contexts, and this is the starting point for decision making. It may be appropriate to advertise in newspapers or other kinds of directed, focused publications, and then establish ways for making decisions about whom to invite. The more quickly such action can become personable with potential participants, the better.

Just as we begin relations with other people in the course of our daily lives, so we begin relationships with research participants. For those whom we do not know we often engage in a discourse that seeks out commonalties and interests as much as distinguishes pertinent demographic features or experiences. We each locate or ground ourselves according to personal (as well as professional) markers or features or intentions. As at the beginning of any relationship, in the researching enterprise individuals engage in a kind of "coming to know" dance. Researchers need to find mutually meaningful ways to "come to know" research participants for whom the new relationship is as a blind date or an old acquaintanceship revived. Concerted effort is required.

Extensive debates and explorations of issues associated with researcher-participant relationships are found in literature on feminist research methodologies (see, for example, Herz 1997; Olesen 1994, 2000; Reinharz 1992). Above all, we acknowledge that the research relationship must be authentic. To fulfill this quality requires foundations of mutuality and common purpose, including trust, respect, acknowledgment of roles, appropriate experience for the task at hand, willingness to reveal, and time and energy to put into the activity. It requires that each party be committed to the task of relationship building necessary for the research. Whichever way we examine the participant-researcher relationship, it is the researcher who, ultimately, has the main burden of responsibility (with the exception of participatory action research processes, where the researching purposes come out of individuals' community defined, collective, and common experiences and motives). Along with energies to proceed with an inquiry is an obvious commitment to relationship building and mutuality of purpose.

If we make the assumption that we are about to begin exploring a subject matter or issue that has a defined focus and that represents or is connected to us as researchers in very "real" ways, then it is probably safe to say that we will carry our researching ideas around with us wherever we go. It is amazing how often our research interests happen to come up in casual conversation. Why not make such conversations a starting point for locating potential participants? Who knows where such conversations might lead?

Recall how Gary described his initial introduction to Thomas (see "Beginnings" chapter): they met as they traveled on the same ferry to the same small, remote island; they struck up a conversation precipitated by their obviously similar status as "outsiders" to the island; through the course of their initial and subsequent conversations, they discovered several points of commonality in experience and interest; they decided to collaborate on a life history study of Thomas' experience as a professor. As Gary put it, "He was at a crossroads. I had the time": the intersection of two people!

4

"Doing" Life History Research

- *Gathering information through guided conversations*
- *Exploring the "context"*
- *Collecting artifacts*
- *Ongoing reflexivity and responsiveness*

When we make a decision to research from a life history perspective we opt for depth over breadth. Our inquiry places us with a small number of individuals for an intensive exploration, rather than with a large number for more superficial engagement. Given the heavy investment of time and energy required for substantial life history work, it is generally not possible to involve tens or hundreds of people in information-gathering activities. Some researchers do, however, perhaps by working in teams, perhaps by spending a lifetime so doing, or perhaps by electing to "skim" lives rather than deeply inquire into them.

We encourage involvement with fewer rather than more participants. Examples of life history explorations of single lives are found in *Translated Woman: Crossing the Border with Esperanza's Story* (Behar 1993); *Nisa: The Life and Words of a !Kung Woman* (Shostak 1983); and *Mama Lola: A Vodou Priestess in Brooklyn* (Brown 1991). In each case the complexity of the life is rendered so fully that the richness and understanding of that one life in context leaves readers satisfied and not yearning for more "cases." These kinds of stories allow for many points of intersection between the reader and the life portrayed. It is important to keep this notion in mind as we work in unison with research participants.

Our task with each participant is to try to get as close as possible to apprehending, understanding, and rendering elements of a life as it is influenced by and intersects with pervasive and subtle forces or influences of context. This is a considerable responsibility, but one that can be shared, to some extent, by research participants.

Given that it is the participants' lives being explored it makes sense that they might have some ideas of how to go about the exploration. In saying this, we are deliberately challenging notions of hierarchy and power that place researchers exclusively in charge of the information-gathering phase of researching (and, therefore, responsible for all decision making regarding process, especially, in the early phases). We are also continuing our attempt to demystify the research process, to treat it more like a commonplace endeavor of thoughtful, reflexive, and systematic action than a highly specialized, complex undertaking requiring particular knowledge and skills in "scientific" procedures. As far as we are concerned, there is no protocol, no neatly defined way of proceeding, no template, no cookbook for sound, innovative life history research.

We trust that the participant, knowing the general intentions of our scholarship and being comfortable with us and secure in the researching relationship, will comfortably reveal telling information. As we say this we hear critics calling loudly, "Bias . . . they will contaminate the findings . . . they will tell you only what you want to know. You'll not uncover . . ." We answer by reminding the critics of the quality of the relationship and its sustained nature, not to mention the value of reflexivity for uncovering deep-seated meanings of experiences, and the "utility" of working with people who are highly informed about the process and the intentions of the inquiry. We are, quite naturally, honoring the participants' intelligence and integrity. We are trusting them. (Our belief is that it is very difficult for participants to intentionally mislead. Eventually contradictions within stories appear and we have opportunities to question. But we don't go into relationships with this in mind. We look for the best in relationships.)

How do we begin information gathering and begin the conversations? How do we collect other kinds of information? How do we find out what we hope to come to know and remain open to surprises and turn of events? How do we know how to proceed? How do we uncover the significant, epiphanic events of a life? We have already developed a focus and beginning point to our actions. We have developed ideas about process and we have articulated our fundamental assumptions concerning our work. We know these things inside out but we remind ourselves of the need for flexibility. We have already located participants. Now we begin the conversations and relationship building.

GATHERING INFORMATION THROUGH GUIDED
CONVERSATION

When we speak of "guided conversations" we emphasize the conversation part of the term. As researchers we come into contact with participants in a number of ways. In chapter 3 we suggested some of the ways and some of them rest in knowledge of the participant before the fact. Familiarity with a participant before the "guided conversations" begin is, obviously, potentially helpful in striking up conversation about the focus of the work and the life. To speak of the inquiry as "work" is to acknowledge the energies expended by both the participant and the researcher; this requires, as we have urged, ongoing attention to the relational—the essential ingredient for the successful completion of guided conversations and the larger research project itself.

As researchers we also have an agenda that is the focus of the inquiry. Invariably the assumptions and conceptions behind the focus of the work have been played out numerous times in planning the inquiry; ideas have been articulated and rearticulated, refined and refined again. Then the focus remains with us, firmly situated within our minds. It is this element of preparation to gather information that provides the "guiding." Because the inquiry work is personally as well as professionally meaningful to us, the gathering of information becomes a conversation between "friends" rather than as an interview with a stranger.

When gathering information through guided conversations we work at not making our interactions and our side of the conversation so blatantly purposeful that mutuality and authentic engagement is lost. We need to be ever mindful that a healthy relationship is built on mutuality and commonality.

So, what distinguishes a guided conversation from other conversations? Not much. The guiding part of the conversation comes about because we do have a purpose and we usually have limited temporal and spatial resources. We intend to end the conversations at some point in the future, at least for research purposes. After all, there usually has to be an "end," if not for the information gathering, then for the research report—the book, article, thesis, or dissertation, or other representational form or summary for the participants or funding agency or other interested and invested parties.

One way to proceed includes generating areas to explore by clarifying purposes with the participants and helping them to see that the telling of stories about their lives is important. Often people downplay the value of telling about their lives; they imagine their lives to be mundane. From this point we might develop together a list of topics to discuss or we might use an already generated list—one developed as part of the conceptualization process or as part of an ethical review process.

In the teacher education professor study, described by Ardra earlier in the book and to which we will refer again later in this chapter, Ardra identified four main areas she wanted to explore: personal and career histories, early experiences of being a university faculty member, the university context, and issues associated with teacher education reform. In each of these areas she generated a few guiding questions or potential ways to explore the topic. For example, for the topic of personal and career history, she suggested the participants might develop a career history map or timeline and name significant events or pivotal points along the line. Some of the questions posed for conversation were: How/why did you decide to pursue graduate studies? Can you tell me about making the transition from your prior work context to the university? What was your family's response to your decision to become a professor of education? The questions were deliberately open-ended and based on the principle of "less is more" in the belief that broad, open questions that help frame an issue or event or circumstance, and allow wide latitude in responses, yield rich insights. Ardra shared the questions with the participants at the outset of their information gathering, and together they discussed the questions and suggested others. In some cases, participants decided to address more fully some of the topics on their own between research meetings.

Developing questions to frame a series of conversations is more difficult than it first appears. Questions need to be sufficiently broad to allow space to roam but not so broad or vague that the focus of the research is easily lost or participants are uncertain about how to respond. Wording is important; questions need to be as free as possible from suggestion so that the conversations are not led in a particular direction. Similarly, and obviously, they need to be phrased in a way that is likely to elicit extensive responses rather than simple "yes/no" answers.

In just about any book on qualitative research methodology, considerable attention is given to the development of interview guidelines or schedules; indeed, some (for example, Kvale 1996; Seidman 1991) define qualitative research *as* interviewing. While some authors (Bogdan and Biklen 1998; Glesne 1999; Seidman 1991) lay out a set of general guidelines or principles for developing interview questions, others (Kvale 1996; Maykut and Morehouse 1994; Merriam 1988; Patton 1990; Spradley 1979) present detailed and highly structured typologies or taxonomies specifying categories of questions to include in research interviews. Our preference is to develop questions based on a set of guiding principles. This approach is more consistent with our notion of research as a more natural than scientific process. The principles of reflexivity, relationality, mutuality, care, sensitivity, and respect guide the development of questions for conversation just as they guide all other aspects of life history inquiry. And common sense is a prevailing source of wisdom.

When developing questions to guide life history conversations, the most important thing to keep central is the focus or purpose of the research. The research conversations are intended to elicit information and insights related to the focus of inquiry. While this seems like an obvious point, it is easy to lose sight of the main purposes for information gathering. Generally, it is helpful to identify areas to cover that are subsumed under the main focus of the research (as illustrated above with reference to the teacher educator study). Then it is easier to develop a tentative guide for the research conversations. It has been our experience that the clearer we are about the focus of the research in general and the purposes of the conversations in particular (that is, the areas we want to be sure to explore), the easier and more natural the conversations are. Knowing, for example, that an important area to explore through conversation is the participant's career history leads naturally to some open-ended questions related to this part of her life. During, and perhaps following, conversation, clarifying questions and requests for elaboration in particular areas of experience or conduct naturally emerge.

The principle of mutuality is also important to honor when developing conversation guides. Chances are that, if the participants are clear about the focus of the research and the more specific purposes of conversation sessions, they will have suggestions about the kind of information they might contribute. One of our practices is to generate a tentative list of areas or topics to explore and to share it with the participants in advance or at the outset of a research conversation. Inevitably, the participants recognize their shared role in decision making and willingly and helpfully contribute to the development of conversation guides. This approach of identifying areas to explore through a few open-ended questions—which are mutually agreed upon as appropriate for and relevant to the research focus—also engenders a more informal and natural process, unlike that which is more likely to eventuate when a researcher begins a research conversation with a long list of highly structured questions and accompanying probes. This latter stance is also more likely to place control over the conversation with the researcher, a role that is antithetical to the principles we advocate.

One very helpful way to work through some issues associated with developing conversation guides is to arrange a mock conversation session with a friend, colleague, or even potential participant. Listening to a tape recording of this session is likely to reveal invaluable insights into the process of conversation facilitation—the tone established, the levels of comfort and formality, whether and how the questions or guides "worked," conversation flow, and so on.

Fewer questions rather than more and broad questions rather than narrow then are the starting points. When we ask questions, we do so and get out of the way. We listen and respond as any good listener would do when personal stories are evoked. Still, we prompt, or gently suggest directions, and we ask clarifying questions or give responses at appropriate times. We work at being attentive. We listen a lot, and carefully so, for this is the first phase of our information analysis and interpretation. We "try out" our interpretations in the comments we make, the responses we give, and the questions we ask. None of this excludes the possibility that we will at some point, in fact, ask very "narrow" questions, ones quite demanding or challenging, but these are not our starting points, nor do they reflect our general mode of inquiry. We are respectful as we are with any "friend." The conversational enterprise within life history work is simply not a barrage of questions. It is as much about creating an atmosphere of security, intentional meaning making, reflexivity, and genuine interaction around topics that are at once intensely personal yet vibrantly interesting to both parties. Indeed, we work hard at creating the conditions where stories can be meaningfully told.

Clearly the settings we mutually create are crucial and the consideration of the physicality of the place of conversation is as important as all of the relational preparation. Locations where there will not be interruptions or distractions, and that are emotionally and physically comfortable, are likely to be ideal contexts for guided conversations. Wherever the conversations take place, it is important to mindfully listen and observe how the atmosphere might be influencing the conversation. If the venue is not quite right, it needs to be changed.

Varying the venue of the guided conversations also offers the possibility of yielding quite different kinds of information. Different settings prompt different memories or evoke different responses or questions. Having conversations in a person's workplace is likely to reveal stories far different from those evoked in the home of the participant or in a cafeteria, restaurant, park, or other recreational setting. Not only will the surrounding "artifacts of a life," as in a home or office, prompt particular questions, but these settings are also likely to call forth stories that reflect responses to those environments. Also, certain settings invite certain kinds of conversations. For example, in an office space or room set up for an interview with a tape recorder placed in the middle of a table, the conversation is likely to be more formal, or less easy, than a conversation that takes place seated side by side on a park bench or during joint food preparation or some other shared activity. So it may well be productive to vary the conversational context. Locating conversations in varied contexts, especially homes or work places, has an added advantage of opening access to other pertinent information in the form of photographs, personal documents, and other memorabilia.

In the following example, Ardra recounts her first meeting with one of the participants in the life history study of teacher educators described earlier in the book. Her account hints at how issues of tone, setting, and relationship influence the nature and quality of research conversations.

It is a bitterly cold winter's evening—dark and silent except for the crunching sound of my heavy boots crushing billions of tiny snow and ice crystals with each step. I quicken my pace, scanning the exteriors of the row of architecturally similar houses, searching for the right number. Across from the church she had said, I reminded myself, encouraged by the multicolored glow of a large stained glass window just ahead. Interior lights, subdued behind heavy winter draperies, look warm and inviting; they beckon me. I estimate which beacon marks my destination. With each exhalation, my breath is momentarily suspended in a smokelike billow before it dissipates into the frigid night air. My toes and fingers threaten to detach themselves from my body. Finally, Number 34. Side door, she had said. I turn into the narrow walkway, pass the late model four-wheel-drive vehicle that is parked in the driveway and that, I notice, is plugged in for the night to keep the engine from freezing, and, with keen anticipation, press the lighted doorbell.

Dinner preparations are well under way. The warm air, filled with a sweet, pungent aroma of familiar herbs and soft tones of piano music, enrobes me like a cozy blanket. With introductions out of the way and friendly chatter about the weather—how she loves it and I don't—we settle in to an easy, comfortable conversation about our work. While she moves between cupboard and dining table, setting our places for dinner, I chop salad ingredients lined up on the cutting board. We tell each other of writing projects we are in the middle of, interesting books and articles we've recently read, and, inevitably, we move to talk about the difficulty of finding time for either amid all of the other demands placed on us. "Which, I guess, brings us to this project," she says. I am aware of how paradoxically natural it all seems—my being here so comfortable in this strange place talking so openly with someone I barely know, about to invite her to "tell all."

We move to the dining table, plates in hand heaped with steamed rice and stir-fried vegetables. Salad, bread, and wine await us. We are set for the evening. As an awkward reminder of the reason for this meeting, I retrieve my shoulder bag from beside the door and produce from it a small audiotape recorder, pretested and ready to go, pad of paper, pencil, and a list of topics or areas that I want to be sure we cover at some point in one of our conversations. (We had agreed that this would be the first of several.)

"Is it okay if I set this here between us? We can just let it run while we talk and if there's something you want to remain off-the-record you can just press the pause button here on the side." I clear a space large enough to hold the audiotape recorder and the list of our conversation "guides."

"I hope you brought lots of tape," she laughs, moving over to switch off the CD player. "I have a feeling that once I get started it will be me, not the tape recorder, you'll want to turn off. I've been thinking a lot about this project. It's important work. Those of us who are trying to do things differently, to make teacher education programs better, are fighting an uphill battle. That story has to be told. So where should we begin?"

"Maybe a natural starting place right now is your current position—how you came to be here, the nature of your work, what it's like for you, and so on. It's a big area to cover but let's just see how we go."

"Okay, well. . . ."

There may be occasions when using a tape recorder is neither appropriate nor possible. In these instances the alternative is to make notes along the way. The challenge of course is to be present *to* the conversation and take notes *on* the conversation at the same time. Also, it is very difficult to accurately capture words and lengthy passages of oral narrative, which will be important to have for later analysis and representation. So relying only on note taking and memory is not a preferred method of recording conversations. When other means are not possible it is vital, therefore, at the conclusion of the conversation to make a detailed account of it, including reflexive responses to the time spent together. The reflexive journal is the venue to record wide-ranging responses to the conversation and the circumstances surrounding it, comments on the inquiry process along with preliminary analyses or attempting to make sense of the event.

The chances are that, after each conversation, many questions or issues will arise. These will come with reflection on the process and through rereading any notations ("field notes"), journal writing, or other responses (including visual or other artistic representations), or through listening to an audio recording or reading a transcript of a recorded conversation. Sometimes a quick telephone call to the participant or an inquiry via e-mail or a short meeting can clarify some small points. Invariably, though, the larger questions or issues or thoughts that emerge through reflection on each conversation provide a starting point for the next face-to-face encounter.

Each subsequent conversation, then, becomes a building block. Each time we meet with a participant we review our agenda and revisit elements of previous conversations. In this way the focus of the inquiry work is always at the forefront of our minds and serves as a kind of marker or reference point within the conversations.

How long should each conversation be? That depends. The length of each conversation is a delicate thing. Individuals' energies expire at different rates and available time on each participant's part may determine conversation length. We tend to favor long conversations simply because there are fewer start-up or warm-up times involved than when participating in many short talks. Participants are able to gauge their abilities to remain focused; the emotional intensity of the subject matter, the conviviality of the setting, the time of day, physical comfort levels, and the general health and well-being of the participant will influence how long conversations should last.

Inevitably a burning question remains. How many conversations? There is no easy answer. Sometimes there are temporal and resource restrictions to the research process and these have to figure into the answer. Generally, though, the number of conversations is a reflection on the "newness" of the information provided by the participant each time and over time, and whether the main topics or areas identified at the outset have been sufficiently explored. We generally converse with people until we begin hearing stories or issues repeated. We reach a kind of saturation or an intellectual or narrative exhaustion. Nevertheless, one of the hallmarks of life history research is that the work with the "owners of lives" is substantial and sustained over longer periods rather than shorter ones. These, though, are decisions that are ultimately a reflection on the research focus and the people involved and the complex intersection of resources and energies.

As teachers we often talk about a "teachable moment" as one presenting ideal possibilities to illustrate an idea or concept, or an opportunity to craft and facilitate a special kind of experience for learners. Similarly, in researching human lives there are "researchable moments." These are the moments to seize. Life history conversations are likely to be engaging and authentically interactive because two lives have intersected. Under ideal circumstances the connection between these two lives is sparked by the possibilities of interaction and the exchange of experiences—and a meaningful researching conversation eventuates.

To be enterprising in life history researching is to be alert to possibilities and opportunities for meaning or making sense. For example, when a research participant presents an opportunity—be it a hint of telling a particular story or a description of a seemingly key event or a clarification of an idea or an apparently contradictory remark—the researcher must "seize the moment." These instances often become celebratory turn of events in the context of inquiry processes and progress.

"Researchable moments" are serendipitous. By their very nature they are happenstance. They cannot be predicted. They present opportunities to connect with others, to see into the inner reaches of the meaning of a life. The intensity of two lives intersecting (far beyond the limited nature of the conversational process for gaining information) presents unique opportunities for surprise. Of course, in reality no more than snippets from the complexities of a life lived are ever possible to be conveyed in such mediated, conversational contexts. Even under the best of circumstances, life history researchers have relatively limited access to the lived experiences of another. Researchable moments have to be seized and "played out" to the fullest. The roles of serendipity and surprise in life history research are significant. In life, serendipitous moments often become turning points or moments of transformation. In research, serendipitous leads often result in significant understandings.

EXPLORING THE "CONTEXT"

So what does it mean to explore the "context"? We have already talked about the meaning of context and here we articulate a sense of process that might be involved in connecting understandings of lives with the contexts in which they are situated. Ethnographers typically spend extensive periods of time (sometimes years) observing, participating in, and studying particular contexts or cultural groups from the "inside"; that is the focus of ethnographic research. This is not what we are suggesting to life history researchers. Life history researchers need to have an in-depth understanding of the focal context within which participants' lives are situated but the context itself is not the "unit of analysis"; context is a reference point, an essential backdrop that helps us understand an individual's life and experience. We, therefore, gather contextual information in a variety of ways. Explorations of context might involve asking "contextual" questions during research conversations, engaging in a period of observation of the participant in situ, gathering information about the research milieu or context through other means such as having conversations with others or accessing documents containing information about the research context.

Gathering Contextual Information through Conversation

Some contextual influences that typically bear exploration in life history studies and that might be revealed through conversation are:

- Family heritage, including racial background and ethnic and familial cultures
- Family and individual health and well-being
- Socioeconomic conditions of family and community

- Religious influences and practices
- Influences of gender
- Educational background and the influence of educational institutions, such as formal schools, churches, and community/recreational organizations
- Political conditions, such as the climate of political decision making and the state, or not, of democracy and free speech, as well as the state of local and national politics
- Fundamental, personal assumptions about the relationships of self to context in all its forms

These influences shift, merge, and blend over time. "Accepted facts" and perspectives on family heritage, for example, may be questioned by family members who hold "revisionist" views of their own family's history that contrast with those held by parents or siblings, for example. Matters of sexual and physical violence, or other intergenerational patterns of dysfunctional behavior, come to mind as often being covered in cloaks of silence or obscurity. Each of these influences, considered over a life span, are at once historical and contemporary, and they represent the broad understandings of what it was like to be living at any given point or span of time within any particular society and community. The life history researcher's role is to sift out the meanings of these influences as they play out in the experiences of those whose lives are being explored. This is the history part of the life in question; not only do life history researchers create histories of lives, but they also reference those lives to history. To uncover the historical forces on a life is to synthesize the influence of the health, socioeconomic, religious, educational, and political conditions during that life.

To explore context at the conversation phase of information gathering is a fairly easy endeavor. Lives are always lived within context and it is our role, as researchers, to seek out participants' articulations of the obvious and not-so-obvious connections with the world, society, and community surrounding their experience. "Tell me what else was going on in your family at the time?" might be an obvious question. So might, "If your parents were really into practicing their religion, and went to services on a regular basis, what was the influence of the church—say, its dogma, and the priest, and your church friends—on your thinking and actions? Try and fill in the complexities of your experience for me. . . ." It is important to seek clarification of as many background and life influences and contexts as seem pertinent to stories being told in conversation. The first step to understanding the role of context, then, is to ask the research participant about its place of influence.

In the teacher educator study, for example, Ardra identified institutional context as one of the four main topics to explore with the research participants. Over the course of conversation she asked several open-ended questions intended to elicit information about the participants' perceptions and experiences of the institutional contexts within which they worked. Some of the questions were: Can you tell me what it is like for you to be a faculty member here—expectations of you, your roles and responsibilities? What can you tell me about the culture of the faculty or your department? How did you find your way around in the first year(s) of your employment? How did you negotiate physical, bureaucratic, relational environments? What is your sense of the relationship between the faculty of education and the university?

To find out about the contextual influences on a life may require asking questions that are more direct than others asked in conversation. Such questions are often generated by the contextual leads dropped in conversation. These questions request specific information or inquire about the details of a particular story. We rely on participants to sift out the relevant details, remembering that what is essential for us is that they help to construct the meaning of their experiences, the meanings of their lives in context.

In addition to gathering information about participants' experiences of and in context, it may be important, depending on the focus of the research, to gather contextual information first-hand by spending time in situ.

Gathering Contextual Information through Observation and Direct Experience

To write about lives in context requires various kinds of knowledge about a setting or site of inquiry, some of which can be acquired best, perhaps only, through experience. Spending time in a setting—an institution, home, or workplace—can provide invaluable insights. Hearing a research participant describe a place or assign qualities or characteristics to a context provides an important perspective; actually seeing and experiencing that place, getting a feel for it, can take a researcher's understanding to another level and, in turn, enhance her ability to render the context to a reader (or viewer).

Life history researchers are likely to spend time in research contexts for different reasons and in different ways, depending on the purpose and focus of the research and the role that context plays. It may be important to focus attention on some or all of these elements of context: the physical or geographical location and arrangement of a home or workplace; cultural nuances or ethos of an institutional setting; aesthetic arrangement of a space; dynamics of an occupational work group or the relationships among colleagues; processes involved in particular

activities of the participant (for example, familial, educational, religious, and occupational); and activities that take place and help to define the character of a context.

In situ knowledge of context might be gathered by spending time
"shadowing" a participant for a period of time, following him through a
day's or week's activities. It might be appropriate to arrange more formal
observations of a participant engaged in particular activities relevant to
the inquiry, such as at work, home, community, or leisure. A guided or un-
guided tour of a setting might also yield useful insights into the physical,
cultural, and relational qualities of that setting. Again, the main purpose
for gathering information through observation or direct experience is to
gain insights into the focal context. Of course, the manner of accomplishing this might vary from passive observation to full participation as a
"friend" or "colleague."

Documentation of site visits is usually in the form of field notes taken
on site, perhaps in a kind of shorthand and elaborated soon after. The extent of elaboration of details and experiences may vary depending on the
purpose of the inquiry work. In some cases, an audio- or videotape
recorder is used perhaps to document a particular event or activity or to
serve as a reminder of particular features of a setting. Direct experience
information on context, combined with other forms of contextual information, provides the basis for enhanced understanding of individuals'
lives and experiences.

Following is an example of one way in which Ardra gathered contextual information in the teacher educator study. She spent time observing
one of the teacher educators teach a class.

> Friday afternoon. And, like most Friday afternoons, the students
> would rather be somewhere else. It has been another long and full
> week; energy is low for intellectual demands, perhaps higher for so-
> cial activity. Scheduling, she says, is beyond her control and the pro-
> gram curriculum is so full that somebody had to end up teaching a
> Friday afternoon class. Given her status as "the newest kid on the
> block" her course was scheduled for that time period.
>
> As we enter the room through a heavy set of double doors I
> am immediately transported back in time more than twenty years to
> my own teacher education program. The university lecture
> theater—low-lit, physically cold, and psychologically uninviting—is
> gradually coming alive as students enter, make contact with friends,
> choose seats, and chatter among themselves. Then, as now, it made no
> sense for eighty-five to a hundred students of teaching to sit passively
> listening to a lecture on methods and issues related to progressive ped-

agogy. I recall, as a preservice teacher myself, how disengaged I was in this kind of learning context. I recall the tension I experienced years later, as a new teacher educator, when assigned to teach classes of sixty to eighty students and when the only space large enough to accommodate such numbers was a lecture theater. Row upon row of stationary seats, with small movable writing surfaces, tiered downward toward a lighted stage furnished with a lectern, overhead projector and screen, and table. I feel temporally disoriented. What decade is this—the 1970s, '80s or '90s? What, if anything, has changed in the way teachers are prepared and in the curriculum they study? How much of what prospective teachers learn or do not learn in the university component of their program is determined by physical and logistical structures that militate against sound and innovative pedagogy and productive learning and teaching? I know from earlier conversations that the physical arrangement of this space, which forces a particular model of teaching, is antithetical to her ideals about learning climate and pedagogical and relational space.

She has made her way down the steps to the stage, chatting along the way with individuals and groups of students who are getting settled. I have taken a place on the left bank of seats, midback. Several students are scattered around me; most are seated in the center block toward the back of the room (up and out of the way?); a few have located themselves front and center. As she spreads out materials on the table beside her and turns on the overhead projector, the class falls silent. After a brief welcome and few announcements, she introduces the topic of the day's class in the form of a question that prompts students to connect their thoughts with their recent practicum experiences. Most students seem content to sit and listen; a few take up the invitation to respond to open-ended questions presumably posed in an attempt to create a more interactive than passive learning situation.

For forty-five minutes she presents material, following an outline projected on the large screen at center stage. Students take copious notes as she elaborates with stories and examples from her own experiences as a classroom teacher. Repeatedly, she invites students to contribute opinions and experiences and to ask questions. Between the note-taking they respond. In spite of the formal nature of the setting there is a relatively high level of interaction between students and teacher—a goal, she indicated to me earlier, that she always tries to achieve—and a pleasant, informal quality to the interactions. Soon it is time for the students to talk among themselves.

As the last point on the outline is covered, she breaks the group into numerous small discussion groups and assigns them the task of "connecting all of this with your own experiences to see how this theory relates to your experience and practice. What meaning do you make of it?" Preservice teachers (the students in the class) move about in an attempt to locate themselves in positions that are more conducive to discussion; some sit on steps and in the aisles, others twist around in their seats, still others perch on backs of chairs. Noise level is high with so many simultaneous conversations taking place. The group with which I sit tells stories of their experiences in schools; their conversation is only tangentially on topic. Students join and leave groups; some leave the room altogether. I don't really understand what is happening. I do know that this way of teaching is very difficult to facilitate in this kind of space and with so many people. I recognize this as yet another of the tensions we spoke of earlier between pedagogical goals and structural constraints.

A few minutes later the teacher education students are called back to the large group for a debriefing session; an individual from each group is asked to report highlights of the group's discussion. Before all groups have had a chance to report, students begin to fidget and surreptitiously, though not unnoticed, begin to gather materials presumably in preparation to leave. It is a cue. With apologies from the teacher educator to those who don't have a chance to report, and a promise to continue and bring closure to the topic next time, class ends with threads left dangling.

Gathering Contextual Information through Other Means

Apart from inquiring of research participants about the influence of context and spending time in situ, there are other ways to develop insights into the influence of context. In some situations it may be appropriate or possible to access others connected to the person whose life is being studied. Parents or children, work associates and others may provide additional, perhaps different or converging perspectives on contextual influences. The point of asking others for contextual information is not to corroborate or validate what the participants have said but to enhance understanding through the provision of information from yet another perspective.

Other sources for gaining understandings about the influence of context on a life are found in pertinent literature available through libraries or community organizations such as churches and schools. Yet other sources are in artifacts or documentation that may be made known at various public and private institutions such as historical museums (often local ones), municipal archives, church and school archives, corporations, art galleries, community organizations, and the like where the historical is deemed relevant. In these cases, the role of the life history researcher is like any other library or resource researcher: it requires the development of skills in following leads and scrutinizing details. It requires perseverance.

Leads are usually discovered in conversations where scant mention of a topic or influence triggers a realization that any one of many contextual influences is relevant. Perusal of historical family photographs with a participant, for instance, is one way to signify the place of the historical in understanding a life.

COLLECTING ARTIFACTS

"Artifacts are the stuff that break cases," a character in a recent forensic science movie proclaimed, as he smugly sat back in his chair congratulating himself on successfully prosecuting a case. While we are not forensic scientists we also acknowledge the important place of artifacts in life history work. We use "artifacts" loosely, since the term itself is a holdover from the days when archaeology and anthropology were as much involved in the collection of specimens as they were in understanding ancient, foreign, or "primitive" cultures. And the "model" of qualitative research—one emanating from ethnography—that has gained universal acceptance is one that relies on a threefold approach to information gathering: interviews (or conversations), field notes (or observations), and artifacts (or documents). This is the "triangulation" that anthropologists and other qualitative researchers speak about—the use of three or more forms/sources of information or data.

What do we mean by artifacts? Documenting a life is the purpose in collecting artifacts and their value is that they may enrich insights and clarify questions or perplexing issues. An artifact is a physical object. It is something that can be handled and observed. It usually has a temporal quality, meaning that it "speaks" of actions at a particular time and place. Often an artifact has meaning much larger than its obvious meaning or use. As a way to understand the values and place of collected artifacts in our work we informally categorize them in a way that helps us see their utility:

• **Artifacts that are primarily information or data about a life.** Depending on the purposes of the inquiry, these include artifacts that purport to present "facts" about a life, such as biographical, documented information (birth certificates, school and other educational reports, medical or health records, criminal records, driver's licenses and records, military service records and documents, passports, property deeds, financial records, marriage certificates and records, occupational records, résumés or curriculum vitae, family heritage records, death certificates, and so on, some of which may be difficult to obtain because of privacy laws or because they are not normally kept on hand); family or personal heirlooms, keepsakes or memorabilia; family or personal photograph albums, home movies or videotapes; personal writing, including business correspondence, personal letters, personal journals, diaries or logs, poetry or prose writing; and public writing, such as that done for schools or universities, published materials such as theses, dissertations, books, and journalistic articles (in newspapers, magazines, and newsletters), or documents created in the course of one's vocational activities. Often family photographs or other related documents may yield valuable insights. Photographs often remind us of both superficial and more complex differences between "then and now." To interrogate photographs is to try to reconstruct the moment captured by inquiring into the circumstances surrounding that moment. While these artifacts may also represent a life, in that they suggest qualities that frame some characteristic of the person under study, their foremost value is in the weight of the insights they shed on a life. They are "new" information.

• **Artifacts that are primarily representations of a life.** These are usually physical objects or documentations of a life as lived in the present and are often created or produced at the urging of a researcher. Examples include: photographs, videos, or films taken by the researcher or those taken at the time of the research by the participants and/or their families; personal documents such as journals, diaries, or log books that are kept specifically for the research (which may also be regarded as "gathered information"); and photographs or objects that symbolize or synthesize elements of a life often because of their simplicity or singular utilitarian function, purpose or place in the life of the person or persons represented. While these artifacts may have most value as re-presentations of a life lived, or as portraits or illustrations, their qualities as information or data are not as compelling. Nevertheless, all artifacts can be scrutinized for their documentary or informational value.

• **Artifacts that are related to the context within which a participant's life is situated.** These could include: historical documents that locate a person in a particular time, place, or era (for example, V-E Day, post-World War II Nuremberg Trials, the assassination of John F. Kennedy or Martin Luther King Jr., the fall of the Berlin Wall, the collapse of the Soviet Union, or at the time of a natural or unnatural disaster, local, or family tragedy); documents related to the life of an institution within which a person is located (for example, records documenting the founding of an organization, promotional or public relations information about an institution, university calendars, financial and other reports, mission statements, and articulated goals and plans); and information related to individuals' experiences within institutional contexts (for example, employee programs, student extracurricular programs, recruitment, hiring, and retention policies). In addition, family and school photographs may yield insights into contextual conditions. The place of the photograph, the action, and the dress all speak of contextual influences.

While we have talked about the nature of artifacts we have yet to explore their place or purpose in the research process along with processes that might unearth them from attics and closets and mantle pieces and coffee tables and work spaces, not to mention libraries, museums, and other repositories of public and personal archives. How do we know or sense that there are artifacts worth exploring or that may illuminate a life? Intuition plays a part, but so does observation of the research participants in their private, public, and work spaces, as well as analyses of conversations and any documentation that may have been requested as part of the most obvious, direct phases of information gathering.

Perusal of personal spaces where conversations are held is useful for finding hints of the existence of artifacts. Most homes have photographs on the walls or other personal memorabilia to which a participant conversationalist is bound to point or refer or that an observant eye will discover. There is also the possibility that, during conversation, ideas will emerge about artifacts that merit further examination. Common sense also will help identify artifacts or documents related to the inquiry focus that might be useful to obtain. Moreover, if we ask research participants to identify potentially illuminating artifacts they are likely to name at least a few.

How do we make use of artifacts? How do we analyze them? In part, these are similar questions. Our reference point here is context. We "interrogate" artifacts as we might formally interview participants under a more traditional mode of life history or qualitative inquiry and as we might seek out connections with or understandings of context. We ask questions about the relationship of the story lines of a life told with the "evidence" of a life documented. In life history research, artifacts take on important roles in the understanding of a life. We try to ask questions about the artifacts that will uncover their meaning at the time of their importance or significance in a life. To inquire of the meaning of artifacts is to ask the participant to tell about their importance or to ask about the

events and circumstances surrounding them. What else was going on in
your life at this time? How was [the artifact] viewed at this time? Are particular meanings attached to this document or memento? What happened
next? How do you view this experience now? We address analyses of information, including artifacts, in chapter 5, but these kinds of questions
initiate the framing of analyses.

One of the most important things we can say about artifacts is that they
have the capacity to illuminate a life in unanticipated ways. The biggest
challenge will be to curb the collection of materials. We can never assume
that individuals will have a paucity of materials to offer. The most mundane of objects and documents may illuminate issues or themes in a life
that are defied by strings of transcribed words on a page. In the following
account, Ardra identifies some of the artifacts she collected in her work
with the teacher educators and the role they played alongside the other
information sources.

Somewhat reluctantly she closes her office door, sending a nonverbal "Do Not Disturb" message to the steady stream of students that
has been washing by all morning. "I almost never do this. My door
is usually only closed when I'm not here and that is seldom. Maybe
that's why my writing gets done only at home late at night and on
weekends. I guess I feel that they're the reason I'm here and so I
make myself available almost all the time. But," she continues, in
response to my unspoken apology, "if I don't close the door, we'll
be dealing with constant interruptions."

Spread out on the small, round, caféstyle table in front of us are
large three-ringed binders filled with course [curriculum] materials, her appointment book, which she says chronicles her life, and a
stack of papers—published and unpublished writing and grant
proposals—that she has assembled in preparation for our meeting.
The audiotape recorder, set in the middle of the table, is running,
recording sounds of shuffling paper and intermittent movements as
she continues to collect items that "might be helpful" from the filing
cabinet, shelves, and a paper-laden desk. These sounds and her running commentary will help me reconstruct this meeting and remember the significance she attaches to the various materials. I am particularly intrigued by her appointment book, knowing the story my
own tells of an overextended, overly scheduled life. "Can you walk
me through a bit of this?" I ask. "Maybe take me through a 'typical'
week?" She begins. . . .

She has invited me to sit in on one of her classes later in the day.
She flips through the volume of course materials contained in

one of the black binders on the table, trying as she goes to help me understand the context and purposes of what I am likely to observe. Course outline, notes, printouts of what I imagine have been made into overhead transparencies, readings, assignment activities—all detailed and organized. I recognize how much thought and work is reflected in this binder of materials. Her passion for and commitment to teaching and teacher education are evident both in the assemblage and in her voice as she embellishes the sparseness of some of the outlined text. Her pedagogical philosophy, goals, values, and ideals are contained in her printed and spoken words. As if reading my mind, she pauses midsentence and offers, "I can make copies of anything here you think you might like to have." I nod in gratitude and relief, knowing that I will have time to spend with this material and anticipating how much it will help me gain insights into who she is as a professor of teacher education. She continues. . . .

ONGOING REFLEXIVITY AND RESPONSIVENESS

As we have said many times, we research who we are. We express and represent elements of ourselves in every research situation. The questions we ask, the observations we make, the emotions we feel, the impressions we form, and the hunches we follow all reflect some part of who we are as person and researcher. We emphasized in chapter 2, and in Gary's account of Thomas in the "Beginnings" chapter, the importance of understanding the personal history-based origins of our interest in a particular research topic and the prior experiences, preconceptions, values, beliefs, and social location that help to grind the research lenses we wear. While this kind of heightened awareness is crucial preparatory work, it also is essential throughout the research process. Indeed, one of the standards of "good" qualitative research is the visibility and acknowledged presence of the researcher in a research account. This presence is commonly referred to as "researcher subjectivity"; acknowledging and "monitoring" one's subjectivity throughout a research process is an extension of reflexivity.

Peshkin (Glesne and Peshkin 1992, 104) describes researcher subjectivity as a virtue in qualitative research:

My subjectivity is the basis for the story that I am able to tell. It is a strength on which I build. It makes me who I am as a person *and* as a researcher, equipping me with the perspectives and insights that shape all that I do as researcher, from the selection of topic clear through to the emphases I make in my writing. Seen as virtuous, subjectivity is something to capitalize on rather than to exorcise. (Emphasis in original.)

He goes on to explain the importance of understanding the role and influence of one's subjectivity and describes a process of coming to know his own subjectivity through various research projects. He characterizes his subjective presence as a set of subjective "I's," each one expressing a part of himself that is knowingly brought to bear on a research process.

We wholeheartedly endorse Peshkin's views and widen his focus on subjectivity to intersubjectivity. It is important to understand one's own subjective influences; when research is characterized as a relationship, the subjective lens is widened to include another. If we accept that the process and product of researching are an expression of the intersection of self and other, the reflexive process honors that intersecting, relational space. As Lawrence-Lightfoot (Lawrence-Lightfoot and Hoffman-Davis 1998, 86) puts it:

> This balance—between documenting the authentic portrait of others and drawing one's self into the lines of the piece, between self-possession and disciplined other regard, between the intuitive and the counterintuitive—is the difficult, complex, nuanced work of the portraitist [researcher]. In many respects, it is *because* the self of the portraitist is so present in the work, *because* she is the instrument of inquiry and the lens of description, interpretation, analysis, and narrative, that it is crucial that her voice be monitored, subdued, and restrained (though never silenced). The voice of the portraitist is poignant with paradox: it is everywhere *and* it is judiciously placed; it is central and it is peripheral. (Emphasis in original.)

Our point, then, is to highlight the vital role that reflexivity plays throughout the research process.

While researchers operating from a more conventional stance would claim that good "interview schedules" and "observation protocols" are void of subjectivity, that "testable" hunches or hypotheses are grounded purely in the data uncontaminated by researcher bias, we make no such claims. We cannot, nor do we want to, "bracket ourselves out," as a phenomenologist might say. We do, however, need to understand our presence.

During the information-gathering phase of research, a reflexivity journal or field-note record is essential. As soon as possible after a conversation, site visit, or meeting with a research participant, it is important to somehow record impressions, thoughts, ideas, questions, and puzzles arising from those sessions. Whether by talking into a handheld audiotape recorder, writing in a logbook, or using a word processor, the idea is to review as much of the research encounter as possible. Through the process of reviewing there will likely emerge elements of subjective presence to be noted or monitored. For example, say time spent observing in a classroom raises questions or feelings about how a teacher handled a particular situation with a student, or, say time spent in the workplace of a health care professional raises questions about patient treatment. Based on limited observation-based knowledge and lack of sufficient time or opportunity to explore the situation with the teacher or health care professional, it would be inappropriate to prematurely draw conclusions or make judgments. Nevertheless, the event did evoke certain responses that, if left unchecked, are very likely to influence subsequent interactions and perhaps influence the entire direction of the inquiry. The research journal is the forum to record and work through these issues.

Similarly, listening to or reading transcripts of taped conversations can also be revealing. The kinds of clarifying questions asked or the gentle nudges given, that take the conversation in a particular direction, reflect particular assumptions, hunches, or lines of thought. Being aware of these forms of presence is critical. The following example, taken from an account written by Radford (Radford 1996, 89–91), about her research with children and their experiences of power relationships with adults, is illustrative.

> During my first exploratory interview, with ten-year-old Ellen, I confronted perhaps one of the most insidious barriers to gaining knowledge about the lived experiences of children. It was during the interview that I was forced to acknowledge the influence of my "adultness" over a child and, in turn, the child's compliance. Furthermore, my questions were more directed at the belief that children are powerless in their relationships with adults, than at my interest in documenting the child's personal understanding of her social reality. Uncovering the dynamics that occurred during that first interview and discovering the reasons for my uneasiness was a difficult personal process that taught me an invaluable lesson about the tendency of adults to shape and name the experiences of children. My journal entry detailing this insight follows:
>
>> Thinking back, I remember feeling myself growing very distant from the discussion as Ellen told me that her parents did not impose rules on her. Ellen's insistence on this point was not in keeping with my adult knowledge of how adults make the rules where children are concerned. From that moment on, as hard as I tried to return to the discussion, it was impossible for me. During that exchange, I determined that the interview was not working out as I had anticipated—actually I wanted to stop. Throughout the remaining 45 minutes I repeatedly asked myself why she was denying her own oppression; why she refused to name the power her parents had over her; and why she was protecting adults' right to this power. I became busy in my own mind going over the possible reasons for why I was so miserably failing to elicit the expected themes. I wondered whether this truly was Ellen's reality. Could it be that she, unlike other children, was not exposed to the rules and regu-

lations of parents and teachers? Could it be my line of questioning was unclear to her? Perhaps she had never before taken the time to question the limits placed upon her as a child. Or maybe she was unable to confront her own powerlessness, much the same way as many women are unprepared to name their daily oppression as they continue to walk along streets in fear. Explanations for her response continued to preoccupy my thoughts; meanwhile, the incongruity between Ellen's personal reality became greater with every question. I continued to try to elicit disclosures of powerlessness. In turn, my interview questions became more and more leading. Ellen began to respond to my questions with nothing more than a curt "yep." I became frustrated. Why was she not offering more detail? I was initially elated when Ellen changed her opinion at the end of the interview when I asked her what would be different about her life once she became an adult: "Like, I don't know but my parents wouldn't set rules for me because then I'll be an adult." Finally, I thought, she admits the truth. Looking over the interview afterwards I realized that I was unable to determine whether Ellen's words were a reflection of her enlightenment, brought about by the conscientizing effect of the interview, or whether she was simply saying what my questions and tone seemed to indicate I wanted to hear. Although I thought I was simply asking questions, now I see that I was actually demanding her compliance, her validation of my understanding. Ellen had no option but to bow down to my superior knowledge as an adult. The interview illustrated for me a child's skill at reading the subtle tone and intention of an adult. In all honesty, I think that I was subconsciously aware at the time of the interview that it was mostly my adultness that was getting in the way of Ellen's truth. In retrospect I see that I failed because I was not able to honor Ellen's understanding enough to relinquish my own adult viewpoint.

By journaling about this relational experience, I was forced to face my adult privilege and my implicit authority to affect children's responses. . . . I needed to accept that children might reject my hypothesis, my understanding, and to instead focus my attention on finding more appropriate ways of exploring children's own construction of their social reality.

Because of her sensitivity and attunement to her role as researcher and her relationship with the research participants, and because of her commitment to reflexivity and responsiveness as essential guiding principles in research, Radford took extra care and effort to explore and be responsive to her presence as researcher. For another example of the role of reflexivity in research, refer to chapter 2 and Ardra's account of reflexivity from her vantage point as a research participant.

5

Preparing to Make Sense of Gathered Life History Information

- *Revisiting research purposes*
- *Organizing materials*
- *Analysis processes and issues*
- *Coming to and exploring preliminary understandings*
- *Imagining possibilities for representational forms*
- *Identifying audiences*

The shift in mindset and action from gathering information, to translating and transforming it for purposes of knowledge development and communication, is quite marked. There is a point of transition that entails both mental and practical or technical preparation. It is usually the case that, once it is decided that sufficient information is gathered, most of the research work continues in the absence of the research participant. The intellectual and moral responsibilities attached to the final phases of the work are enormous. In this chapter we focus on this transition. We take time to pause and consider the importance of the tasks ahead and ways to prepare for them. We begin this process by reminding ourselves that the principles of relationality, mutuality, reflexivity, care, sensitivity, and respect must continue to guide and inform our actions. The relationship continues to develop, perhaps even deepens, through intensive interaction with the "life texts" entrusted in our care. This work continues to focus our attention on the ethical dimensions, even more so.

Preparation and planning for the intensive processes of analysis and representation involves reviewing the purposes of the study; organizing information gathered; considering processes and issues related to analysis; exploring preliminary understandings; imagining possibilities for representational forms; and deciding on and considering the audiences we want to reach with our work. These are not sequential activities; nor are they tasks that we have just begun. Such considerations are the backbone of solid, research-informed scholarship.

REVISITING RESEARCH PURPOSES

It is not as though we consciously forget the goals or directions of the researching endeavor but that we must constantly bring them into consciousness so that they can inform the work in a consistent and cohesive way. This deliberate action is also an acknowledgment that, in truly responsive life history work—as in other similarly informed qualitative research—where the patterns of interaction with participants and collection of information are recursive and reflexive, the ultimate goals or directions and tone of the inquiry may subtly change because of myriad decisions made along the way. The task, then, is to acknowledge changes in process or focus as a result of cumulative decisions made. On some occasions the focus may change dramatically. For instance, when a researcher, working in the field, believes the emphasis in the pertinent literature or in conventional wisdom is at odds with "street wisdom" and that the inquiry might be better served by shifting the focus to some other element of lives or contexts, then a changed focus may be pertinent. The challenge for many researchers is to be comfortable altering the direction of an inquiry when alternative opportunities, compelling field evidence, or even intuition suggest an inherent wisdom in so doing. Such actions will ultimately influence how information is prepared for analysis.

Even if the research purpose, or focus, is not changed, it is easy to lose sight of it during the analysis process. Embedded in the considerable amount of material gathered are numerous possible directions to follow, some of which may lead away from the original purpose or direction of the research. It is often the case that life history researchers end up gathering far more information in one research project than is possible to use; it is difficult, despite the best of intentions, to know at the time what is and is not directly relevant to the research focus. It is, therefore, important at the outset of and throughout the analysis process to keep the purpose of the research clearly in mind and to set aside, for another time, thematic leads that are not related to this purpose. Once again, this is a fine line to be walked.

ORGANIZING MATERIALS

We are not advocates for using high technology during the analysis process but we do urge sound organization of the various information gathered. Meaningful organization of information, along with ongoing, responsive preliminary analysis, is a good omen for developing insightful life history accounts. Of course, we assume that the quality of information gathered is eventually reflected in the power of analysis and in the representation of lives lived. We simply cannot, as if by magic, develop insightful accounts of lives without useful organization of extensive and sound information as the starting point.

There is another purpose for and value in attending to the organization of information gathered: it is a period of reconnection with substantive amounts of material gathered over time. In a public lecture, Pulitzer Prize-winning author Carol Shields once told a story about the collection and organization of artifacts of her writing life. In preparation for a move to a much smaller residence she came upon numerous boxes and bags of writing notes, draft manuscripts, letters, and other documents and artifacts related to her writing life that had been relegated to a storage cupboard. Faced with the reality that there was no room for this material in her trimmed-down abode, and with the unhappy prospect of disposing of it, she contacted a public archive only to discover that her almost-disposed-of material would be openly and gratefully received into the public archives collection. Shipping arrangements were made and the materials were sent off. Several months later, she inquired after the materials and was invited to visit the archive and to see for herself what had happened to them. She found that every item—every note card, letter, manuscript, notebook, even paper serviettes on which she had scribbled ideas—had been cataloged, labeled, and filed for preservation. The treatment of these materials attributed a level of respect and significance that honored her, her writing life, and her artistic process.

Our task as life history researchers at this point in the inquiry process is similar to that of an archivist. We have to understand and categorize researched information in ways that make sense both to us and to those being researched. Like an archivist, we have to "deposit" information in a way that makes sense for future "retrieval" and rearrangement. The schema developed for this task is probably located somewhere on a continuum between a basic system of organizing materials, such as by chronology/life phase, category/type of information, or by source types and a more complex one that reflects unique elements of a life. A really workable system will emerge only by coming to know that particular life. There are no ready-made templates.

One of the tasks, then, is to organize gathered information in a way that maximizes access and ongoing visitations of that material. One way to categorize material is according to how it was generated. So, for researcher-generated information such as field notes or journal reflections, audio- or videotapes or photographs, and transcripts of conversations, for example, we may wish to first organize the items of information in a chronological fashion so as to facilitate easy notation and cataloging, future access and merging of categories, and future photocopying or duplication. Every day of the information-gathering process will likely mark another "deposit" in our "system." The process is, in its simplest description, analogous to a storekeeper maintaining inventory records. First there is a chronological record made that mirrors the time the goods were received. Then the items are distributed to the shelves, or racks, and are placed in categories that articulate the focus of the storekeeper's energies, the basic goals of her business. At stocktaking time, at the end of the fiscal year, items are categorized according to type or kind, a process that reflects the activities of the store. Using this analogy, all of the various kinds of data are interleaved according to the dates of the research activities over a period of time.

Another alternative for organizing researcher-generated materials may be to categorize according to source types—field notes, journal entries, logs, audiotapes and transcriptions, photographs, and so on. In each case a "table of contents" and, ultimately, an index are important to create so as to aid information retrieval. An index presupposes that all of the material has been examined and reexamined in detail with regard to its substance and quality.

Another category includes participant-generated materials such as work logs and diaries, e-mail, personal writing, or other written documentation (such as work- or occupation-related documents integral to participants' productivity), artwork, photography/film/videotape, artifacts, and memorabilia, which are not institutionally mandated, fabricated/manufactured, or controlled. Chronological organization of these items within each category is useful, and alternative frameworks for their arrangement may follow.

Other-generated materials are found at sources beyond that of the researcher and the researched. They are predominantly artifacts and include the many kinds of personal records kept by public institutions or government agencies (such as those pertaining to motor vehicle licenses and registrations, military service, police records, land titles and deeds, births, deaths, marriages, and many others). Nonpublic institutions such as banks and churches also contain such information. School and university grade reports and transcripts, and media-generated profiles of a life or career also fall into this category, along with medical reports. Other-generated information also includes context informing materials and information that may be the result of long hours of library or archival work—notes, photocopies, duplicates of photographs and artwork of various types, frames from videotapes or films, quotations/citations, microfiche or Internet Web site printouts, and bibliographic references. Here, thematic organization of information may be best for making access easy and workable. Topical or thematic information may also be readily categorized according to historical time.

The form that the organization of life history information takes is also likely to be an intersecting expression of both the researcher as person and the participant as person. The focus of inquiry is a reflection of the researcher, as Denzin (1994, 503) aptly points out ("The Other who is presented . . . is always a version of the . . . self"), and the organization of information reflects the intersection of lives. In essence, evidence of a fundamental understanding of the experiences of a research participant is first found in the manner in which gathered information is organized. A question worthy of consideration is: What makes organic sense in light of this life or these lives?

Several other organizational activities may help tie all the information together and set the conditions for exciting outcomes. Creation of a time line of the information gathered, emphasizing the varieties of information forms, their sources, and their relation to each other, may give a sense of the completeness of this phase of the inquiry project. It is akin to developing an index for a book. Or, it is like creating a memory or cognitive map where the explicit purpose is to show the relationship between each element of the life and the gathered, context informing material.

For example, in gathering life history information from parent-educators suspicious of the intentions of educational and research institutions, and especially researchers, Gary compiled individual sets of information for each family studied. Each set consisted of the individual parent's autobiographical account, which had been completed at his request; transcripts of audiotape-recorded conversations; observation notes made during home visits and during conversations; curriculum and other materials (or documents) from parents (including school records, family photographs and, in one case, published youth novels and, in another, a published book on home education); and notes or other documents regarding the "general" locational or situated context of the study (including local newspaper articles, transcripts of radio broadcasts or interviews with home educators, and data from school boards/districts regarding home-education students). Simply knowing the scope and the quality of gathered information was important, and Gary preferred to arrange the material in a chronological fashion for each participant. Material of a general or collective nature was filed separately but was indexed along with everything else. In addition, there were his own reflexive notations (located in a journal-like document); where applicable, this was filed as a kind of summary for each participant. The task was to try to illustrate—through the manner and form of organization—the complexity of the lives and families and the interrelated nature of all the information in the documentation. Gary was already familiar with pertinent popular and research-informed literature and so this organizational aspect of the process was less important.

Gary ended up with several extensive files on individual families. He began each family file immediately after collecting information. For the most part, each file contained parallel information. While all of the text-based information, with the exception of published books and curriculum materials, was transferred to a word-processing program, it was not necessary in the end. On the advice of a colleague he had planned to use a computer-assisted analysis program but found that it was far too unwieldy and that the process removed him from experiencing the stories and the information in a personally satisfying and meaningful way (an issue we explore in greater depth in the following section). A careful compilation of materials, and their organization into manageable files, is an important element of analysis and goes hand-in-hand with the completion of information gathering. Our sense is that, while a chronological location of each piece of information is helpful, other possibilities may make more sense given the project in question.

It may seem like we have belabored the point of information organization; we do so to underscore the importance of developing a system or scheme that will make manageable the potentially overwhelming amount of material a life history researcher is likely to accumulate. Such a system, developed at the outset of information gathering and refined throughout, in effect, can set up a construct for later, more in-depth analysis. Attention to the organization of information in an ongoing and systematic way, so that it informs both the subsequent information-gathering and analysis processes, describes what Miles and Huberman (1994) refer to as the "iterative cycles" of research. It is also reflected in Glaser and Strauss's (1967) "constant comparative method" and is part of the interpretive dialectic commonly described by most qualitative researchers. (Miles and Huberman, and Glaser and Strauss, advocate tightly controlled and instrumental processes of researching; it is important to acknowledge that, overall, their perspectives contrast with those that we advocate.)

ANALYSIS PROCESSES AND ISSUES

It is usually at the point of transition from the information-gathering phase to the analysis phase that researchers, especially those new to life history research, set out in search of a set of tools, techniques, or "tried and true" methods to aid in the analysis process. The search is fruitless; the results are disappointing. There are no formulae or recipes for life history analysis and writing. Plummer, in his book *Documents of Life: An Introduction to the Problems and Literature of a Humanistic Method* (1983, 99), describes the analysis of life history data in a way that accurately captures the process:

> In many ways this is the truly creative part of the work. It entails brooding and reflecting upon mounds of data for long periods of time until it "makes sense" and "feels right," and key ideas and themes flow from it. It is also the hardest process to describe: the standard technique is to read and make notes, leave and ponder, reread without notes, make new notes, match notes up, ponder, reread, and so on.

Unlike in statistics-based research, where preparation for analysis requires learning a computer program or locating a service that can provide analysis assistance, preparing for analysis of life history material requires a kind of mental readiness to understand and accept the complexity of the task, the creative nature of the process, and the requirements of time, patience, and commitment to a sometimes convoluted and chaotic process. This is yet another reminder that, in qualitative research, the researcher is the "instrument."

In the search for straightforward and efficient methods for data analysis, researchers are often seduced by the prospect and promise of computer software developed for qualitative data analysis. Opinions on the role of computer-facilitated analysis range widely (for discussions of this issue, see, for example, Lincoln and Guba 1985; Richards and Richards 1994; Tesch 1990; Weitzman 2000; Werner and Schoepfle 1987), usually in accordance with authors' orientations to qualitative research. The stronger the commitment to the intersubjective nature of the researcher-participant relationship, the less likely it is that a researcher will invite a computer program into that relationship. In contrast, the stronger the claims of objectivity, the more likely it is that a researcher will see significant advantages in using computer-assisted analysis. For example, the following data analysis procedure was described in an article (McAuley, Travis, and Safewright 1997) published in the journal *Qualitative Health Research*:

> A content analysis of the transcripts was performed using the Hyper RESEARCH software program for qualitative analyses. . . . The software provides a concrete method for describing the reasoning chain for coding the data and permits reliable, verifiable conclusions to be obtained. . . . One member of the research team coded all transcripts and generated a list of 257

discrete codes. A second reader . . . was given the aggregate list of codes and asked to use the list to independently code a set of random pages drawn from each of the [twenty-eight] transcripts. . . . The list of codes was returned to the first reader, who reviewed the codes and revised or eliminated confusing choices from the list. . . . Each code was then categorized into [one] of [ten] mutually exclusive response categories. . . . This list was then given to a third reader . . . who was asked to agree or disagree with the first reader's coding on a sample of six complete transcripts.

Contrast this description of the analysis process with that given by Plummer earlier in this section. The language used in this description is a distinct marker of the assumptions guiding the researchers' approach to qualitative research. Clearly, their perspective and attendant commitment to computer-assisted analysis are at distinct odds with the position we advance in this book. Reductionist, positivist assumptions underlying process are antithetical to the perspective we portray.

When computer programs for qualitative analysis were first introduced, a colleague, seeing Gary staggering under the weight of material gathered in his life history study with home-educating parents, suggested that a software analysis program would alleviate much of the burden. Unfamiliar with any such program and eager to understand its possibilities, Gary located an appropriate software program and went about using it. His relationship with computer-assisted analysis was short-lived; his expectations of the program were too great. He expected to be able to rely on the computer program to make thematic connections and engender important insights but quickly realized that, while the program was useful for organizing and managing data, it was not able to engage with them and "think" about them in a sufficiently meaningful way. The preliminary analysis required before entering the data into the computer so that the program could perform its "mechanical" operations yielded more satisfying results than those generated by the computer program. The organizing constructs generated by the analysis program never seemed to meld with Gary's own messy analysis and he was more inclined to trust his own judgment and intuition. He knew that analysis decisions were based on more than just the information provided. He was additionally informed by what Polanyi (1958) would call a "tacit" understanding of the participants and by his intimate relationship with the data. Later efforts with similar analysis programs only highlighted their limitations, the most significant being the reductionist, segmented nature of the analysis and the exclusion of any emotional and intellectual responses to the data derived from the intensity of his relationship with the participants and the information gathered. More revealing was the acknowledgment that Gary's modes of analytical work are more visceral than any program can help him to be.

COMING TO AND EXPLORING
PRELIMINARY UNDERSTANDINGS

While first insights usually occur as we are engaged in conversation, or experience an event, and play out in the ways in which we respond physically and verbally, the second wave of analysis occurs as we transcribe, reflect on, and/or read and reread conversation records, or observations, and as we engage with the documentation gathered. We become enmeshed in a life. Our thoughts and feelings about the information gathered comprise an important element of our ongoing analysis. It is really a matter of perspective, trying to look at the data from many different sides, trying to make meaning from it, trying to envision the lived life. We do not see this as a process of mythical or mystical proportions (although it can be if the information-gathering phase has no well-defined end), nor do we see it as one with a rigidly defined structure.

In most guides to qualitative research, it is suggested that analysis preparation involves developing a system for sorting, classifying, categorizing, and coding data in order to take it from its raw form through an analysis process to a sophisticated level of theory development. Many researchers, especially those who seek a holy grail of qualitative research analysis, look to computer-based analysis programs for such fortune in developing emergent theory. Others are content with simply coming to know the information in a highly personal and complete way. While the analysis process does require systematic and disciplined attention to the information gathered, and is, in a sense, a reductionist activity; it does not require researchers to devise and strictly adhere to a rigid categorization system or analytic scheme. To do so would be to risk the parts for the whole. Understandings of participants' lives in context can never be truly whole or complete; however, we must strive to honor the richness and complexity of lives lived. We do so not by taking information and slicing it into discrete bits and storing the pieces in separate containers, but by trying to understand, in a holistic way, the connectedness and interrelatedness of human experience within complex social systems. The analysis process is not one of dissection but one of immersion. We become surrounded and washed by the material, we bathe in it, live it, and breathe it. Like getting to know a very good friend, because we have spent so much time together and come to know so much about her, eventually we begin to think, just a little, like her. In part 2, chapter 18, Maura McIntyre recounts elements of her process of working with interview transcripts and other research texts. She elucidates the intersubjective nature of the interpretation process.

All of the enabling and relational conditions established during the early phases of information gathering are but preliminary to being able to "listen" with both head and heart to the information accumulated about the lives lived. We try to feel the depth of emotions yet step back, just a little. We allow our subjectivities to surface but we consciously take note of them, eventually articulating them clearly and unapologetically in the final account of our inquiry work. We aim to reason the actions and empathize with their consequences. We surround ourselves with the lives of these individuals. We try to imagine their experiences. We try to walk in their shoes. We work rationally as well as intuitively. We try to relive elements of the life or lives told to us. As much as is humanly possible we try to embody their experiences—a notion that is often highly enervating in its realization. It requires much work, much dedication to the tasks and to the participants. The scope of gathered information is sometimes overwhelming; its cumulative extent and complexity can be surprising.

Just as we intuitively follow leads in conversations, or allow our intuition to guide the direction of other information gathering activities, in the meaning-making process we continue to heed that subconscious part of our knowing. To allow intuition to play a role in the process at every point is as important as anything else we will do in the period leading up to our final analysis. These early analyses provide the opportunities to check the meanings of our researching actions in tandem with the tone, tenor, and quality of the gathered information. This is also the time to bring to specificity all the questions and issues that we wish to clarify as we conclude the major phase of our information-gathering work.

In being responsive in our researching actions, and in the ongoing process of making meaning from the complexities of participants' lives, we honor participants in a way that, we hope, is taken in the spirit with which it is given. By paying careful attention to the details and complexities of their lives, participants will know of our authenticity and integrity as researchers. They will know of our intention to sensitively represent them. They will know of the moral fiber of our commitment to their experiences and of our mutual purpose. They will feel comfortable placing the analysis and representation of their lives in our care. Such conditions and exhibitions of trust, which enhanced the quality of the information revealed, will continue to enrich the analysis and representation processes.

IMAGINING POSSIBILITIES FOR REPRESENTATIONAL FORMS

One of the most exciting elements of researching lives is imagining the possibilities for representing them. Readers are drawn into a good and gradually unfolding story. Viewers are compelled to consider the implications of a provocative and aesthetically or intellectually challenging image. Audiences are aroused by vivid, intriguing, soothing, perplexing, provocative, and even shocking portrayals of all kinds.

The power that lives may have for others is found largely in their forms of representation. The extent to which representations allow readers (or viewers) to enter these constructed life texts (those that draw on conventional scholarly forms or literary, visual, poetic, dramatic narratives, or some combination) reflects the researcher's moral purpose in relation to her intuitive and rational frames of portrayal, her technical skills and institutional, political confidence, and her intentions with respect to public access and political action.

To craft a life is to engage in making art. The powers of imagination and metaphor are crucial ingredients for the process of sensitively crafting elements of a life—and the crucial meanings of it—for others to discover. How we do this is at once a beautiful mystery and a relational, rational act. To conceptualize representational possibilities is to be thoroughly alert to the various alternatives that resonate deep within our creative and epistemological frameworks. It is to be vigilant and responsive to the metaphorical cues that lives offer to onlookers. It is to be informed by that life or lives and to be open to the most "sensible" and resonant alternative (or many, presumably) with which to communicate about it. To embrace the potential of art to inform scholarship is to be open to the ways in which the literary, visual, or performing arts—and the inherent methods and processes of those various art forms—can inform processes of scholarly inquiry.

Development of an artful representation is dependent on the soundness and complexity, perhaps even the "messiness," of all the preceding phases of the inquiry and relies as much upon the imagination of the researcher as it does on the formal and obvious connections between contexts and lives. Artful representations often emerge from intuitive responses to complex and messy interpretations. In actions leading up to such representations we make analytical decisions that most strongly resonate with the data—and, therefore, the life or lives—given the intersection of the life or lives with our own. Since we are the "instrument of understanding," our interpretations and eventual representations of lives will reveal some of the "essential truths" of a participant's life and some of the most impermeable elements of our own life. Life history researching is, at its most fundamental, a complex interaction between the lives of the researched and the researcher—a point discussed in several of accounts in part 2 and particularly by Avi Rose in chapter 12 and Maura McIntyre in chapter 18.

In research as in life as in art, there is no possibility of completeness, certainty, or closure. Representations of life, in research and in art, can be only partial. For contemporary artist Martha Rosler, the task of the artist is not to strive to, and perhaps make claims of, exact representation but rather to draw attention to the inadequacies of all forms of representation. Eiblmayr, writing about Rosler's work, states, "She does not claim to tell the 'truth,' but, on the contrary, to work on the 'inadequacy of descriptive systems'" (1998, 160). We suggest that researchers adopt a similar stance for their representations of lives in context. As we imagine possibilities for representational forms, with this idea in mind, we allow ourselves to think about analysis and representation activities in a way that is different than the way we would think if we were to strive for one-on-one correspondence between lives lived and lives represented. In part 2, chapter 19, Ilze Matiss explores the evolving and dynamic nature of lives lived and the importance of research representations being acknowledged for their indefinite, moment-in-time quality.

There are a number of issues to consider when illuminating and portraying a life: the fundamental meanings of experience held by participants given the focus of our inquiry; the work's moral and political purposes; the audience to which the research-informed understandings are directed; our own technical skills and abilities with regard to developing representations, whether in conventional forms of scholarly text or any appropriate alternative; and our interest in stepping outside the box of conventional scholarship forms. (The latter point is larger than it first appears because it embraces questions about ready acceptance into the academy and questions about authority of process and groundedness in a tradition of inquiry—issues that some members of the academy are hesitant to consider and, even less so, to act upon.)

During research conversations with professors of teacher education in the life history study described earlier, Ardra became acutely aware that some of the experiences being recounted were so imbued with emotion and poignant illustrations of the often-dysfunctional relationship between academic institutions and individual faculty members, that conventional forms of representing these experiences seemed inadequate. Frequently, the teacher educators used graphic language to create images or metaphors to describe elements of their experience. They struggled to find words to adequately convey the passion and emotion imbued in certain issues and experiences. A search for appropriate words to convey interpretations revealed the inherent limitations of language, especially when crafted in conventional academic prose. In an attempt to find more authentic and meaningful representational forms that would more closely render the aesthetic of lived experience, however partial, and afford readers better opportunities for their own resonant interpretations, Ardra turned to multimedia and to the tableau art form. She was drawn to the tableau form as articulated by the U.S. contemporary artist Edward Kienholz, who devoted a good part of his life (1927–1994) to producing large-scale, provocative works.

Kienholz's life-size, three-dimensional, multimedia interpretations and renditions of the human and social condition are often raw and shocking. His use of confrontational realism is deliberate as he compels viewers to face and be implicated in the bold cultural and political statements he makes through his portrayals. According to Raskin (1996, 43), Kienholz's art invites us "to judge our present social conditions and then we are begged, through a visual scream, to create another reality, one that celebrates human dignity." For Kienholz, the reality of human suffering is best expressed through art with the use of absurdity, exaggeration, or distortion that forces the viewer to become an active participant in the representation.

The experiences recounted by the teacher educators, and the themes and issues embedded in those experiences and in the telling of them, inspired the conceptualization and eventual creation of a series of multimedia representations. The images rely on shock value and exaggeration to draw viewers in, to connect with the truths expressed, and, it is hoped, to precipitate the creation of a more humane and generous reality for teacher educators in the academy.

In conjunction with three other life history researchers Ardra developed a three-part multimedia installation (Cole et al. 1999a, 1999b, 1999c). The title, *Living in Paradox,* reflects the overarching theme that emerged through analysis. The three parts of the installation each represent a predominant convergent theme that defines elements of the teacher educators' experiences as pretenured faculty members in university-based teacher education programs. "Installation I: Academic Altarcations" represents one of the most striking and prevalent self-contradictory yet "truthful" expressions made by the teacher educators—the paradox of sacrifice. The dichotomous demands of the institution and the profession of teaching and the life of schools create incredible pressures, and the teacher educators said they felt as though elements of their lives and careers were sacrificed. The installation is made up of a three-dimensional, life-size "altar." The altar is surrounded by a simulated blackboard and other images of the university: an ivy-covered wall, a men's room, a professor's office door, and adjacent message board. On the blackboard are words and phrases depicting the professors' emotion-laden perspectives about the power differentials within institutions. Other issues and expressions are faintly printed as in previous chalk writing that has been erased. Symbols of the academy and tenure are laid on the altar. An electrically driven, near bloodred conveyor belt carries, on small white satin pillows, symbols of personal sacrifice to the altar. These are the losses. These are the sources of these professors' pains. Piled on the floor at the foot of the altar are more pillows. Background music of Gregorian chants is contrasted with audiotapes of "chants" composed from the professors' words—words that rationalize their sacrifices: "I love teaching. . . . I want to make a difference. . . . I care about teaching and teacher education. . . ."

"Installation II: Wrestling Differences" is a commentary on the gendered nature of the academy. It presents particular problems for women in colleges, schools, or faculties of education where the arena of change extends from within the faculty to the broader university context (a context, perhaps, applicable to other professional schools in the university whose members in the field are predominantly women). Within education faculties women struggle both for acceptance by their male counterparts and against the norms and values on which the dominant male culture is built (even in a feminized profession). For many women teacher educators, this is the paradox that defines their struggle. The installation is a simulation of a wrestling arena with large, World Wrestling Federation-syndicated toy action-figures pitted against a much smaller (perhaps barely visible to some) female figure. She appears vulnerable yet defiantly resistant. The black ring emblem-embossed, is set among a crowd of cheering onlookers. Poignant narrative excerpts (from transcribed conversations) recounting elements of the teacher educators' experiences are projected onto the arena's spotlighted and smoke-filled painted backdrop. More phrases are written on the installation's bleacherlike supports.

"Installation III: A Perfect Imbalance" is less complex than the others. It depicts the dual mandate of teacher educators' work that requires them to serve both the academy and the profession and that keeps their gaze focused on the fulcrum of their lives striving for balance. The problem for most teacher educators, especially those committed to change in teacher education, is that no matter how hard they try the scales are impossible to balance because the weights are uneven to begin with. According to the values and standards of the university, teaching, service, professional and community development, and other activities that have mainly local or personal implications and that demand inordinate time and energy commitments, do not carry much weight. The heavy weights from the university's perspective are those activities that result in intellectual and financial prestige and international acclaim. For most teacher educators, it seems, any balance that *is* possible to achieve is always imperfect. The installation is a simple balance scale weighted on either side with foam blocks that represent the many and varied roles and responsibilities of teacher educators' work and lives. On one side is a high tower of blocks, each representing a different activity or role required of the professors of teacher education; on the other side is a single, multifaceted block that represents the activities the university deems most meritorious. This single item, a foam block, is weighted on the inside so that the scales will balance only when the entire pile of blocks identifying teacher educators' work is in place. The result begs the question of whether the scale is, indeed, balanced.

The information gained through this project demanded an alternative representation; this is an example of how one can be developed following the lead of participants' talk. It is a responsive interpretation. Ardra also wanted a direct and evocative vehicle to raise awareness of these seemingly obvious, dysfunctional contexts and issues associated with them. At major conferences and other venues, teacher education professors and other members of the academy have expressed strong resonance with this exhibit. The installation has evoked ranges of emotion: from tears to expressions of affirmation (a realization that one's experience is not unique); from unfettered anger to rational reflection; from silence to recounting new and similar stories of experience. This installation work is complemented by more traditional texts about the experiences of pretenured professors (see, for example, Cole, 2000a, 2000b; Cole, Elijah, and Knowles, 1998).

So, what are the representational possibilities for life history work? They remain, perhaps, enormous. Always, though, a compelling, well-told story is imperative. Consider predominantly text and page-defined forms, for instance: booklike or articlelike texts that embrace research as story. Some of the many alternatives include conventional formats of text, those perhaps couched as case studies or narrative, thematic accounts of a life or lives. The advocacy for narrative and thematic articulations of research findings are numerous. Fictionalized accounts, even poetic ones, or combinations of the two are possible. (For discussions and examples of some of the text-based possibilities see, for example, *Composing Ethnography: Alternative Forms of Writing* [Ellis and Bochner 1996] and *Daredevil Research* [Jipson and Paley 1997].) The key is to embrace the text-based representational possibilities with an open mind. After all, the goal is to make use of an illuminating representational form.

IDENTIFYING AUDIENCES

During the 1990s arts-informed representations of researched lives entered into the legitimate scholarly work of the academy. (We are not overlooking the considerable contributions of visual anthropology and sociology. Rather we are speaking of something with a very different orienting purpose, although elements of their information gathering/documenting processes may be applicable. For insights into the anthropological perspective, see, for instance, Banks 1998; Banks and Morphy 1997; Collier and Collier 1986; Loizos 1993. For sociology, see Becker 1998; Chaplin 1994; Harper 1982, 1987, 1997. *Image-Based Research: A Sourcebook for Qualitative Researchers* [Prosser 1998] offers views into both fields and has application for the kind of arts-informed life history work we advocate, as does *Writing Strategies: Reaching Diverse Audiences* [Richardson 1990].) Documentary filmmakers and screen writers, drama directors and playwrights, fiction and nonfiction writers, not to mention curators, galleries, and artists, have a long history of tackling society's pressing sociopolitical concerns and confronting the willing and not-so-willing public with their messages. The most powerful of these works of art influence readers and onlookers because of the works' intellectual and emotional pull. For us it is not simply enough that a "good" or sound piece of researching work has been done. It is simply not enough that an inquiry is intellectually solid, that peers respect the processes, that the findings are insightful, and that the researcher has developed certain wisdom about the topic. How has the life, or how have the lives, been changed for the better? How has the process cast light on problems and their resolution within individuals, families, and communities? How has the work been heard by those whose influence is great and far-reaching? How has the work made a difference? So what?

The question "So what?" runs deeper than what may be immediately obvious. The answer demands the acceptance of a moral ethic and responsibility whose veins not only run deep into the motivations and potentialities for life history work—and the traditions associated with it that reside in the academy—but also strongly pulsate into the affairs of the world at large. This world is the one inhabited by politicians and policy makers, legislators and governors, media workers, and citizens of all stripes. It is to this broad (or even narrow) audience, whenever applicable in the most basic sense, that the work of life history researchers must be communicated and, then, through the substance and form of that communication, readers and viewers must be transported to new understandings. This is the goal toward which we strive. Our work must count for something. In part 2, chapter 15, Jeff Orr explores the advocacy role for life history research in his work with First Nations and Aboriginal communities. He identifies the political agenda of his life history research as a central driving force. For him, as for Renee Will in her account of researching in the context of nursing (chapter 7), life history research approaches and representations offer a counternarrative to the dominant discourse on how knowledge is defined and constituted by professional or societal communities. In chapter 8, Gary also notes that "counting for something" is located in his responsibilities to the home-education communities.

Ultimately the strength of our work is judged by others outside the research process. Such judgment was once performed by peers alone. Contemporary scholars and communities and society now weigh in on the scales in very different ways. As politicians and communities demand greater accountability of researchers, as the limits of conventional scholarship are made more apparent, and as the moral accountability standards of researchers (to "the researched" and communities and society) are heightened, the calls for alternative representations of research increase in volume. Once it was good enough to do research that was interesting only to a small and exclusive population—academic journal readers and like-minded academics. Now this kind of interesting research in and of itself is not good enough: the value of work is more embodied in the ways in which that research may reach a wider audience. Besides, the morality and purpose of life history researchers go beyond the utilitarian value of a good story. Still, a good story is absolutely essential. It is the crucial evidence of sound work. Many life history researchers are morally and ethically bound to make a difference in the communities and lives with whom they work. Life history scholarship may be judged, therefore, by the way it influences contributing communities of the researched.

That inquiry work may be deemed relevant and accepted beyond the entrenched communities of like-minded scholars is as much a reflection on the political astuteness of researchers, the fickleness of the media, or the potential power of politicians or policy makers as it is on the artistic and scholarly merits of the work. We recognize the labyrinth taken in politicizing researching outcomes. We also know that the extent to which good scholarship is taken up in the seats of political power often has nothing to do with the veracity of the work. Rather, we sense that, although good stories are listened to, and their power recognized, all too often the power of numbers is what sways the vote—especially in legislative bodies. And here is a major contradiction. While demands are made that researching activities be more relevant or community-centered, that research outcomes often have potential for "bottom-line enhancement" (whatever that means in corporate communities or in contexts of economic rationalism), and that it be accessible to society at large, the calls for evidence usually go little beyond cries for numerical evidence. This presents yet another challenge for life history researchers. How can we make the findings of the work we do more noticeable in the best sense?

We know firsthand of the difficulties and complexities of getting sound research sensitively presented in the popular press or noted on radio and television. Thirty-second sound bites serve little purpose. Artistically informed work—meaning that which embodies an aesthetic and form of process and "end product"—honors lives in unique ways, and tells "the story" with emotional and intellectual power, acknowledges the holistic and multidimensional nature of intelligence as well as knowledge and knowledge production. Theoretical insights that emerge from such work are not happenstance and are a result of expressions of work and

subsequent insights that really get at the heart of the matter being studied. The media, meanwhile, is more interested in the sound-bite version
of the "research story" than the long, convoluted, potentially illuminating
version. We live in a society that demands synopses of nearly everything
complex, which flies in the face of the very tenets of what we advocate.

The forms of the arts, broadly defined, offer modes of representation
and communication that have been traditionally excluded from formal
social science research. Yet, even literature, poetry, visual and installation
art, drama, dance, and music—while loudly touted by literature-savvy or
music- or dance-hall, theater- or gallery-going academics as revealing of
the human condition and provocative in their suggestions—offer not in-
considerable challenges to scholars wishing to employ them. There is at
once the task of becoming competent in the technical elements of these
various art forms, and at home in and with them, and that of being able
to connect with artisans who can truly influence the quality of the work.

Perhaps the most pressing issue, when completion of the analysis is
within grasp and considerations of the communicated form are being
made, is that of audience. None of these decisions (about representational
and communication forms, and audience, for instance) bears any resem-
blance to a linear development of process. Each must be considered simultaneously. Indeed, the question of audience is something to be considered at the outset of the inquiry work.

Having broadly identified some issues worthy of consideration when
developing representations and communicating life history work, there
are related and pressing matters to consider. Here are some questions that
often occupy our thinking: To whom and to what purpose are the understandings of the work directed? What are the values of this audience and
how can we facilitate the intersection of the lives of the researched with
those of the audience? What kinds of evidence does the audience typically
expect? What is the scope of representational forms that may capture their
attention? Are there possibilities for shock or other "extreme" means to
grab the audience's attention? How can the emotional and reasoned be
fused?

Other questions are connected to the potential influence of the work:
What influence may or can the audience have with respect to the moral
purposes of our research? What are the potential political outcomes of our
inquiry work and how can we assure that their value is recognized? How
can we assure ourselves that the work, indeed, is of value to audiences beyond those of the academy?

It is simply no longer savvy to put enormous energies into life history
work without being mindful, at the very onset, of the links between
moral purpose, audience, representational forms, and the level of commitment to working either inside or outside the traditional boundaries

of researching within the academy. Innovative scholarship that draws inspiration from the arts and relies on alternative forms of representation is an artwork in itself—crafted by an artist who has a love and dedication, as well as a social and political commitment, to the subject matter. This is about work of a life or lives and it deserves commitment of lives to bring it fully to fruition and into view. We refer once again to chapter 17 and Gary Knowles's and Suzanne Thomas's research with high school students as inspired by the work of a photographic artist. One of their commitments is to communicate research-informed perspectives on the students' experiences to audiences beyond the academy. They wanted to engage parents, teachers, and other community members in conversation about students' realities of school.

6

Making Sense of and Representing Lives in Context

- *Participants' and researchers' roles in interpretation and representation*
- *Levels and processes of analysis*
- *Realizing the possibilities for representational forms*
- *Issues of rigor in life history research*

In this chapter we bring the researching cycle to a close; yet we know that the representations of lives will evoke many more questions in our (and, it is hoped, the readers') thinking that may inform future work. Because there is no one or best way to make sense of and represent lives in context, the most we can do here is to provide some signposts to guide the analysis and representation processes and raise some issues for consideration. We seek optimum resolution of process. We acknowledge the rational, systematic, and yet at the same time complex, messy, intuitive, and serendipitous nature of these crucial, final phases of researching work. As researchers live with information gathered and give ample time for reflexive and reflective examinations of it, the network of themes and patterns in a life become evident. Insights gained through a reflexive sense-making process, involving different levels of analysis and varying points of perspective taking, are revealed.

The role of participants in the interpretation and representation of their lives and the researcher's role and responsibility in these phases of the work are a reflection of the relationship between the researcher and the researched and, also, of the researcher's stance on this issue. Inherent in this concern are political, ethical, and relational complexities.

112

Issues of rigor will surface, as well, when others engage with our pub-lished or communicated research text or with other forms of our research representations. But rigor is difficult to define and we prefer to do so on our own terms. As an artist prefers to exhibit her work to the viewing public in the most favorable way, so do we. That means, perhaps, helping viewers or readers to understand as much of the "behind the scenes" or studio work, and the conceptualization of process, so that reasonable judgments can be made about the artistry and its subject matter. So an artist frames her work by means of an "artist statement"—usually a text that illustrates or notates the fundamental concepts and processes behind her work. She lays down the criteria that governed its conception and pro-duction. She wants to make known the soundness of her thinking as well as the basis for the passion that went into the work. She is interested in both evoking and provoking understandings of her unique process, artic-ulating her idiosyncratic perspective on the work, explicating her distinc-tive style, and making visible her signature approach. These qualities of purpose are often implicit in the display of the artistry. Further, exhibiting also means that she illuminates her work in the most favorable fashion, controlling the manner in which it is viewed. She is concerned with the evocative implications of its arrangement and setting. In a sense, issues of rigor are about the central or essential conceptualizations of process and how meanings are made and represented.

PARTICIPANTS' AND RESEARCHERS' ROLES IN INTERPRETATION AND REPRESENTATION

What are the roles for the participants in these phases of the research? How do participants take up the challenge of working for mutual benefit? What are the elements of relationality that may be important for partici-pants? How do notions of mutuality and relationality change the face of life history inquiry?

In the final phases of the research process we maintain our commitment to participant involvement, albeit in a different way because, usually, par-ticipants are not physically present for most of what takes place during this time. We continue in our work based on the premise that participants have much to say about their lives and, through their words and actions, we can make sense of their individual and collective experiences. In this regard, as in the many other phases, our task is quite different from that of a researcher working within a positivistic model based on natural sci-ence methods. As Bertaux (1981, 38) observes, when researching human beings, scientists who are used to working with and manipulating objects have "no other way than first to reduce them to silence." As life history researchers, our stance is in direct opposition; our challenge is to find ways to make participants' voices heard, to let their individuality show and shine, to make their stories sound loudly. The extent to which we do this is in direct relation to our moral and ethical commitment to the central intentions of our inquiry work.

At the same time as we make known lives, as researchers, we do have an important role to play: in our commitment to ensure a central role for the participants' voice, we do not muffle our own. As Lawrence-Lightfoot (Lawrence-Lightfoot and Hoffman-Davis, 1997, 85) puts it:

> The portraitist's [or researcher's] voice . . . is everywhere—overarching and undergirding the text, framing the piece, naming the metaphors, and echoing through the central themes. But her voice is a premeditated one, restrained, disciplined, and carefully controlled. Her voice never overshadows the actors' voices (though it sometimes is heard in duet, in harmony, in counterpoint). The actors sing the solo lines, the portraitist supporting their efforts at articulation, insight, and expressiveness.

Along similar lines, although more subdued than we may advocate, Langness and Frank (1981, 99) assert:

> Life history may be seen as a kind of double autobiography in which two personal configurations are fused: the writer's (mainly through such elements as choice of topics and tone) and the subject's (through what is usually thought of as the content of the book).

Of course, there is no way one way to conceptualize life history research but there may be instances when a researcher chooses to harmonize a life history exploration with a (self-) reflexive examination based on life history processes. In such a case the researcher's voice may have "equal" weight with one or several participants. It may even be that the researcher's reflexive voice speaks loudest. The weight given to each voice is a decision that rests in and reflects the purposes of the inquiry and the representation itself.

There is considerable debate over whether and how much researchers need to interpret or translate participants' life texts or, in instances where alternative forms of representation are used (such as visual images, poetic text, fiction, or creative nonfiction), whether and how much researchers need to translate or explain their own renditions. Likewise, the visual artist exhibiting her work in a gallery has the same dilemma. How explicit she should be in a personal statement, in her explanations of her artistry, depends on the context, the subject matter, the medium, the audience, and the time. As life history researchers, it is our position that, because of the broad purpose of our work—to understand and make explicit as best we can the complex relationships between individuals and the contexts within which they live, work, and develop—we have a responsibility to provide a level of translation and theoretical interpretation. What this means in practice is for each life history researcher to understand and articulate.

By virtue of our roles as researchers, and our access to a collection of information rather than to a single personal story or viewpoint, our interpretations are differently informed. We have the capacity and, we emphasize, responsibility to make and render collective meaning. In saying this, we are not intending to suggest that researchers' interpretations are the only ones possible for a given life, and we are not meaning to suggest that researchers should strive toward neat and finite conclusions. Rather, we are suggesting that researchers have a unique position and perspective that enables them to identify and make explicit themes and connections that give a particular shape and meaning to a body of material. In this way, we see the role of researcher in interpretation as similar to that of a curator in a museum or art gallery.

Curators, like those engaged in sound and substantial life history analysis, seek to uncover the fundamental elements, themes, complexities, and conceptualizations behind the artwork and the artist's life. They display the works in a manner that provides a level of understanding yet evokes questions and notates points of interest. Depending on the degree and framing of their critical perspective, their fundamental values about life, art, society, culture, and even civilization (Western, though it may be, since the notion of curatorship is a Western construct), curators will arrange and talk about the artworks in different ways. They seek to tell a story or to have well-told, well-known stories questioned. They attempt to provoke audience response. They want viewers to leave thinking differently than when they arrived at the viewing place. They want their arrangement of the artist's or artists' work, and the viewing/experiencing of the work itself, to make a difference in the life of people. Hence, in reading research texts, as in viewing art, the reader/audience member has an active rather than passive role in interpretation. We refer again to Maura McIntyre's writing in chapter 18 about the role of the reader in interpreting research texts.

LEVELS AND PROCESSES OF ANALYSIS

In his book *Transforming Qualitative Data: Description, Analysis, and Interpretation* (1994), noted educational anthropologist Wolcott uses the concept of transformation to describe the researcher's task of doing something with the vast amount of material collected so that it can be communicated in a coherent way to a larger audience. For us the term has a somewhat mystical tone. (It also reminds us of the enthusiasm for trans- former toys that lasted a short while: menlike action figures that suddenly, with a twist of the wrist, become something else—a space rocket, an armored vehicle, a bomber. "Lives"—or "bodies"—are transformed, re-presented.) Transformation is about change, especially change in form. It is about changing the appearance and form of a life told as surely as it is about revealing the heart and substance of that life. But the title and substance of Wolcott's book does capture the essence of the tasks of this phase of life history work. Wolcott's delineation of the analysis process into the constituent elements of description, analysis, and interpretation is also helpful for understanding the complex and multilayered processes of making meaning.

The three levels or phases of analysis involve different ways of reading or working with the research material and represent different levels of meaning making. While it may seem that we are describing the phases in a distinctive and definitive way, we are actually endeavoring to illustrate the concept of a multilevel, recursive process with coherent and intercon- nected elements. As we work with research texts we read them with in- creasingly penetrating lenses. First readings may reveal insights that help us to sketch a profile of an individual. From a second, deeper reading might emerge some patterns or themes that help us to begin filling in and adding shape and texture to our understanding of the individual. Read- ings of contextual information, material about the person-in-place, will likely add other dimensions and perspectives. And eventually, as Plum- mer (1983, 99) insists, the "brooding and reflecting upon mounds of data for long periods of time" will begin to "make sense" and "feel right," and "key ideas and themes [will] flow from it." Plummer reminds us here also of the role of intuition.

Without wanting to make too much of the analogy, we are reminded of the role of detectives. In order to catch or apprehend a criminal, or to make a case for prosecution, it is important to try to understand the crim- inal's thinking. The investigator pieces together scraps of information about the life of the suspect in order to infer potential action (so as to out- maneuver him, for instance) or explain his behavior and actions. Intu- ition, coupled with evidence of all kinds, is the vehicle for insight, and in more than one movie or television show, or real-life drama, we have seen the line between the criminal and detective minds to be very thin. In a sense, as researchers, one of our analysis goals is to try to emulate the thinking of research participants so that we can understand the meaning of their experiences. In a sense, we are attempting to relive elements of an individual's life so that we can authentically portray that life. At the same time it is important to acknowledge that, no matter how authentic our portrayal, it is *our* portrayal. It represents a retelling, a re-presentation, filtered through time and enhanced by articulation and interpretation.

Engaging with research texts at different levels and representing each of these levels are important for both researcher and reader. Through a descriptive analysis and representation we come to know the individuals—like being introduced to and coming to know characters in a compelling literary work. In composing this part of the analysis, the researcher stays close to the gathered information. Through a process of deeper analysis and representation the researcher and reader see themes and connections that provide structure and meaning—the story begins to unfold, the plot line is revealed. At this level the researcher's lens is clearly evident as she seeks to make meaning of participants' lives in context. From her unique vantage point, the researcher has the capacity to stand back and, through a wide-angle interpretive lens, consider the meanings revealed. In so doing she offers a broader and more contextualized interpretation. She conducts an exegesis of the literary work.

In life history research, where the stories told and the meanings attached to them are central, deciding on a form and structure of the telling is vital to the quality of the work. Decisions about how to introduce, present, depict or describe the participants are crucial. The descriptive level of analysis and representation provides the foundation and organizing framework for the subsequent levels of analysis and the ways in which the meanings derived are represented. The manner and tone of an introduction to a participant's life is crucial for framing the analysis and representational work of researching. For example, a description (or profile, portrait, or account) might be in the form of an expository account, based on information gathered, that introduces the participant or participants and hints at essential elements or key themes from her life or their lives that are relevant to the research focus. This kind of introduction could be relatively brief or quite lengthy and might include excerpts from research conversations. Mainly, though, it is likely to ring of the researcher's voice.

In direct contrast to an expository account of a life lived is a descriptive introduction that appears entirely in the words and voice of the participant (see, for example, Behar 1993, and Orr, chapter 15, this volume). To prepare such an account the researcher selects, organizes, and edits transcribed text. The effect created by this kind of descriptive representation is substantially different from that created by the previous kind of account. Also at play here are issues related to the politics and power of "voice." Etter-Lewis (1993), in her book *My Soul Is My Own: Oral Narratives of African American Women in the Professions*, provides excellent examples of this kind of descriptive account as well as an extensive explanation and discussion of the analysis and representation processes. She describes, among other things, how grammatical voice can be, and has been, used to express aspects of power. With respect to representational form, presence of the first person, active voice of the participants communicates an element of power that is quite different from that communicated when the researcher subjugates the participants' words.

Another form of descriptive account is when researchers take literary license with participants' words. For instance, in poetic transcription (see, for example, Glesne 1997, 1999; Richardson 1992, 1994), words of participants are carefully selected, ordered, and placed by the researcher to communicate a particular meaning or image through poetic or poemlike form. The voice of poetic transcription is neither the researcher's nor the participants' but a third voice that emerges through creative dialogue between words and structures. According to Glesne (1997, 213), participants' words are "shaped by [the] researcher to give pleasure and truth." The notion that research "reports" can be pleasurable is alluring—and they can be.

Yet another form of descriptive representation is that of researcher-created fiction. In their book *Fiction and Social Research: By Ice or Fire*, Anna Banks and Stephen Banks (1998, preface) assert: "If scholarly research is genuinely a pursuit of the researcher's mind and heart, it is the expression that makes the research come to life and connect each of us to what we have learned, to a tradition, and to audiences." Banks and Banks go on to say, "Whenever the aim of the research is to evoke in audiences a feel for the subjective experience of others, fiction can be the mode of representation" (1998, 18). Given that we have rejected the pursuit of one Truth and the representation of objective facts as our research responsibilities, we can now devote our attention to forms that evoke, resonate, and communicate.

Fictional forms present an array of new possibilities for research representation and connection with human experience. Although not a life history inquiry, Kilbourn, in his book *For the Love of Teaching* (1998), explores, through an essay and a novella, the complexities of teaching, learning, schooling, parenting, and writing. His use of nonacademic prose, including fiction, allows him to evoke emotion and empathy, create tangible, vicarious experiences, and stimulate a deeper, more thoughtful reader response than is engendered through conventional academic text form. In a similar way, Dunlop wrote *Boundary Bay: A Novel As Educational Research* (1999), a well-received novel (the first accepted as a doctoral thesis in education within Canada) that explores the lives, work, and passions of beginning teachers and university educators as they are played out within institutional and societal structures. For Dunlop, "fictions are not the unreal side of reality or the opposite of reality; they are conditions that enable the production of possible worlds" (1999, ii). Similarly, brenda brown (1999, ii) wrote "a fictional tale spun from the imaginary realm, held within theory, while engaging in a collaborative relationship with art, story, and lived experience." Her "true story with lies" made possible a telling about childhood sexual abuse. In part 2, chapter 11, Ardra explores the role of fictionalized telling as a way of honoring participant safety. Gary's accounts in "Beginnings" and "Endings" also speak to this issue.

All telling is an interpretation regardless of whose voice is heard; all interpretation is a fiction despite reliance on "facts." No matter what we do and how we do it we are not representing Truth (with a capital T). What *do* we want to represent and communicate? This is the important question. Perhaps it is one of the most important questions that can be asked once a study is under way. Another important question: How close to the "data" and true to the original form is it important for us to stay? And, further, what are the considerations that help us to answer these and related questions?

If we accept the premise that all memory is selective, a reconstruction or perhaps a creation of mind and, therefore, a fiction, then we should assume that the remembrances selected and told earn their status as memorable and significant events for good reason. The stories we remember and tell about our lives reflect who we are, how we see ourselves, and, perhaps, how we wish to be seen. As Langness and Frank (1981, 109) state, "If memory is selective, then there must be a prior structure of personal identity that provides the template by which certain events are cast as images significant enough to be stored." In other words, when participants reveal elements of their life histories, they are revealing elements of their identities. In a sense, it is as though the participant engages in the very first level of analysis. They sift out, from their wealth of experience, stories to tell us. They abbreviate or condense even their most rehearsed versions of events or experiences. No matter how much time we spend in conversation with participants their revelations to us are always constrained or limited. This is the nature of retelling experience. One of our tasks is to understand the thinking or meaning making—the conceptual framework, as it were—that induced a participant's analysis of experience and the selection of stories told to us. In an overarching way we seek to understand a participant's conception of self. As life history researchers interpreting and representing lives, we use these identifying elements as organizing constructs, foundational themes, or root metaphors. Kohli (1981, 65) reminds us that "life histories are . . . not a collection of all the events of the individual's life course, but rather 'structural self-images.'"

Denzin (1989a) and others have used the notion of epiphany to describe the major, life-marking events that shape a person. Epiphanies hold strong sway on our actions and play out in surprising ways within the minor and grand schemes of our lives. While the religious connotations of the term may be irrelevant for our purposes, the notion of epiphany still has a particular utility for us in the messy, interwoven, sometimes mind-boggling tasks of meaning making. (The term "epiphanies" is akin to the "critical incidents" or "critical phases," for example, that Sikes [1985] and Measor [1985] talk about in their work on teachers' careers, the "critical interactive phases" to which Becker [1966] refers and, similarly, the "periods of strain" that Straus and Rainwater [1962] note in their work on the lives of chemists.)

Individuals have profound experiences of many kinds—events that turn lives around or, less dramatically, mark the passage of the years and the tone, tenor, and influence of a life. These are the events and circumstances to which we return when reconstructing the past and making sense of our lives. These are epiphanies. For a researcher wading through thickets of information about a life—sifting though piles of notes and text, images and artifacts—the notion of epiphany is useful. Just as epiphanies shape the major decisions and meanings that individuals ascribe to a life, so too are they found in the process of inquiry.

Invariably, for the researcher struggling with the task of analysis or narrative meaning-making, epiphanies become organizing points around which lives can be retold. They are like flashing neon signs blazing in the night. They illuminate. They become text or image markers. Ultimately, they can become the story lines that hook the reader. In their power to convince they provide authenticity and substance to the convictions of a life lived. Unearthing epiphanic events of a life lived often become epiphanic research moments for one engaged in research analysis. In turn, they become the pivotal points around which the story of that life is told.

Discovering epiphanic moments in an individual's life or central elements of a person's identity comes as a result of intensive engagement. It requires listening and looking hard and deep into words spoken out loud and between the lines, searching for underlying constructs that give shape and meaning to individuals' lives in context. Following Eudora Welty (cited in Lawrence-Lightfoot and Hoffmann-Davis, 1997), as life history researchers we need to listen *for* a story rather than *to* a story as we engage with participants in conversation and later with information gathered.

Making decisions through the processes of making meaning and interpretation involves several important considerations. First, as researchers we need to look and listen for the root metaphors, life-defining themes, central truths, or epiphanies that can provide an organizing construct for a participant's life. These constructs will also figure centrally in the broader interpretation and in the organization of the account. Second, the way the story is told must also reflect the guiding research principles of relationality, respect, care, and empathy. In other words, the representations of meaning must be full of respect and care and they must reflect the reflexive and reciprocal qualities of the research relationship. Finally, as researchers, we need to find a form and structure that best reflects and upholds the integrity of participants and ourselves and attaches a deep level of authenticity to the meanings expressed.

REALIZING THE POSSIBILITIES
FOR REPRESENTATIONAL FORMS

We know firsthand that the really difficult work in this final phase of life history work is realizing the previously imagined possibilities for representational forms. (Similarly, making connections with what others have written about similar topics and lives is also difficult but it follows "naturally" from that which we choose to represent.) Sound research conclusions, even generation of theory, are made or not, according to the form of representation employed (not to exclude the political and editorial influences that come with being connected to some academic journals or publishers and their editors, or to others who control exhibition or alternative communication media, spaces, or events). From experience and perusal of many qualitative research reports we believe the element of representation is given less consideration than it deserves. The tendency is that adherence to a method, and one's articulation of it, is given more attention by researchers. It is hoped that the importance of representational form is clear from reading chapter 5.

Researchers tend to procrastinate and slough off considering representational possibilities because they raise the possibility of difficult and even more time-consuming work. It is also, generally, outside our frames of reference and experience—it is not what we, as university-based academics, were "trained" to do! Given that conventional scholarship is largely embedded in traditions of dry, disengaged reporting, there are usually few alternative models for new, emerging scholars to follow. Perhaps, mostly, it is common for much weight to be given to the "conclusions" or the "results," and the manner of their presentation is given less attention than each of the previous phases of the work. The institutional and peer pressures to publish, which often places value on quantity of publications over quality, is a disincentive to ponder long and hard about representational forms. (Besides, within the institutional reward structures of merit pay and promotion at universities, there is little space for acknowledgment of creative endeavors that may be represented by some of the alternative representational forms we have mentioned. "Best to wait until after you have tenure before trying out wildly creative texts or representations," we know, is commonplace advice for new tenure-stream scholars. As creative researchers these are the kinds of institutional disincentives we ought to challenge.)

In life history research, however—as in other forms of qualitative research where researchers have a particular commitment to pushing the boundaries of form and audience—we view representational form as central to the achievement of research goals. As Eisner (1993, 6) puts it, "meaning is shaped by the form in which it appears." In other words, the form, itself, has power to inform. Representation, according to Eisner, is "the process of transforming the contents of consciousness into a public form so that they can be stabilized, inspected, edited, and shared with others. . . . Meaning is shaped by the form in which it appears."

It is helpful to remind ourselves that our research reports—in whatever form they appear—are the main vehicle through which our scholarship becomes known and, for that matter, widely accepted or rejected by peers. Still, as we write or represent "differently" we are also subject to possible rejection by some of those very same peers. We, too, in the past have given less attention to this element of our scholarship than we care to admit. Our position now is that it is a significant element of our work on which our scholarship and contribution to our respective professions or fields of inquiry will be judged.

In contrast to more linear approaches to research representation, where writing is interpreted as "writing up" the data and analysis, in the kind of research we advocate, writing (or any mode of arts-informed representation, for that matter) is an integral part of the analysis process. We write *for* meaning rather than *to record* meaning. Edel, in *Writing Lives: Principia Biographica* (1984, 15), claims that the quality of a written life "resides in the art of narration, not in the substance of the story. The substance exists before the narrative begins." This assertion acknowledges the significance of the decision making around form and structure and the responsibility inherent in the writer's task. Acknowledging the complex and messy nature of lives, he goes on to say, "a writer of lives must extract individuals from their chaos yet create an illusion that they are in the midst of life— in the way that a painter arrives at an approximation of a familiar visage on canvas."

ISSUES OF RIGOR IN LIFE HISTORY RESEARCH

What are the qualities of rigor? What are the evidences of it? How important is it? How do life history researchers ensure its presence? One of the hallmarks of qualitative research is the transparency of the research process, what Kilbourn (1999) describes as "self-consciousness," which makes clear the researcher's connection between method and meaning.

When we talk of rigor we are referring to standards or criteria used to make judgments about the quality of a research piece. Research grounded in a positivist tradition relies on validity criteria primarily associated with methods of measurement and the accuracy with which those methods are able to represent and make predictions about the objective world. These criteria of validity (internal and external), reliability, and generalizability (to populations) have become what Kvale (1995, 20) calls "the methodological holy trinity of psychological science." But these constructs, as revered as they are by some researchers (and in fields beyond psychology), are simply inadequate for judging the goodness of research that falls outside the positivist paradigm. Every report of research contains knowledge claims and every report of research must provide evidence to support these claims; however, judgments about how any piece of research does both of those things must be fundamentally tied to the epistemological roots of the research methodology. To use the criteria of validity, reliability, and generalizability to assess a life history study, for example, would be like examining the contents of a barrel of apples in order to decide which orange to buy (or examining the apples for their quality and freshness but applying knowledge about oranges and their desired qualities). To extend the metaphor, within the veritable fruit market of qualitative research, each variety must be judged on its own merits. The veracity of knowledge claims is tied to purpose and method. Throughout and beyond analysis and representation researchers are guided by a set of standards or qualities by which their work can be judged. Because those standards are context- or method-dependent, it is essential for each researcher to decide *how* her work can best be judged. To use another analogy, providing a map for the journey will help readers or viewers follow the trail, have a sense of the destination, and understand decisions made along the way. To provide a sense of how this might work we draw examples from a variety of writings about qualitative research methodology.

It is noteworthy that researchers, within the broad qualitative research paradigm, have varying levels of comfort with or at least take varying degrees of issue with the language used to describe qualities of methodological rigor. These range from employing the language of positivism but assigning new meaning to the words, to assigning one-to-one correspondence to the language of positivism and post-positivism (for example, external validity equals transferability), to an explicit rejection of positivistic language and constructs in favor of terms that more appropriately reflect the paradigmatic roots of the research.

Drawing on the work of several qualitative researchers, Merriam (1988) offers detailed guidelines for establishing sound qualitative, case study research. Triangulation, member checks, length of time in the field, peer examination, involving participants in all aspects of the study, and declaring researcher biases are all listed under the heading "internal validity." These are strategies for ensuring that the work is "truthful."

"Reliability" is used synonymously with "dependability." Strategies for ensuring reliability in qualitative research are triangulation and transparency of the research process, both in terms of the perspectives and assumptions informing researcher's decisions along the way and a detailed accounting or "audit trail" of the research procedure. Finally, the strategies of providing rich, thick descriptive accounts, establishing how typical the case or account is compared with others, and conducting cross-site or cross-case analysis are each listed under "external validity" as ways to enhance generalizability.

The above strategies for enhancing the strength and quality of a study are quite typically cited by qualitative researchers. As evidenced by the language of one-to-one correspondence with positivist-based constructs and by the intentionality of some of the strategies, these standards still smack of positivistic thinking and are, therefore, not appropriate for making judgments about qualitative research that is conducted from other paradigmatic vantage points. For example, while a piece of research represented as fiction *could* be tested and pass according to these criteria, the constructs and language are simply not appropriate. As Kilbourn (1999, 31) asserts:

> The strength of a piece of fiction lies in its structural corroboration—its coherence with the human condition and credible possibility. . . . The power of fiction is its ability to show . . . the qualities of experience that we . . . recognize as true of people and situations.

Kvale (1995, 37) suggests that a validity paradox has been created by the persistent quest for certainty and legitimation, and that we need to find a way out of that paradox of "legitimation mania and validity erosion." He offers a useful reframing of the concept of validity so that post-positivistic research is judged according to the quality of its crafting, the nature of its communicability, and its pragmatic value. He argues that research attendant to these qualities would make questions of validity superfluous because it would be so powerful and convincing in its own right that it would be inherently valid, like a strong work of art.

Wolcott (1994) lends further support to the idea that the concept of validity itself is problematic for qualitative researchers. At the end of a lengthy discussion of ways in which he attempts to "satisfy the implicit challenge of validity" in the conduct of research, he admits, "Validity neither guides nor informs my work. What I seek is not unrelated to validity, but 'validity' does not capture its essence and is not the right term" (1994, 347, 356). He goes on to assert that "We have labored too long under the burden of this concept (are there others as well?) . . . [and need to] look elsewhere in our continuing search for and dialogue about criteria appropriate to qualitative researchers' approaches and purposes" (1994, 369).

Lawrence-Lightfoot and Hoffman-Davis are among those who choose different ideas and words to think and talk about the quality of their work. For them "good" research results in "a seamless synthesis of rigorous procedures that unite[s] in an expressive *aesthetic whole*" (1997, 274, emphasis in the original). The criteria or qualities inherent in this work are resonance, authenticity, and coherence.

Barone and Eisner (1997), operating from within a particular approach to arts-based research, lay out seven features of arts-based educational inquiry that might be used as design elements and/or to determine the extent to which an inquiry can be characterized as arts-based. (We prefer the use of the term "arts-informed" research because it suggests that the processes and forms of researching and representation are *informed by* the arts, instead of being *based in* them or even, perhaps, being about them.) They are the creation of virtual reality; the presence of ambiguity; the use of expressive language; the use of contextualized and vernacular language; the promotion of empathy; personal signature of the researcher/writer; and the presence of aesthetic form.

It may be useful to follow up on any or all of these (and other) brief references to how various researchers address issues of rigor. Our main point in presenting this brief overview is to highlight the relationship between research quality, purpose, and method. If the proverbial shoes fit in style, size, color, aesthetic appeal, and so on, then they can probably be worn for the occasion of judging research quality. If, however, they are ill-fitting in any way, then new ones are in order, even if it means personally designing and hand crafting a new model. Always, though, internal consistency between process and form, between intentions and "outcomes" (not a word we like), between epistemology and practice, between methods and "standards" of judgment are essential for developing satisfying and sound life history research accounts—no matter what form they may be.

The life history research approach, described and illustrated throughout this book, reflects several distinctive features. Judgments about the quality of an inquiry that is informed by this approach must necessarily honor these defining features. We, therefore, delineate a set of eight elements and associated features that can serve as standards or criteria by which life history research—which places central the notions of *self, relationship,* and *artfulness*—can be judged. For each element we also pose questions that might usefully guide the evaluation process.

Defining Elements of Life History Research

Intentionality. All research has one or more purposes but not all research is driven by a moral commitment. "Good" life history research has both a clear *intellectual* purpose and *moral* purpose. Life history researchers have two intentions: to advance understanding about the complex interaction between individuals' lives and the institutional and societal contexts within which they are lived; and, through consciousness raising and associated action, to contribute to the creation of more just and dignified explorations and renderings of the human condition that, in turn, lead to the enhancement of qualities and conditions under which lives are lived. Ultimately, the research must stand for something.

Researcher presence. A researcher's presence in life history research is evident in a number of ways throughout the research account (and by implication throughout the entire researching process). We especially infer a degree of self-consciousness in the procedural elements of the work. The researcher is present through an explicit *reflexive self-accounting*; his presence is also implied and *felt*; and, the research text clearly bears his *signature* or *fingerprint*. Life history research texts explicitly (although, perhaps subtly) reveal the intersection of a researcher's life with that or those of the researched.

Methodological commitment. The life history research approach we advance is guided by a set of articulated principles that are reflected throughout the inquiry process. Sound life history research reflects a methodological commitment through evidence of a *principled process* and *procedural harmony*. These qualities evidence a deep reflexiveness about processes grounded in a set of coherent ideological principles. The principles, as articulated in chapter 2, are rooted in notions of relationality, mutuality, empathy, care, sensitivity, and respect.

Holistic quality. From purpose to method to interpretation and representation, life history research is a holistic process and rendering that runs counter to conventional research endeavors that tend to be linear, sequential, compartmentalized, and distanced from researcher and participants. A rigorous life history research account is imbued with an *internal consistency* and *coherence* that represents its seamless quality. Such an account also evidences a high level of *authenticity* that speaks to the truthfulness and sincerity of the research relationship, process of inquiry, interpretation, and representational form.

Communicability. Foremost in our approach to life history research are issues related to audience and the transformative potential of the work. Life history research that maximizes its communicative potential addresses concerns about the *accessibility* of the research account, usually through the form and language with which it is written. For other than printed, text-bound representations of research, accessibility is related to the potential for audience receptiveness and response. A life history account is also written or revealed with the express purpose of connecting, in a holistic way, with the hearts, souls, and minds of readers. It is intended to have an evocative quality and a high level of resonance for audiences of all kinds.

Aesthetic form. How insights about lives in context are conveyed is as important as what insights are conveyed. In life history research that has an artful quality, attention to the aesthetics of form is important. Here, we are concerned both with the aesthetic *quality* of the research account and its aesthetic *appeal*. By the former we mean how well the form adheres to a particular set of artistic processes and conventions. For example: Does the chosen form—say, a novel—follow the conventions of that genre? Is the process of visual art making explicitly honored and adequately represented in the work? By the latter we mean how well the form "works" as a mode of communication.

Knowledge claims. Research is about advancing knowledge, however "knowledge" is defined. As researchers, we make claims about what we have come to know through our work and we do this in a variety of explicit and subtle ways. Our stance in life history research rejects any notions about the possibilities of an absolute and objective truth and relieves the researcher of any responsibilities for making knowledge claims that are conclusive, finite, and universal. Any knowledge claims made must reflect the multidimensional, complex, dynamic, intersubjective, and contextual nature of human experience. In so doing, knowledge claims must be made with sufficient ambiguity and humility to allow for multiple interpretations and reader response.

Contributions. Tied to the intellectual and moral purposes of life history research are its theoretical and practical contributions. Sound and rigorous life history research has both *theoretical* potential and *transformative* potential. The former acknowledges the centrality of the "So what?" question and the power of the inquiry work to provide insight into individual lives and, more generally, the human condition, while the latter urges us as researchers to imagine new possibilities for those whom our work is about and for. We are not passive agents of either the state or the universities or any other agency of society. We have responsibilities toward fellow humans.

SOME FINAL QUESTIONS TO CONSIDER AS INDICATIVE OF THE DEFINING ELEMENTS

The answers to the following questions (and there are many more to be added) are integral to the development of sound, defensible scholarship grounded in a consistent and coherent life history perspective. It is hoped that they will return us to the beginning of the process of life history work and remind us of the important goals with which we began.

They are (in no particular order apart from some semblance of chronological sequencing):

- What is my purpose? What is the personal, theoretical, and social
  value of the work? Where is the place for the moral and intellectual
  purposes within the inquiry endeavor? What are they?
- What are the fundamental personal and professional perspectives
  that drive my work? How does this inquiry work fit with my worldview?
- Is the method appropriate to the purpose? In process, am I true to the
  method?
- Is the process informed by a set of coherent principles?
- Am I true to my principles throughout the inquiry process?
- Is my presence felt and known throughout the work? Will others
  know that the work is mine while the life told is of another? How
  have I told of or represented the intersection of lives?
- Does the form of representation make inherent sense? Is it extended
  to its full capacity, given the constraints of resources or energy?
- Does the work authentically represent the participants?
- Does the substance of the work ring true to the participants, to me,
  and to a wider audience? Who makes up the audiences for this work?
  How can I best reach them?
- Do all elements of the work—from purpose to interpretation and
  representation—cohere and work together?
- Are my knowledge claims (however they are articulated) consistent
  with the perspectives and principles that guided the research?
- Have I honored the reader's role in interpretation?
- To what extent is my work an expression of self, relationships, and
  artfulness?

2

EXPERIENCING METHOD

7

Lessons from Nurses' Lives

Renee Sarchuk Will

Writing within the context of nursing and nurse education, Renee Sarchuk Will challenges the status quo conception of nursing knowledge as narrowly defined by theory and clinical practice. She argues that the complexity of nursing knowledge that is expressed in nursing practice is substantially informed by individuals' life histories. This chapter elucidates the role of life history research in delineating a professional knowledge base. In so doing, it illustrates one of the broad purposes of life history research as discussed in chapter 1 and how it is evidenced in the field of health sciences, particularly nursing. An earlier version of this account was presented February 19, 1999, at the First International Advances in Qualitative Methodologies Conference, Edmonton, Alberta, Canada.

When I was thirteen, my paternal grandfather died. My brother and sisters and I were staying with my grandparents while my parents were away. On Monday of the Labor Day weekend, feeling unwell, my grandfather washed, shaved, and dressed in a suit, as he had every day of his adult life, and drove himself to the doctor's office. He was immediately admitted to the hospital, having suffered a major heart attack. Four days later, he put down the book he was reading and died alone in the intensive care unit. I clearly remember my grandmother and aunt leaving for the hospital and, later, my father's breaking voice on the telephone, telling me they were on their way home, and then my grandmother coming into the hall.

Later I learned that my grandfather's body was moved to the morgue before my grandmother and aunt arrived at the hospital. They learned of his death by finding his bed empty when they entered the room. I remember, in the midst of grief, being dumbfounded at the callousness of this act. How could the nurses and physicians have let this happen? Why didn't someone stop them, take them aside, and tell them?

As I recall and write this story, I realize it has affected me differently at different times of my life. As a child, I knew this experience as the loss of a beloved grandparent. As an adult, I recognize that it profoundly affects the way in which I understand the death of a family member, of how I *know* that phenomenon. And as a nurse, I believe the impact of this life experience extends to the way in which I *know* nursing and conduct my practice.

In 1975, right after graduation, I went to work on a terminal care unit. Today, these wards are palliative care units, but in 1975, our predominant focus was revealed in the name: terminal care. I worked there the first time for fifteen months, eventually being present for hundreds of patients' deaths, but only the first one remains clearly etched in memory; his name, diagnosis, and room number, 209. He was about seventy-five years old and had cancer of the bone. Surgeons had excised his cheekbone, the orbital fossa, his right eye, and his upper mandible. The result was a huge crater that became an awful, foul-smelling wound. Dressing changes were a nightmare because of the smell and the fact that it took about forty-five minutes. No one wanted to be assigned to this patient.

For some reason, I took to him. I would traipse down to his room, set up my tray, and we would chat about a whole variety of topics, forgotten now, while I did the dressing change, and I guess I became quite attached to him. Eventually, he was dying. I wanted to sit with him but was told by the head nurse to attend to my other duties. The chaplain was with him. Despite my low status as a "novice" nurse, I argued with her, believing it my responsibility to be with him. In 1975, arguing with the head nurse was an exercise in frustration. I was not present when he died. She did, however, assign me to the postmortem care with a young, new orderly. I think he was more scared than I, but not much. Part of that job is packing up belongings. In the man's bedside table I found a bus pass with his picture on it, a picture of him before cancer and surgery had changed him into someone almost unrecognizable. Showing it to the orderly, I started to cry, overwhelmed by what this man had experienced and that here he was at the end of his life, alone with two strangers putting his things in bags.

At the time of this man's death I was a very new nurse with only a few months of clinical experience. This was, in fact, my first "professional" experience of death. I had taken no courses in my nursing program about death or palliation. In fact, I do not even remember having a single discussion about the end of life in four years of nursing education, so my knowledge of dying did not arise in my nursing education or clinical experiences. I was very certain, though, that I had to be present for this man's death, that I had a part to play in his dying.

These stories of my life, recently written, compel me to strive to understand how a nurse's nonclinical life experiences inform nursing knowledge. In my life history study, therefore, I am both researcher and participant, engaged in conversation with one other woman who nurses on a palliative care unit. The impetus for this work is twofold: reflection on my own life experiences and what significance they have held for my nursing practice; and my belief that many nurses are reluctant to reflect on how their nursing knowledge might be informed by experiences outside the realms of theory and clinical practice.

Nursing academe has concentrated on the development of an empiric knowledge base, only recently exploring knowledge embedded in clinical practice. Consideration of nurses' lives outside the clinical realm is a neglected area, even though we invest a great deal of who we are in our relationships with patients. Many nurses struggle with this personal investment, caught up in contradictory messages of nursing education. "Nursing sought to teach me to maintain both separation and linkage in my practice—separation, 'you must remember that the other is a stranger,' and linkage, 'you must think and act as if he [sic] were not'" (Dunlop 1986, 663). This pursuit of separateness is revealed in the words of a nurse, caring for a patient with the same diagnosis as a family member. "Because my own mother had [breast cancer] . . . personal feelings can get into it. You have to really ignore that, leave your feelings at home" (Will and Fast Braun 1997, 12).

For nurses, leaving our feelings at home is, in reality, virtually impossible. As this nurse's words reveal, we engage with other human beings at profoundly intimate times, often providing care and support in circumstances similar to that we have personally experienced. These experiences produce a particular and subjective way of knowing a life event; a way of knowing that is further delimited by the experience's context. Our lives are deeply contextualized, lived as they are in the foreground of a variegated backdrop of family life and tensions, cultural, educational and religious influences, and institutional settings that may or may not honor and respect unique ways of knowing. The depth and breadth of contextual layers suggests that there are also particular and subjective ways in which a nurse's life experiences will find their way into her nursing knowledge and, subsequently, her nursing practice.

Where the nurse works is a good example of the power of influence. Settings vary from technology-driven operating rooms and intensive care units, to patients' homes, including homes located in hotels and on the streets. It is critical to choose a research method that not only discloses these and other contextual features, but also begs examination of them, enabling the researcher and participant to appreciate their impact in a fuller sense. Failure to do so is to assume life is context-free, that we are in no way touched by events and relationships that transpire around us. Life history is a vehicle for this understanding, as it allows for the exploration of the intersection between an individual's life and the context within which that life has been and is lived.

Exploration of the juxtaposition of life and context necessitates two key decisions: where to locate the study and, within that context, who to invite to participate. I chose to locate my study in palliative care as it is the predominant context of my own practice and because it is an emerging specialty, only now being recognized as requiring a body of knowledge and skills different from other practice areas. I invited a nurse to participate in the research expressly because her work is with dying people. The personal and subjective nature of knowledge arising from life experience necessitates a thorough, intense picture of the life and the context within which it is being and has been lived. I was able to achieve this depth of understanding by focusing my attention on this nurse.

A review of health sciences literature demonstrates that research using life history method has tremendous clinical significance. Saillant (1990), a medical anthropologist, focuses our attention on context, particularly the context within which an individual experiences illness. Her poignant life story of a woman dying of cancer depicts an ever-widening gap between the patient's experience of illness and imminent death, and the context of an oncological discourse of hope and survival. The woman's increasing alienation, as she moves beyond the prevailing discourse, impresses upon us the need to reveal how her and others' experiences are shaped and informed by the events of life.

Miller (1994), an assistant professor of psychiatry, explores borderline personality disorder from the patients' perspective. In this work, the descriptions of patients' lives are so rich that details not previously shared with therapists are revealed, perhaps because participants perceived that they and the researcher were involved in a more collaborative and egalitarian relationship than if they were in a therapist-client relationship. Miller hypothesizes that information is seen as helpful to others rather than detrimental to self, as may be the case when sharing is linked to treatment decisions.

This notion of life history method as a therapeutic intervention is debated in occupational therapy. In Larson and Fanchiang (1996, 247), it is described as a means to assist therapists in "better understanding the complexity and contexts of the client and his or her experience in the therapeutic process." Burke and Kern (1996) claim life history method as a legitimate part of occupational therapy practice and propose that therapists who separate life history from their regular work are failing to account for unique and complex needs of each patient.

In nursing, very few examples of the life history method are available for consideration. Bramwell (1984) suggests life history's value lies in the holistic perspective that nurses can obtain of individuals and their lives. Use of the method as described is limited, however, because Bramwell only perceives it being used with older people. King (1989) documents the life health history of an eighty-five-year-old woman through the use of a life health-care history protocol proposed by Leininger (1985). Here again, the method is utilized in a limited way, exploring a single aspect, the health history, of a long life.

The use of the life history method in nursing research has the potential to be, in reality, broader and richer than is revealed in these limited examples. It gives us the capacity to reveal aspects of nurses' and patients' lives that are not well represented, their life experiences outside of the clinical practice environment in which they meet. It provides a means of illuminating and exploring how these life experiences frame the way in which they know or make meaning of experiences of health and illness. It can, therefore, be used to reveal the lives and practices of nurses: who they are, what they believe their knowledge to be, and how they understand the contextual landscape of their nursing practice.

We can look beyond the curricula of educational programs and the knowledge arising from experience in particular clinical practice settings, to knowledge arising from life experience; experiences of birth, health, illness, and death that we share in our lives and that affect us in ways we seldom consider. How do these milestone experiences become part of what we know about the human condition and about nursing? The method provides an opportunity to engage with nurses in the reconstruction of their life histories, and in shared exploration of how those histories inform their nursing knowledge.

Further, the life history method can explicate the difference between traditional and societal expectations of nurses—and any individual nurse's unique history—and has the capacity for interpretation and molding future action. Nurses are "tested" on a daily basis through the fundamental and varied beliefs (their own and others, as well as those that are institutionally sanctioned) about what constitutes "nursing care" and how it will be accomplished. The institutions in which they are employed, the physicians with whom they work, and the public for whom they care, all have different expectations of what nurses can and will do. What these expectations are and how nurses perceive or define their nursing practice have not been well investigated. Through life history method, the opportunity exists to explore these relationships of institutional culture, social structure, and individual lives.

Any attempt to portray nurses' contemporary situation must therefore begin "by recognizing the changing context within which [their] work is undertaken" (Ball and Goodson 1985, 2). Politically mandated health reform and restructuring illustrates the importance of considering context. In health reform, closure of institutions and beds, aimed at reducing health-care costs, has resulted in the deletion of thousands of nursing positions. Nurses have been retired, laid off, declared redundant, and "bumped" throughout facilities, out of specialized practice areas in which they have developed considerable knowledge and expertise. Nurses in hospitals grapple with increasing patient acuity and technological complexity that necessitates both greater time commitments and different knowledge. Nurses in community settings cope with the impact of shorter hospital stays and caring for much sicker people unmatched by resource availability. Diminishing dollars has led to increased numbers of unregulated, minimally trained staff replacing highly skilled and experienced practitioners, a strategy that increases a nurse's workload by expecting her to monitor what service is provided.

What is the significance of this context of health reform for nurses' lives and work, for the expression of their nursing knowledge? How do they understand the rapid and dramatic changes that seem to be overtaking their nursing practice? How can their knowledge contribute to the process? These are just some of the questions I wonder about when I listen to my colleagues talk about nursing. Research using the life history method can contribute richness and depth of understanding about these and other questions, thereby broadening our comprehension of the complexity of nursing knowledge and practice.

8

Responsibilities to Community: Relationality and Mutuality with Home-Educating Families

J. Gary Knowles

Gary Knowles draws on his research in the area of home education to explore three issues related to the process of researching lives in context. Knowles describes the personal history-based roots of his research in home education and how the principles of relationality, mutuality, and empathetic regard for community are articulated in his involvement with home-educating parents and their families. Foremost in Knowles's account are the principles guiding life history research as discussed in chapter 2.

Lives have wonderful ways of being led: sometimes by forces unknown, mysterious and energy-giving forces; sometimes by principles developed, profound notions that inspire allegiance and the refinement of a life; sometimes by events of local, national, and global significance, events that carry one's life headlong into the unknown as in uncontrolled movement within the press of a crowd; sometimes by the power of an influential other, a close, dear friend or family member, one whose energy is compelling and instructing; sometimes by opportunities of happenstance, events that shape and inspire new experiences as if by chance. "Happenstance" best describes the beginnings of my involvement with home education but it fails—and by far—to describe my commitment to the individuals and communities I have met as a result.

In this short account of elements of my life history researching experience I dwell on three interrelated issues. The life events that led me to explore home education is one issue, and the tone of receptiveness expressed by home educators to my work is another. The notions of relationality and mutuality come to the fore when I articulate my involvement with these parents and their families. Together, and for me, these raise issues of responsibilities to community.

MY LIFE INDUCES A RESEARCH TEXT

The source of my interest in home education is a story worth elaborating. I know this because, in numerous educational institutions I have visited over the past fifteen years or so—as teacher, presenter, or merely just an observer, a passer-by—whenever it is discovered that I am a researcher of "home schooling" lives the questions begin to flow, and they flow thick and fast. Often emotions flare. Anger, frustration, and rationalized objection have all been cast at me on different occasions. Barbs of criticism, too, have been fired. These are often the emotions of educators or other professionals who profess to know—never, though, as in the systematic knowing of an inquirer or the experiential knowing of a participant. Casting my work as a researcher helps to calm the emotive responses. Many of these individuals think of researchers as distant, unbiased, and objective. Other times there's just plain inquisitiveness about the topic—nothing political, nothing too emotional, nothing too charged. Just individuals asking, "So, what do they do?" "How do they do it?" "Where do they do it?" "When do they do it?" and "Why?" The classic questions. The fundamental questions of "scientific inquiry." The questions of research. Then they ask, "Why you?" "Why do you research it?" "When did you begin . . . ?" "What do you research?" "Are you an advocate?"

My responses are varied. This is personal stuff. I try to create a living image. I usually trace my life backward to the days of my youth, then forward to the present—a kind of oscillation of a life. I try to weave a cloth of experience. I tell of the strong ties to alternative expressions of pedagogy and curriculum. While my education was received at the hands of public school teachers in New Zealand during the 1950s and 1960s, I had a good number of them who worked well-outside the standard pedagogical boxes. Experiential learning and outdoor learning were some of the elements of these actions. And these notions continued to be as much part of my explorations of the mountains as they did of university classrooms and geography field trips. I talk about self-directed learning. I tell some more. . . . Then I get to the point about becoming a teacher in secondary schools. I tell about my involvement with kids who were on the outside, kids who were not "mainstream," kids on the margins. I was kind of on the margins also. . . . Years pass in my life. I often go against the grain, as I always have. . . . It's a habit of mind and spirit.

I tell about my involvement in a remote secondary school in a South Pacific island country. I am the principal. I tell about the fact that I am now a father and there's no accessible classroom for my two young children. I tell of our grappling with how to formally educate them. Then I tell listeners that we home-educated. We taught our two rambunctious kids at home. Time passes. We moved from that island nation, and then they attended formal schools.

Five or so years later I'm studying for an advanced degree at the University of Utah, Salt Lake City. There's a major court case occupying the minds of those who produce the media. It is the case involving the wife of John Singer. In an "ambush," Singer had been shot by sheriff's deputies in Summit County, supposedly because he home-educated and was a polygamist. It's a long story. . . . And then there are some myths . . . about the man, his wife, and their children (see, for example, Fleisher and Freedman, 1983).

The media's stories, however, shock me. They are off base. They reveal the near hysteria toward home education that surfaced in the late 1970s and early 1980s in the United States. Then, the courts were full of cases that illustrated the feverish objections of public school educators and the public alike (see Knowles, Marlow, and Muchmore 1992).

My story gets a little convoluted when I try to tell of my interests as a public and formal school educator. Public education doesn't mingle with home education, so I'm told. I tell my captive audience at the time that I'm completing a doctoral degree in education. I'm "supposed to be aligned with the schools," so the education professors suggest. But my resonance with these home-educating families under media siege persists. I know that parents are being misrepresented, maligned. While I have differences of opinion with the ideological orientations of highly conservative, Christian parents, I understand their issues. I've been there—or somewhere near! I intuitively know why they and their pedagogically driven peers went underground for a time. I know why many taught behind drawn shades. I know of the practical issues they face. I know of the instructional challenges. It's damned hard work. And I know that there is virtually no research on the topic but am surprised to find it out (just a handful of publications, mostly statistical or suspect in quality).

It's the early 1980s. Most of what is written about home education, if it is not advocacy journalism or damning criticism, is light. It doesn't get at the heart of why these parents do it and under what conditions. These are, it turns out, the questions that begin to fuel my fire. Very simple questions. Questions that arise from a happenstance intersection of lives.

As an emerging professor I wanted to get inside parents' experiences. I wanted to understand their actions. I sometimes stop my story about here. Other times I recount some of my subsequent experiences—had

over a couple of decades—of working with home educators. The happenstance occasion of the court case and my presence in Salt Lake City ce-
mented my researching interest in home education. A rare intersection,
and I found a purposeful focus that continues to motivate me. The text of
my own life begins to be interleaved with the text of researching home educators. And it has continued (see, for example, Knowles 1989, 1991a,
1991b, 1998; Knowles and Muchmore 1995; Mayberry et al. 1995).

RECEPTIVENESS TO RESEARCHING

Without being overly dramatic, years of withstanding media and legal
barrages forced many parents underground. Suspicion of "outsiders," especially professional educators, became the rule of the day—even while
there were slow increases in the numbers of parent-teachers and their
children who had "exited" from formal, mostly public schools. So, not altogether unexpectedly, when I first approached families requesting to
work with them it was a difficult pitch. Suspicions evaporated somewhat
when they discovered that I'd been "one of them," that I'd home-
educated. My philosophical orientation—my ideology—was unimpor-
tant to them. I'd done it! "But you will show the good side of home
schooling," they implored. I'd smile, not promising anything.

My goal in this early work was to come to understand the rationales
that parents had for engaging in the home-education enterprise (see, for
example, Knowles, 1989). I figured that there were deep-seated motives
behind their "exiting" actions and that the superficial reasons given in
both the scant research literature and the media were misleading. Biographical explorations seemed to the point, a perspective that took a
whole-life view of the meaning of experience, particularly early or prior
experiences of family and school and learning.

Underneath parents' cautious agreements to work with me floated an
ephemeral yet palpable quality of apprehension and expectation. New
parent-teachers, especially, looked for the possibilities of a mutually satisfying relationship. They knew of my teaching interests. They knew of my alternative education perspectives. All of this I'd revealed as a way of establishing rapport and comfort between us. I'd tell parents the story of how I
came to research home education. Given their chosen independence from
formal schools I wanted to reflect elements of that independence in the research process. I also wanted to respond to the new parent-teachers' appre-
hensions about the course of their new-found responsibilities.

Looking for a vehicle to give the parents greater authority over the
kind of information that I wanted to gather, I requested that they each

write or record an autobiographical narrative. I provided them a loose framework consisting of a series of issues to consider (which I called reflection topics). Alternatively, they could engage with me in conversational interviews. In addition, I spent considerable time in the homes of these families, at first observing from a distance (Why, that's what researchers did, didn't they?) but as my own confidence evolved over time I entered into the learning activities of the day as a full participant (sometimes even acting like another parent-teacher). Observation field notes and reflective notations became the main source of information apart from the life history accounts. All in all, though, my first attempts were more than a little clumsy but that changed as my researching confidence grew. Reflexivity birthed responsiveness and, in turn, relationality and eventually commitment to community. As I experienced the highly personal contexts of these families' affairs and educative actions it was hardly surprising that notions of relationality and mutuality surfaced as being crucial to my work.

The parents expected to get something out of my participation in their homes and in their highly personal, educative endeavors. Without realizing it, I was immediately thrust into a context where relationality and mutuality were valued. They weren't explicitly stated, though. Still, within our many conversations, there were obliquely unarticulated expressions of relationality as there were expressions of mutuality. The parents expected to gain in the relationship. I'd be another set of eyes and ears. I'd be a sounding board. I'd be a resource person. I'd temper discussions about public and formal schools. So, what happened?

As it turned out, many parents elected to write autobiographical accounts based on the reflection topics I'd suggested. Their accounts were often very extensive, several being more than a hundred pages of hand- or typewritten narrative. In conversation these parents told me of the value of reflecting on their lives. They told of the revelatory power gained from weaving together strands and patterns of a life of decision making connected to families and learning, and being in schools. And there were also patterns of going against the grain.

Parents were enthusiastic about the insights of self that they'd gained. Essentially, these new perspectives were often the very same interpretations that I'd derived from their accounts. Further, in their conversations with me about their experiences or perspectives they often made midsentence exclamations such as "Oh . . . I've just realized how my experiences in school added up to my terribly negative views of schools and teachers . . ." or, "You know, given my lifelong experiences, I'm not surprised that I've taken this road . . ." or, "My attempts at cocooning have just been revealed; I thought I was doing this solely for my kids' benefits . . ." or,

"This reflective process is invaluable as it has helped me make the links between all of my experiences and beliefs and they sort of come together, in a haphazard way, which has made me think more about what I do, so this is good."

Paradoxically, by the end of the 1980s, there was another perspective on researchers and the place of research on families' teaching efforts with which I had to contend. Networks of home-educating families had sprung up in North America, especially in the United States and, beginning in the early 1980s, many networking, home-educating families were solicited for participation in mail surveys/questionnaires. Over a short period of time, clusters of populations who had become overly researched, usually at the hands of graduate student researchers and others who used relatively simplistic but time-consuming surveys. Home education networks also engaged in researching their membership and students' educational performance, some being captivated by test score results and intent on "proving the value of [their] actions."

Kaseman and Kaseman (1990) were among the most vocal of home educators who challenged what seemed to be the extraordinary interest within the "research community" on exploring the lives, processes, educational achievements, and experiences of families. The backlash from these various institution-sponsored research activities was the considerable resistance to the idea of being "the researched." Kaseman and Kaseman recognized the insidious "research and run" perspective typical of some researchers. Many families committed their resources to researchers only to receive little or nothing in return. Ethically responsible, responsive, and reflexive qualitative inquiry evokes a different relationship between the researcher and the researched but this was antithetical to their experiences and stated position.

One of the outcomes of these and other objections and cautions, born of the burgeoning collective savvy and communicating powers of the networks, was that many established home educators became highly informed about issues of researching. They expected reciprocity. They expected to develop relationships in the researching process. They wanted to control, if not influence, the researching outcomes. They were interested in other than the superficial and perennial issues (that is, beyond the "why" and "how" questions that many new researchers couldn't get past) and had interest in developing their "professional understandings" of the pedagogical, curricular, legal, vocational, and lifelong implications of home education. These were not unexpected issues, given that home education is not a responsibility entered into lightly. Neither were parents unreasonable, given the private nature of the educational activity.

RELATIONALITY AND MUTUALITY AS "NATURAL" PROCESSES

The manner of my ongoing interaction with parent-teachers has evolved out of the genuinely respectful relationships that were established, and continue to be established, in part because of our similar pathways. But there's more to it. Being a bona fide member of the community—albeit at a geographical/physical distance—afforded me a level of acceptance and respect. But more than that, by an accident of good fortune I never assumed to be the "expert," whether it was in my teaching days or my previous professional work, and this aided in building relationships. Indeed, the principles of experiential learning, which have guided much of my professional work, were expressed in the conversations I had with parents. I worked hard to be a keen observer and an astute listener. I brought my teacherly problem-solving skills to bear. I was also informed about schools and teachers, and about teacher preparation, and this, too, became a point of engagement. I endeavored to provide illumination of issues through discussion and questioning in a "nonthreatening" or "nonhierarchical" manner. Indeed, on reflection, my natural inquisitiveness led at least some parents to question some of the fundamental assumptions on which they'd based their educational actions. From my perspective as a teacher, this is always a healthy sign. It's also something that I appreciate others doing for me.

RESPONSIBILITIES TO THE HOME-EDUCATION COMMUNITY

The sensitivity of researchers to their source communities is central to morally responsible research. That the parents with whom I research have a degree of authority and control over aspects of my work with them is not the issue. I have made a career as a researcher through their goodwill and respect. We have mutually benefited. I have participated in various home-education conferences, provided workshops and discussion sessions. I have attempted to give back some of what I've been given. Consistently, though, parent-teachers know of my philosophical position, they know of my role as "questioner of assumptions and practices," they know of my unwillingness to compromise my own fundamental principles of action as a researcher and as a teacher, especially as a pedagogue.

I have acted at times as an observer and listener, reflecting through "thick description" what I have seen and heard. Other times I'm asked to engage more with very particular problems, thinking aloud and through the various elements of the issues. At these times I act somewhat like an expert because I facilitate their engagement in what we configure to be the heart of the problem.

On reflecting on my researching participation with home-educating families it seems obvious to me that my ongoing interactions are guided by the very same principles on which I have shaped my life. For me, there seems to be little distinction between the modes, tone, and central tenets of my researching and personal life. Others may differ in opinion as to how well these are fused into my actions but they cannot argue with my intentions. I seek not to make the distinction between the ways in which I develop rapport and relationships with potential friends and with potential parents with whom I may more formally work. Relationships, no matter in what arena, require mutuality of purpose and wholesomeness of respect.

Journalists often contact me for interviews about home education. These interviews are frequent and far-ranging in scope, depending on the journalist's familiarity with home education and the context in which she is located. They contact me because they believe me to be a "home school research expert." I often shudder at the possibilities and the expectations, not knowing of their political or ideological orientations and purposes. Inevitably I am concerned about presenting a thoughtful account and observations about the educational practices where I am able, mindful of my need to be respectful to individual families yet cognizant of the larger world in which children grow and flourish. I am interested in pushing the boundaries of practice and of thinking about that practice, and I endeavor to do this through my researching work. My intentions are to continue working within a critical yet relational- and mutual-building frame of mind and professional practice. Hopefully home educators know this is my theory and practice. They're the ones who can tell.

9

Research as Relationship

Jacquie Aston

In chapter 1 we describe the centrality of relationships in the process of life history researching. In chapter 2 we further explore this notion with a focus on the relationship between the researcher and research participants. Jacquie Aston conducted a life history study of how women shape their lives to accommodate career and motherhood. In the following account, she describes how attention to the researcher-researched relationship throughout the study enriched both the research experience and contributed to the quality of the insights gained.

At the heart of life history research is the relationship between the researcher and the person being researched. The researcher is interested in understanding as fully as possible the experiences of others and the meanings they make out of their experiences (Yow, 1993). A good rapport with the person being interviewed facilitates an openness to explore experience and to cocreate meaning. In the context of a conversational-style interview, or a "grounded conversation" (Cole 1991, 197), the researcher develops connections with people (Reinharz 1992) as they share their stories and ideas. As a female researcher interviewing other women, I also experienced a resonance through our shared gender. In this account I intend to explore the relational aspect of research, from my experience as researcher. I illustrate points with examples from my own research.

My research explored how women shape their lives to accommodate career and motherhood when these aspects are equally salient (Aston 2000). I gathered experiential information through conversational interviews with eight women from a variety of careers and professions. The

life stories of the women were woven into broad themes that were expressed largely in the women's voices. Each theme concluded with some
reflective comments that represented my dialectic analysis.

Development of rapport was a crucial first part of the interview since I
wanted to create an environment in which the participant would feel comfortable in talking about her life. I also indicated a genuine interest in her
life story. Each of the women had misgivings concerning the value of her
contribution. I gave some reassurance that every story has value and that
we can learn much from other people's lives and about ourselves as we tell
our stories. In fact, in telling their stories, several of the women in my
study made a point of mentioning that it was a rare opportunity to recall
and make sense of the scattered events of their lives. I was amazed at the
openness of the women and the depth they went to in telling their stories.

As researcher, I wanted themes to emerge that seemed to hold importance for each participant in the way she shaped her life. I wanted
to be as unobtrusive as possible but at the same time to be in tune with
the needs of the individual woman. Some liked the guidance of specific
questions, while others were happy to talk about their lives. Any questions were broad and open-ended, such as "Tell me how you chose your
career." I used "positive minimal responses" (Yow, 1994, 131) as well as
nonverbal responses as encouragement. I would sometimes ask them to
describe more fully an aspect that seemed pertinent to the research
topic, especially if I perceived that we were straying too far from the
topic. I wanted to be as nondirective as possible while also maintaining
focus on the question.

A RELATIONSHIP OF TRUST

One of the participants in the study, Paige (a pseudonym, as are the names
of the other participants), described her life as being "full of hardships."
As she talked about her life, she became completely immersed in the
events as they started to come into her consciousness. She recalled her
parents' separation when she was ten years old. Because there was little
money available, she and one of her sisters moved with their mother to
Ontario to live with their maternal grandmother, leaving their father and
three other siblings in British Columbia. The father was the more nurturing of her parents and so he was sadly missed. The grandmother was a
hard taskmaster and she instilled a strong work ethic into the girls.
Mother and grandmother both worked at low-income jobs to support the
family. Paige recalled the unhappiness she felt at this time. She also talked
about an early marriage to a man who seemed to be her "Prince Charm-

ing" but who turned out to be a very demanding and jealous man. He left the marriage and their two young children, both of whom were born with congenital problems.

The stories that Paige shared in our first meeting held a lot of emotion. My custom was to provide complete transcripts of the conversations shortly after each conversation. When Paige saw in words what she had shared, she was concerned as to whether she had been too negative about some people in her life. We looked together at how she might modify the text without changing the essence of the meaning and how she would want to represent different people in her life. A sense of trust that stories will be treated with sensitivity is essential in this style of working with people. A relationship of trust also provides opportunities for participants to explore deeper meanings and to gain new insights (Measor and Sikes 1992).

Through our conversations, Paige realized that it was in going through some tough years that she has developed a tremendous inner strength. After her husband left she took more control of her life than she had before. She progressed in her career as a teacher, becoming a "special educator." Because of her difficult life and because she had two children who had some early disabilities she felt a particular empathy for disadvantaged children. She said of the children she works with, "These are little people [who] have feelings, and some of them come from lives of hell and their time with me is going to be the best time it can be." She had found meaningful work, and six years later she married a man who is more of a partner to her than her first husband was. She shaped her life in a way that brings her satisfaction and contentment. I, as researcher, provided the occasion and the safety to explore her experience. She enjoyed piecing together her story, finding the richness of her life.

RESONATING THROUGH SHARED GENDER

I was interviewing professional women from the same subculture I was part of and although they were ten to fifteen years younger than I am, I found myself resonating with their stories. Yow suggests that "women often learned as children to establish an ambience of thinking things through together" (1994, 131) and they establish connections through conversation.

Susan is a woman with whom I "connected" very easily. Traditionally, the researcher does not disclose personal details but, in a conversational style of interview, I believe that a certain amount of disclosure is essential. It facilitates a sense of trust and mutuality and it increases the comfort level of the narrator. Susan and I found some commonalties in terms of our position in our families. We felt on the same wavelength and she felt comfortable in sharing her story with me.

As a single mother of twins, Susan has a particular vantage point from which to observe and experience societal attitudes toward women. Already feeling outside the mainstream of society as a single mother, she is sensitive to the unfair expectations that society places on women. She finds herself in a position of always being "asked to give." The notion that she, as a single mother, might herself need some support and nurture is not considered. When her children were two years old she moved from her mother's place to her own home. She had an uneasy relationship with her mother and thought she and the children would do better in their own place. She also had a very responsible job, with more than thirty staff working for her. In addition, one of the children was experiencing some problems. She described this child as being very troubled and unresponsive to any attempts to pacify her. Susan shared a little of her experience of when the children were young:

> I remember feeling so strongly, "Why won't anybody help me?" I mean, I can't even talk about that. "Why won't anybody help me?" It was terrible, terrible. I really wanted to have a breakdown, but then I couldn't because of the kids. But it was like I thought, "Maybe that will get somebody's attention here, I am in real trouble." I did very well at times. People thought I did, that's that image. But in my heart of hearts, no way. I didn't even know any young mothers. There was nobody that I could call to say, "Come over, I need a cup of coffee and a chat" or whatever. I felt so alone in those early years. I had no opportunity to meet anyone.

She looked to the church for support and found it for a while in a group run for single mothers. But when the leader left she was asked to lead the group. Again she was asked to give. Her comment was, "How much do you bring on yourself because of your natural ability? We are trained into it and it's almost as difficult to back out of it as it is to do it." This kind of comment rings so true to women. It was an example of resonating on a gender level. At work, she finds that her coworkers take their problems to her rather than to a male coordinator. As she said, "I think being female I'm expected to care more. Whether I do or I don't, it's the expectations that are still very stereotypical."

The expectation that women will take care of others and not have the care reciprocated is perhaps a universal experience of women. The isolation that Susan felt because of her lack of support is very striking. She said, "Who do I go to? I am not allowed to break down at work. I've got thirty-two staff, but I can't be friends with them. For me it's very lonely." She highlights poignantly women's position as caretakers.

TWO SUBJECTIVITIES

A life history interview is an interaction between the narrator and the listener. The listener asks, responds, and ultimately tells. In the activity of listening, responding, and telling, a life story can be assimilated into the listener's own life story as it resonates with her experiences and perceptions. Thus the subjectivity of the one merges with the subjectivity of the other through the research process. There is a "fusion of horizons" (Gadamer, cited in Nielsen 1990, 29) whereby the researcher is open to new knowledge while also being grounded in her own perspective. Through the fusion of horizons, one's viewpoint is transcended.

One of the interesting aspects of being a researcher is learning from other people. At the time when my children were young many mothers stayed at home with their children. The women in my study expected to continue in their work when they had children. They had trained in high-profile professions, but had not anticipated the impact that motherhood would have on their lives. I learned from their experiences that the playing field is far from level for women once they have children. This was especially so for these women who took their role of mother very seriously, and also remained highly committed to their jobs. They struggled with some hard choices as they tried to find some balance between these two important aspects in their lives.

One of the women, a physician in emergency medicine, was evaluating the advantages of a career opportunity at the time of our first meeting. Because helping people to heal is a strong motivating factor in her life, she struggles with maintaining boundaries around her work. With three young children, a husband, and a career, she worked hard to find a reasonable balance among the important elements of her life. She said of the career opportunity:

> It's a difficult time for me because I really don't want to upset the apple cart. If there's going to be one commitment and dedication in my life, it's going to be to keep this balance. Even if it's a different career path, I am going to preserve this as my number one.

It is common for a man to have a busy career, a wife, and a family, but the equivalent is not true for women. She could look across from where we were having lunch and see a male counterpart who was ahead of her in his career. His wife takes care of their home responsibilities. But then she has to remind herself of the quality of family life that she, her husband, and three children enjoy.

Tracy, a physician in family medicine, made some blatant compromises. She completed medical school the same year as her brother and they are now in practice together. When she had children, Tracy chose to reduce her workweek to forty hours so that she could have some time at home with her children. Daily she is confronted with where she could have been in medicine if she had been as single-minded as he is:

> I watched his role going through medicine and my role going through medicine. He does the eighty-hour workweek, he does the committees, the meals where they talk about medicine, he writes books, he does drug studies, he does all that stuff. His wife is at home full time with the kids and does some of his paper work, and that allows him a lot of freedom in medicine. Of course, when you do that you don't know the kids as well but, at this point in time, his résumé is far more impressive than mine is, and that's the choice, for both of us.

She has to constantly remind herself that she has chosen a different path. Sometimes it seems a hard choice but most times she feels good about her choice. In entering into their world through the research process, I came to understand from a different perspective the complexity of women's lives.

COCREATING MEANING

In life history research we describe the world from the perspective of the people being studied. As researchers, we enter, as far as possible, the phenomenological field of our participants and work with them to understand to the fullest extent the experiences and the meaning of those experiences to them. We resonate with our participants and frequently find ourselves mirrored in them. Gorelick (1996), speaking from a feminist perspective, cautions, however, that in mirroring ourselves in others, we may be limiting the study by confining it within their perceptions. My responsibility is to bring a perspective that illuminates social structures that are oppressive to women. Interestingly, I found that in working with participants, they sometimes come to their own understanding of underlying structures that spoil the quality of their lives.

Ann worked her way up to a senior management position in a large company. She had her children when she was in her late thirties. At that time, her husband was starting up a new business. She took on the mother role as an "added-on role" because that was what she and her husband assumed would happen. She felt better trained in tasks around the house than her husband did, and with her "can do" attitude that had served her well in her job she thought that she could "project manage" her home. The idea of sharing home responsibilities was not seriously considered. She explained, "Both he and I thought by default I would be the one doing it and while he is very willing, that's not either of our default thinking." She became overwhelmed by what she was trying to do and felt some resentment that she never had time for herself. "From the minute I wake up to the minute I close my eyes, somebody wants something of me." Her image of a harmonious family was shattered. In our first conversation, her disappointment in her family life came strongly across.

By our second meeting, after further reflection on what she had said, Ann had shifted in her thinking and had started to organize their family life in a different way. In referring to her husband she said, "Now I am saying, 'Well, no, we are partners in this.'" She started involving him more in family life. She gave him responsibility for the children on some nights so that she could visit her mother and take a self-assertiveness course. She organized activities that involved the whole family. She now says of her husband, "He talks to [the children] more. I think he is finding out that if he had caught on to that sooner . . ."

Through the research process, Ann's eyes were opened to the possibility of managing her family life in a different way. She broke away from ill-serving traditions and experimented with new ways. By the third time we met, she had started taking an architectural course that she described as being purely for fun. As she said, "You allow yourself into that group that has to be cared for." She seemed much happier with the way she was shaping her life. Working with participants can have surprising and, hopefully, positive effects.

SOME CONCLUDING COMMENTS

Because in life history research we are asking people to open up their lives to us, we have to be aware of the possibility of touching on sensitive areas. We need to be careful that in our interest to probe a little deeper into people's stories we maintain boundaries of respect. We need to share in the process with our participants as much as is feasibly possible so that they determine their level of participation and so that we include material with which they are comfortable. Acker, Barry, and Esseveld suggest that "the powerful subject has no difficulty in being active and determining the parameters of the interview" (1996, 82). While this may be so, participants still find themselves sharing material that they may not want to have included in the research report. Respect for those with whom we work must come before research ambitions. It is through working in relationship with participants that we are able to develop research that is relevant to everyday experience. In interpreting their lives as accurately as possible, we can convey to a wider audience the richness of their lived experience. We all can learn from the stories of others.

10

Fidelity and Ethical Ideals

Kathleen Gates, Kathryn Church, and Cathy Crowe

Integrally connected to the principle of relationality, as discussed in chapter 2, are the issues of ethical and moral responsibility in life history research. Kathy Gates, Kathryn Church, and Cathy Crowe highlight the ethical dimensions of a research relationship through an exploration of the criterion of fidelity as it relates to both the process and the findings of life history research. Church and Crowe were participants in a study of social activists conducted by Gates. Together, they outline four ethical principles or ideals that contribute to ethical research relationships.

E thical relationships are the binding matrix of life history research. My research features the stories of women educators who are social activists (Gates 2000b). Each participant answers in her own way to inequalities that she encounters related to age, class, race, sex, and state of health. The merit of this qualitative research is considered according to the criterion of fidelity as it is linked to ethical research relationships. I contend that the exploration of ethical ideals in relationships is key to the understanding of fidelity.

While I am, as researcher, solely responsible for the text that follows and am the reason for writing in the first person singular, I agreed with my two participants, Kathryn Church and Cathy Crowe, that they would be acknowledged in the authorship of any publications that resulted from my intensive inquiry work with them. They were, after all, the cocreators of knowledge within the bounds of my study.

The researcher needs to maintain fidelity in relationships with participants, self, and text. Text includes interview transcripts and other evidence that contribute to the understanding of peoples' lives within social and historical contexts. Participants construct trustworthy renderings of their experience by selecting memories that are salient to the inquiry. They use personal abilities such as creativity, ethics, intuition, and reason. The researcher's reconstruction of meaning is also a scientific-artistic work that aims to accurately reflect the situated stories as told by the teller. In addition to reflecting the participant's perspective, the researcher attempts to be transparent about personal positioning in the structuring of the narrative. It is not necessary, or even desirable, for the researcher and narrators to construe meaning in the same way. It is crucial, however, that participants feel that the meaning of their personal stories is honored and not violated.

In this chapter, I explore the criterion of fidelity as it relates to both the process and the findings of life history research. The criterion of fidelity in narrative inquiry is linked to its use in art and social science (Blumenfeld-Jones 1995). Blumenfeld-Jones maintains that fidelity and ethical relationships are inextricably linked, and this account extends that idea by exploring four ethical principles or ideals that contribute to ethical relationships.

Fidelity is a way of being-in-relation that is grounded in the four ethical ideals of autonomy, nonmaleficence, beneficence, and justice. Principles are not rules to prescribe behavior but rather intellectual ideals that "are the final methods used in judging suggested courses of action" (Dewey, cited in Johnson 1993, 105). Fidelity involves the development of a trusting researcher-participant relationship in which the partners cocreate knowledge in an atmosphere of mutual respect. An ethical research relationship provides the foundation for structuring life histories that re-present the practical wisdom embedded in contextualized lives. Fidelity is important. Its pursuit is a worthy guide for the researcher, its presence provides a safe place for the participant's contribution, and it promotes findings that are authentic histories of both the participants' and researcher's lives.

CONTESTING CONVENTIONAL ORDER
TO PROMOTE EQUALITY

Struggling for the well-being of the underdog has been a compelling interest of mine since I was a young child. My white, Anglo-Saxon, working-class parents, who lived through the Great Depression, became adamant supporters of the Saskatchewan socialist party that first introduced universal health care in Canada. My family saw politics as a way to secure every Canadian's right to the basic necessities of life. My research quest arose quite naturally from these and other narrative strands of my life.

While working within health-care and educational institutions for more than three decades, I have been frequently discomfited by happenings that undermine the well-being of patients, clients, and learners. Recently, for example, I worked extensively with patients with dementia and their families. The diagnosis of dementia carries with it a devastating label that exacerbates the effects of the disease and diminishes quality of life for the person and the whole family. Family caregivers perceive many service barriers to quality of life for their loved ones (Gates 2000a). People with dementia are often deprived of opportunities to use their preserved abilities because insufficient resources are directed toward their care. The protection of vulnerable people, such as those with dementia, is the work of the social activist.

Social justice work is not value neutral; it requires a moral consciousness. To remain passive in the face of official power is a choice (Goodson 1995). We can choose to remain quiet or to contest the injustice. In my life history research, I welcomed the opportunity to explore women's experience of contesting conventional order to promote equality.

Seven women educators representing a variety of professions were selected as participants in my research because of their pioneering public work to decrease inequalities related to age, class, sex, race, and the stigma of chronic illness. Cathy Crowe and Kathryn Church, the two participants featured in this writing, are educators who maintain both practice and academic roles in the health-care field. Cathy, a nurse, is engaged in the field of "street health" and works with homeless people. Kathryn is a sociologist who works in partnership with people within the psychiatric survivor movement. I selected these women because, as health professionals, they serve people who have been disadvantaged as a result of poverty and stigmatization. Each woman chronicles challenges to powerful political and professional forces that tend to marginalize poor people and those with chronic mental illness. Cathy and Kathryn portray very different stories in each of their unique constructions, but the quest remains the same: contesting conventional order to promote equality. It is the different expressions of the plot that expand imaginative possibilities for the reader.

USING ETHICAL PRINCIPLES AS IDEALS

My career choice in nursing contributed to my personal and professional growth. A shared humanity is the moral foundation of nursing, and its professional code of ethics provides directives that are concrete expressions of the principles of autonomy (self-determination), nonmaleficence (to do no harm), beneficence (to do good), and justice (fairness). My career as a nurse and a nurse educator began more than three decades ago when obedience to authority was the prevailing ethic; it was difficult for me to reconcile my parents' teachings about equality with the marginalization that I discovered in practice. Today, although the guiding ethic for nursing is client advocacy, many disadvantaged groups are not consulted about their needs. The health-care system remains unresponsive to basic health needs for shelter, food, clothing, education, and work. My research focuses on the efforts of interdisciplinary, women activist-educators to address the needs of groups who have been underserved within society. As a researcher, I strive toward ethical ideals in relationships to achieve fidelity in my life history work.

Autonomy, or self-determination, is the right of the individual to function independently without the control of others. The protection of participants' autonomy requires that the researcher seek consensus and validation from them with regard to the way they are represented in findings. Nonmaleficence is the ethical duty to do no harm. The researcher is bound to a duty of care during the research process that safeguards the participants' well-being. It is incumbent upon the researcher to articulate possible risks and to confer with participants about ways to minimize them. Beneficence, to do good, reflects the goodwill of participants and the researcher who engage in a common interest to cocreate a work for the benefit of self and others. Justice relates to fairness that is reasoned, informed, and equitable. Justice entails credible, believable treatment of the life histories that includes some transparency of the researcher's perspective. The researcher and the participants invest considerable time, and justice also requires that the researcher's findings provide a return for that time and attention.

Autonomy in Relationship

I tried to respect the autonomy of the participants throughout the research process. Initially, I contacted potential participants in person or by telephone to introduce my research project and to invite them to take part. Everyone agreed. I was conscious of imposing on their already busy schedules, so we arranged sets of three seventy-five-minute interviews at times and places most convenient for them. During the first interview, I gave them a written description of the research and a letter of consent for signing. The interviews were unstructured apart from a general focus for each session. The first interview explored concrete, current experiences that related to the inquiry into contesting conventional order to promote equality. During the second interview, participants were invited to share autobiographical information related to their beliefs and actions. The final interview afforded an opportunity for participants to speculate about the educational implications of their work. I promoted their ability to make autonomous choices by providing information about the approximate time commitments required and the nature of the interviews. The participants knew that they could withdraw from the research at any time.

Autonomy ensures that the participant is the final arbiter of the way she is represented in story. The participants decided what to disclose during the interviews and what to include in the interview transcripts and the narrative profiles. Autonomy is integral to the approach of feminist interviewers "whose primary orientation is toward the validation of women's subjective experiences as women and as people" (Oakley 1981, 30). Trust and respect between research partners is critical in the construction of research findings that are attuned to the storyteller and faithful to the story. If mutual understanding cannot be achieved, the participant may choose to withdraw from the inquiry altogether.

In order to be faithful to their voices, I tried to mirror, as much as possible, their ways of supporting the autonomy of others. These story segments illustrate how Cathy and Kathryn promote mutuality in relationship:

Cathy: I am involved in a hospital's reorganization into an integrated delivery system. I said, "I don't want another bus on the streets for homeless people. We need to talk to homeless people and find out what they want."

Kathryn: One of the things I learned from the psychiatric survivors was how to resist. I watched how Pat Capponi [a psychiatric survivor, author, and advocate in Canadian mental health care] tried to facilitate the survivor's speech in public meetings. I interviewed her about the spaces she was trying to open up for speech, the opposition she got, and how that opposition was delivered.

Cathy and Kathryn's relationship-centered autonomy emphasizes the connectedness between the consumer and the service provider. Similarly, I tried to reduce the researcher-researched distance by sharing my own experiences with them and being open and spontaneous in research interactions. Autonomy in relationship fosters a process that opens space for self-expression.

Nonmaleficence in Relationship

I was enthusiastic and curious in my interactions with Cathy and Kathryn. Our conversations were warm and genuine. Cathy and I reflected on issues confronting the nursing profession, while Kathryn and I compared our roots from western Canada. We shared insights and feelings.

I once had a traumatic experience as a research subject, and I did not want to impose the same misfortune on my participants. I had volunteered to be a participant in a research project to standardize questions to be used in family assessment. The interviewer sat in a darkened area of the room reading questions in a monotone voice and under the scrutiny of a video camera. I answered her predetermined and highly personal questions candidly. She did not utter one unscripted word. I was not given any feedback. I left the interview feeling exposed and used, like a microbe on a petri dish. I feared that my videotape would be used for teaching as well as research purposes. Oakley describes an ethical researcher-researched relationship: "Personal involvement is more than dangerous bias—it is the condition under which people come to know each other and to admit others into their lives" (1981, 58). After my experience as a research participant, I was determined to conduct my research in an egalitarian and transparent manner, so that I would do no harm to the participants.

Cathy and Kathryn each acknowledged that their work posed a risk to their health and well-being. The following information warrants sensitivity to the stressors brought on by the research process itself.

> *Cathy:* When you confront conventional order, there are dangers. You suddenly become very public, and open to criticism. It involves criticizing authorities and that's scary. All the talk about my work [during our first interview] made me think more about it.
>
> *Kathryn:* You'd asked me what I had to give up in terms of this contesting, and I said "peace of mind and my health." That's really true. There just aren't very many places of ease, fit, and comfort if my social and political sensibilities are at work.

In terms of nonmaleficence, the issues of confidentiality and anonymity are crucial because their breach could result in harm to the participants. Confidentiality is maintained by securing obtained data and restricting its access to identified people such as a research colleague and audiotape transcribers. Anonymity is a complex matter. It involves protecting the identities of well-known people in published works about them. Because the research participants are public figures whose opinions are reported in the local and national media, it is difficult to fully disguise their identities in the findings. I negotiate with the participants so that they are not exposed to risks that they find unacceptable. I reiterated their right to revise my introduction and profile of them in a letter that read in part:

> I realize that some of my reflections on your words, knowledge, and experience might not conform exactly to the ways in which you might describe yourself, but this, I suppose, is the creative work of a [research report]! In any case,

> I hope you think that the profile employs the interview data in a way that is
> faithful, interesting, and respectful. . . . I will edit any parts you would like to
> see removed or add any information that you believe must be included.

In this way, I tried to prevent psychological or professional harm that could result from re-presentations of participants that lacked fidelity to their self-perception, or self-disclosure comfort.

Another way in which I tried to incorporate the ideal of nonmaleficence into the research methods was to promise not to use the actual data from research participants' interviews in other publications without first obtaining their consent and providing an opportunity for coauthorship. I chose not to use the information in this chapter without their knowledge (Oakley 1981). This plan acknowledges mutuality inherent in the research relationship that is consistent with the equality-seeking nature of this inquiry based on the experience of contesting conventional order to promote equality.

The ethical ideal of nonmaleficence includes the consideration of risks associated with the research process, and the possibility of an unwitting disclosure of information that could be injurious to the participant. Nonmaleficence contributes to fidelity in relationship by attending to the risks inherent in research that employs personal information.

Beneficence in Relationship

Acting out the ethical ideal "to do good" was a daunting task for me when it came to encountering and shaping the vast and rich qualitative data with which I was entrusted. I felt obliged to write accounts that were a tribute to participants and their pioneering work. Their original transcribed interviews exceeded a hundred pages. These were then reduced to twelve-page profiles per participant with two- to three-page introductions. Initially, I listened to and read the transcripts several times. My introduction of participants was a distillation of ideas from oral histories, participants' published works, documentary evidence, and theoretical materials. I used documentary information to "cross-validate participant accounts" (Cole 1991, 186). I wanted to express beneficence by portraying their life histories in a thoughtful manner. Life history is useful in obtaining accounts of "critical incidents or epiphanies in lives" (Cole and Knowles 1995, 141) and I became intellectually and emotionally attuned to these junctures as I dwelt with the data. Keeping copies of the original interviews gave me the assurance that I could revert to that text if I felt that I had overlooked or misinterpreted something.

I attempted to promote beneficence through a careful and deliberate process while reconstructing the stories into profiles. At first I deleted interview data unrelated to the purpose of the inquiry. Next, I reflexively shaped the profiles focusing on Cathy and Kathryn's particular stories of social activism. I asked myself, "How would they like their stories to be told?" (Cole, personal communication, October 1, 1998). I was reassured and challenged that these women would clarify any misreading. I discovered new levels of understanding each time I listened to their stories and reflected on the type of information that I had not heard the first time around.

Eventually, I chose to use the participants' phrases or sentences as headings to organize the story into segments. I sequenced these segments to begin with current experiences and to conclude with formative ones. I believed that the use of these headings, in the participants' words, provided more faithful renderings of their lives and would contribute to the believability of the research. The profiles became verbatim, condensed accounts of their stories. Participants reviewed the profiles and made minor revisions. The phrases are listed below for each participant. Disjunctive moments, identified by an asterisk (*), indicate the disruption of automatic, predictable performance of everyday activity by a problem without a solution. Heidegger (1962) maintains that everyday aspects of being in the world are noticed more when this disruption occurs. The resolution of the problem is denoted by two asterisks (**). Polkinghorne, in elaborating on Dollard's criteria for judging life history, maintains that it is the researcher's responsibility to "mark the beginning point of the story and the point of denouement" (1995, 17).

The itemized lists below identify the key phrases that configure Cathy and Kathryn's stories. I begin with Cathy's list:

1. Would work with the homeless be diverse and interesting enough?
2. I felt unprepared to do advocacy and political work with the homeless.*
3. A group of us talk about how we acknowledge our power.
4. I went to the gym because I knew I had to.
5. We told the story [of the freezing death of a homeless man].
6. I am choosing to take part in events that are risky.
7. It takes a tremendous knowledge base.
8. What's going to make a difference?**
9. I look back on a very ordinary childhood.
10. The Helen Caldicott film was absolutely a turning point for me.
11. Can you teach a heart connection?

Cathy's story is configured by her work with homeless people, and it includes political, self-care, and formative experiences. The resolution of her story is depicted by her question, "What's going to make a difference?"

She chooses to use her formidable organizational and nursing skills to work in areas where she discerns that positive change is possible.

Documentary evidence supporting Cathy's perspective is plentiful. She is a member of a committee that formulated an influential informative document titled, *Homelessness in Toronto: State of Emergency Declaration during the Fiftieth Anniversary of the Universal Declaration of Human Rights* (Toronto Disaster Relief Committee, 1998). This document contributed to a U.N. committee's condemnation of Canada for policies that have "exacerbated poverty and homelessness among vulnerable groups during a time of strong economic growth and increasing affluence" (U.N. Committee on Economic, Social and Cultural Rights, cited in Philip 1998).

In the introduction to Cathy's profile, I compared her approach to Rawl's (1989) position that fairness to all is the basic underpinning of justice. Her beliefs resonate with Rawl's assertions in three significant ways: social institutions have a duty to be fair to everyone; every person has a stake (and should have a voice) in justice as it relates to fairness; and, in limited circumstances, the citizen has the right to engage in civil disobedience. Cathy's social responsibility as a nurse-citizen is action-oriented and grounded in the ethical principle of justice. Her reconstructed narrative is a holistic perspective that includes political, cultural, psychosocial, and spiritual considerations. Holism promotes beneficence because it resists a reductionistic and fragmented view of the person.

Kathryn's story is configured by items that chronicle her personal transformation: "I was embedded in processes of training and education that encouraged establishing relationships of power over people. I was being taught to take control, to know, to be a knower. That is what broke." Through her change process, Kathryn was mentored by friends within the psychiatric survivor movement. Her own doctoral studies provided a background for that activity.

1. I was struggling to fit in.
2. Wonderful and also quite devastating.*
3. I was an unwatered seed for so long.
4. A tremendous shift in identity for me.
5. The illness was a kind of epiphany.
6. I was raised to be compliant to authority.
7. Writing from the "I" is probably going to be my most consistent form of resistance.**
8. Love was incredibly important in that change process.
9. Transcendence happens in sense-making.

Kathryn's change of identity provoked an illness experience at the same time as it enabled her to do "authentic work." Her resolution is to write from the "I": "I'm going to be present as a writer who is both thinking and feeling. I understand very clearly where the survivors are and what I can contribute but my own independence is crucial to me now." She works jointly with psychiatric survivors to prepare proposals and reports that address, among other things, community economic development. Her writings are used within the movement and in academic courses that relate to consumerism, advocacy, and ethics (Church 1995).

In my introduction to Kathryn's work, I elaborate on her dialogic relations with psychiatric survivors as a meaning-making process. She is interested in exposing exclusionary discourses and assisting those without a voice to find one. In essence, she poses Bakhtin's question: "*Who* precisely is speaking and under *what* concrete circumstances?" (1989, 782, emphasis in original). In her profile, Kathryn's consciousness spans the space between wanting to fit into a privileged, hierarchical, externally authoritative discourse, and choosing a relationship-centered, contextualized, "internally persuasive discourse" (Bakhtin, 783). Dialogue promotes equality by decentering privileged authoritative voices in order to include voices of psychiatric survivors that had been previously silenced (Bakhtin 1981). Kathryn's experience of working within the survivor movement enabled her to discover her unique contribution; it was an experience of great tumult and creative imagination.

I advanced the ideal of beneficence by using a holistic lens to reconstruct stories in accord with the participants' understandings of happenings. The integration of documentary evidence and theoretical ideas further substantiates life history research.

Justice in Relationship

Justice is an ideal that contributes to fidelity in relationships by calling for a sense of fairness. This research is about conscious thinkers who embrace citizens' rights in a democracy. Socrates (cited in Saul 1995, 71) defends the examined life:

> If I say "... I cannot 'mind my own business,'" you will not believe that I am serious. If on the other hand I tell you that to let no day pass without discussing goodness ... and that examining both myself and others is really the very best thing a man [*sic*] can do and that life without this sort of examination is not worth living, you will be even less inclined to believe me. Nevertheless, gentlemen, that is how it is.

Saul maintains that the "essence of individualism is the refusal to mind your own business" (1995, 165). This busybody lifestyle does not garner much public approval. Instead, individualism is a way of being that "often consists of being persistently annoying to others as well as being stubborn and repetitive." The participants demonstrate persistence and dedication in the quest for fairness in a world rife with inequalities.

Life history has the power to exhibit a person's unique and contextualized experience in a way that "can make the familiar strange" (Hatch and Wisniewski 1995b, 118). In this case, it provides the reader with a vicarious experience of what it means to be connected to others in a way that opposes their oppression. The meaning of their local experiences illumines a larger reality that has global significance (Hatch and Wisniewski, 1995a).

The analysis of data entails a consideration of similarities and differences between individual participant stories, and then a synthesis of emergent themes. These narratives have relevance not only for healthcare educators but also for educator-citizens who hold democratic ideals. Cathy and Kathryn both exhibit intellectual flexibility that enables them to live with uncertainty, understand issues from diverse perspectives, use empirical knowledge as warranted, and, notably, learn with and from oppressed people. They combine scientific and narrative knowing. George Grant (cited in Cayley 1995) attributes the harmful effects of the dominant scientific paradigm to its disconnection from the notion of the good. Cathy and Kathryn use their narrative understanding to discern possibilities for change, and to strategize practical, imaginative approaches to ameliorate suffering. They often feel the injustices inflicted on others as if they were their own.

> *Cathy:* I hate the word "boundaries." Boundaries are about protecting yourself and not getting too close to clients. It is class-based. A heart connection is about having pain or joy in your heart about their circumstances. The damage that homelessness does to somebody's self-esteem, spirit, and mental health is shocking. I work in this other world that is cut off from and shunned by society. Those trapped in this world have so much talent, fight, imagination, creativity, and personality.
>
> To me, social responsibility is part of being human. Health care is political in terms of hierarchies, access, power, and how dollars are allocated. I don't like oppressed group theory about nurses; nurses have to take responsibility for weakness. Nursing is so silent and conforming.

Kathryn shares a similar perspective. People who were psychiatric survivors mentored her before she began contract work with them.

> *Kathryn:* The ongoing relationships with psychiatric patients were very important to me. I became familiar with their life circumstances: poverty, the impact of treatment, medication, joblessness, instability, and poor housing. The lived experience of the mental patient was very tangible. It is the differ-

ence between understanding it conceptually, and living and breathing and being able to taste and feel it. These people had become my friends. I have learned that I need to work with them on a contract basis. The contract relationship is a far cry from, "I am the professional, you are the patient." Now they purchase my services and if they don't like what I am doing, they don't hire me. I think I became ill as a result of beginning to do authentic work, of having the question about my own legitimacy go deep.

Justice is an ideal that evokes a rigorous research approach to transform data into well-configured narratives and a thematic synthesis. Social activists' life histories can inspire others to struggle for more equal sharing of resources and opportunities. Cathy and Kathryn embody a way of being in the world that resonates with Morales' words (1998, 125):

> Solidarity is not a matter of altruism. Solidarity comes from the inability to tolerate the affront to our own integrity of passive or active collaboration in the oppression of others, and from the deep recognition of our most expansive self-interest.

The criterion of fidelity is addressed in research relationships that incorporate the ideal of fairness to self and others. The findings of this inquiry are intended to open space for the consideration of justice as it relates to citizenship responsibilities.

11

Telling "Inside" Stories:
The Paradox of
Researcher Privilege

Ardra L. Cole

Ardra Cole explores two interrelated issues in her account of researching within the professoriat: researchers' responsibility for participants' safety and the implications of this responsibility for the representation of knowledge gained through research. The discussion of participant safety is set within a moral dimension of research and directly relates to the guiding research principles developed in chapter 2. Cole explicates her struggle for a way of telling participants' stories in a way that preserves their safety and authentically represents their experiences, a discussion that elaborates some of the issues related to representational form presented in chapter 6.

In the mid-1980s, after several years of teaching in a variety of special education settings, I left the public school system to become a university-based teacher educator. I left because my images of what it meant to be a teacher had been shattered. I was dissatisfied with what I came to see and understand as undervalued women's work; bored by staff-room conversations about domestic life outside school and almost constant complaining about the disempowerment of teachers; unchallenged intellectually by what I was teaching; constrained by the rules and routines that ordered school life; and discouraged by the unfairness and inequities of the education system. I moved to the university because I wanted to make a difference; the way to do that, I thought, was to be involved in the initial and ongoing education of teachers.

I joined the professoriat at a time, in Canada, when there were beginnings of a fundamental redefinition of teacher education as both a professional and scholarly discipline that had implications for the profile of teacher educators hired at the university. A discussion paper released in Ontario, which was to have a significant national impact on teacher education program and policy (see Fullan and Connelly 1987; Fullan, Connelly, and Watson 1990) identified faculty renewal as one of the key issues confronting teacher education. The authors raised questions about the role of faculty renewal in the future of teacher education. Fullan and Connelly (1987, 48) state: "An important set of recommendations in this report has to do with the kind of people who teach teachers; the question of theory and practice applies as much to them, and to their theoretical and practical lives, as it does to their students." Similarly, in a review of teacher education in another province, Bowman (1991, 109–110) observes:

> Because it is people who make programs successful, only people of the very highest quality . . . must be engaged in them. It is of the utmost importance that all who teach teachers must, in their varied ways, be fine teachers themselves. And those who engage in teacher education programs . . . must be recognized and rewarded appropriately.

In the United States, review and reform bodies such as the Holmes Group (1986, 1990) and Carnegie Forum on Education (1986) made similar recommendations calling for teacher educators to be both skilled practitioners and committed scholars. All of these calls for change came at a time when demographic trends pointed to a rapid turnover in faculty and "unparalleled opportunities for faculty renewal" (Fullan and Connelly 1987, 30). The stage was set, it seemed, for substantial change in teacher education institutions brought about, in part, by a new generation of teacher education faculty of which I was proud to be part.

As years passed, the harder and longer I (and many others) worked, in a variety of subtle and not-so-subtle pedagogical, programmatic, and scholarly ways in the service of better preparing teachers, the more evident it became that not much by way of change was happening both within my own local context and more broadly. Phrases such as "the predictable failure of educational reform" (Sarason 1990), "the more things change, the more they stay the same," "a dance of legitimacy, not a strategy of change" (Deal, cited in Cornbleth 1986, 10), which once seemed cynical and defeatist, started to make sense to me. What, I wondered, was wrong? If the time was right and the conditions supposedly were set for change, why was change so slow to happen?

After years of research and program development focused on teacher education in universities and schools, and on understanding the learning-to-teach process, it was time to turn the research lens inward to focus on those who teach teachers, design programs, and help shape the contexts within which teacher education and development take place. To date, so much energy had been devoted to understanding and improving teachers and schools and so little was known about the goings-on within universities. Ducharme, in his book *The Lives of Teacher Educators* (1993, 102), described the new generation of teacher educators as those who would "inherit the professoriat." This phrase rang in my mind's ear. What were we (they) inheriting? What was our inherited history? What would that history mean for those of us who were trying to do things differently?

I set out to explore the general question: Who is the new generation of teacher educators? Who are they as persons and professionals committed to change in teacher education? What are their aspirations and commitments to ongoing improvement in teacher education and education in general? Who are they as persons operating within complex institutional contexts? What life and career history influences do they bring to their current practices? How do their life and career histories intersect and interact with contemporary institutional and societal realities? I wanted to better understand the nature of the changes in which pretenured teacher education faculty members were engaged and the personal and contextual (institutional and other) influences facilitating and constraining efforts to do things differently.

This research would not be a straightforward undertaking. The academy is a tricky place to negotiate. Researching inside the academy is tricky business. It is tricky for researchers, especially those who are members of the academy themselves. It is tricky for those being researched, especially those untenured faculty members not securely protected by a promise of academic freedom.

I would be asking untenured professors to talk candidly about their experiences in their institutions. I was well aware, even when they were not, of the political implications of their open participation. They would speak forthrightly under the guise of academic freedom but without its full protection. Besides, is there such a thing as full protection anyway, especially in the academy where much of what happens with respect to faculty hiring and firing is clandestine—opaque at best? I have colleagues and friends who, for no apparent reason, were denied tenure or whose contracts were not renewed. These were strong scholars and teachers, part of the new generation of teacher educators wanting to make a difference. I knew colleagues—outspoken activists within the university passionately committed to affirmative action—who had been called in to the dean's or president's office and "encouraged" to tone down their activities. What would I be asking of the participants in my study? What were the risks for them and for me?

I have a friend and colleague whose husband is a criminal court judge. Because my friend and I are both longtime educators with strong backgrounds in professional development, and because she is married to a judge, and therefore a kind of "insider," we were invited to submit a proposal to develop and conduct a professional development program for a regional judges association. This was tricky business, too, because, as my friend told me, "Judges are untouchable, isolated. They can't afford to let outsiders in and especially to explore issues related to morals, values, and beliefs. It's because of the power they have; they're not supposed to behave like real people."

The situation is not dissimilar to that of university professors. Outsiders are seldom "let in." This is not because university professors have great power or are held in high esteem (or fear) by the community, but because the academy, as an institution, is a politically charged bastion of patriarchal, hegemonic power that has survived for centuries in large part because of the protection offered by its ivy-covered tower. Keeping the public at arm's length and keeping the research gaze trained outward have helped to conserve, insulate, and protect the university from public intervention and change. By moving the microphone and microscope inside the walls of the academy, there was a possibility that I might tug at the roots of the ivy and shake loose a few of the tower's bricks. That would not go unnoticed. While I wanted to know and tell the stories of teacher educators' lives in context, I could not risk their position and well-being (and my own for that matter). I needed to proceed carefully, stealthily, cat-like.

Over a three-year period I engaged with seven teacher educators in different institutions in different parts of Canada. We had in-depth conversations and e-mail exchanges about personal and career histories and their current experiences. I spent time with them in their places of work and, in some cases, their homes. I gathered institutional and personal documents and artifacts, including autobiographical writing, course syllabi, appointment books, and institutional policy documents. The conversations, which mainly focused on their current experiences as professors and which revealed the deep rootedness of their individual commitments, were poignant reminders of the powerful role that history—personal and institutional—plays in the push and pull of change. Individuals, with rich personal and career histories in education and a tireless commitment to making a difference by challenging the status quo, experienced the power of academic institutions to preserve their own traditions and institutional histories. I was mindful of this struggle as we talked, as I read, and as I tried to authentically represent them and their experiences.

"Be careful what you say." "Be careful what you write." These words sat on our shoulders and mediated each conversation, giving wise counsel on the potential implications of what is revealed. The promise of anonymity and confidentiality is vital; yet, how possible is it really? Each

time I sat in conversation with one of the study participants I was mindful of the weight of moral and ethical responsibility I carry because of the
trust they placed in me—one of them; an insider; one who knows the potential consequences of telling inside stories; one who had assured them
that no harm would come. The stories are powerful, evocative, painful,
heroic; they are stories of lives lived out in the academy by people who
want to make a difference. They are stories of frustration, oppression,
steadfast determination, self-sacrifice, and naive optimism. They are stories that reveal the underbelly of the institutional beast. They are stories
that must be told; they are stories that must be told with great care.

How to tell?

The stories as told to me (through conversation, writing, and observation), infused with passion, joy, and pain, have not yet left my care even
after several years have passed. I struggle to know what to tell, how to
tell, and when it might be safe to tell. I have written around and about the
stories in relatively conventional academic prose (Cole 2000a, 2000b; Cole
and Knowles 1996, 1998). I have aggregated the data, so to speak, so that
not only is the participants' anonymity protected, the participants are all
but invisible—their stories sucked dry of life by a syringe of academic
convention and protection. The stories are as yet untold but the stories are
too powerful to remain untold.

In partial response to the need to find ways to tell and to honor the participants' experiences and struggles, I searched for a form of telling that
was both safe and authentic. I looked to the arts for inspiration and constructed three-dimensional, multimedia representations of some of the
predominant overarching themes that emerged through an analysis of the
stories told (see chapter 5, this volume, for an elaboration on these representations and the processes of their development). Although these representations are powerfully evocative and revealing in their own way,
they still represent a small part of a collective story; the individual stories
remain untold.

By virtue of my position as an insider I have been privileged to hear
and hold these stories. By virtue of my position as an insider I am
(hyper)vigilant about the potential impact of the telling of these stories on
the lives of the participants and on the lives of others. Therein lies the paradox. The stories reveal some terrible truths about the academy and they
powerfully elucidate how the university has been able to remain virtually
unchanged in any substantial way for centuries. The stories also reveal
the strength of commitment and unabashed passion of those who challenge the status quo; they are inspirational stories. For these reasons,
among others, the stories must be told. Their telling might, in some small
way, help us to move forward. But, their being told cannot and must not
place individuals at risk. Details and idiosyncratic complexities, which

could surely identify individuals and institutions, must be camouflaged. Particular events and incidents, which both illustrate and reveal, must be presented carefully. Aspirations, commitments, and strategies that perhaps have remained covert except to me must remain so, somehow; I cannot blow anyone's cover.

How to tell?

Informed consent means, among other things, a guarantee of anonymity with an understanding that research participants will be protected from "harm." When it comes to reporting life history research, especially research on lives in "tricky" contexts, such promises are difficult to keep, that is, if researchers rely on conventional forms of representation and reporting. With the form of conventional academic prose, telling safely may mean hardly telling at all. Telling safely *and* authentically—capturing the richness and complexity of lived experience as influenced by the potent forces of context—might require life history researchers to push beyond the bounds of academic convention to find more appropriate representational forms. The search for a safe, authentic way to tell the stories of the teacher educators' lives in context has taken me to the realm of fiction and the genre of the novel (see chapter 6, this volume, for a discussion of the role of fiction in academic writing).

It is a heavy responsibility to research from the inside. Insider privilege makes it possible; the responsibilities associated with insider privilege must be felt and honored. More than the names must be changed to protect the innocent.

12

Going Deep: Intersecting the Self as Researcher and Researched

Avi Rose

In the following account, Avi Rose reflects on one of the key points developed in chapter 3: the researcher's location in a research project. Avi shares some of his early struggles with acknowledging his personal location in his research on adults with learning disabilities. In his reflection on the research process, he explores the central role that reflexivity played throughout his researching endeavor.

From the moment that I first encountered the qualitative research paradigm, I felt that I had found a home. So much of it—the structure of research endeavors, the underlying belief system on the nature of truth and universality, the latitude offered in terms of format and creativity, along with the ethics, sensitivity, and respect given research participants—reflected my own core worldview. Somehow, just hearing about the work that others had done convinced me that I could be myself and do my best scholarship within this context.

Though I saw possibility in many forms of qualitative inquiry, it was the narrative element that struck the deepest chords within me. It is because I both learn from and express myself best through story that I felt so strongly about this type of work. Even my spiritual tradition—rife as it is with parable, history and memory—seemed to find resonance here. So it was that I decided to embark on a research journey that would allow me to collect narratives in a life history format.

The most formidable obstacle I encountered, while trying to conceive of and construct a suitable project, was an internal struggle to understand the place of self in research. Whereas other notions connected with the positivist paradigm fell away almost instantly (since I had never really believed in them anyway), I remained, for a time, mired in the belief that I should avoid anything to do with personally inclusive research. After all, I had been taught over and over that the self had no place in research, or in professional writing of any sort.

Yet somehow, despite my reservations, I knew that I really wanted to "go deep" and incorporate my own lived experience into a research endeavor. As the last step in my formal education, I wanted to sum up my learning and discuss the journey that it had been. Having seen others synthesize essential elements of their being into their research, elements that had always seemed outside the realm of formal research and education, I was further intrigued. I was especially excited to see how others had included works of visual art, poetry, and even dance into their research. I wondered if I might be able to incorporate myself as an artist in my work—a further act of synthesis, since I had long since placed this part of my expressive self on the sidelines in order to pursue "serious" academic work.

As I learned more about the methods and rigor involved in life history research and began to read research accounts that were meaningful, creative, and had much to teach, I became convinced that I, too, could create good research that included my own narrative and artistic experience. It seemed that what was required was a careful set of guiding and operating principles and a willingness to engage in constant reflection at all stages of data collection and analysis.

I chose to examine the lived experience of students (including myself) who had reached the graduate level of formal studies while living with some form of recognized learning disability (Rose 1999). I knew that this experience had affected me profoundly and my review of the pertinent literature suggested that there was little information gathered on the needs and experiences of this population. Soon after, a group of motivated research participants "emerged" and the project began to take on an organic quality that seemed to endorse my decision to travel down this path.

INCORPORATING THE SELF IN DATA COLLECTION AND THEMATIC ANALYSIS

As with all of the work involved in a qualitative project, it seemed important to be prepared internally before approaching the external world. Good process, I learned, made for good product. Preparing to act as both participant and observer demanded an extra level of clarity and forethought. I found it useful to delineate for my readers and myself the delicate balancing act that I was performing in my dual role. I clarified my stance as a constructivist, embracing myself as a subjective being who possesses bias, prejudice, and feeling. At the same time, I committed myself to engage in the struggle for both an internal and external view, never allowing my own perspective to overshadow what was to be learned from the ideas and experiences of others. Though I was starting from within, I was moving outward, to a place of common insight, experience, and understanding. My goal, therefore, was not so much to let go of my self but to allow it to join with the selves of others and to cocreate a truly "intersubjective" understanding of the phenomenon.

I prepared for data collection by setting forth a pattern of interviews that would be identical for each participant but would, at the same time, allow for individual needs and differences to emerge. As I conducted the interviews, I found myself constantly engaging in an internal assessment of boundaries. Was I remaining open to what others were telling me? How did the stories, feelings, and insights affect me, and was this, in turn, shaping the manner in which I asked questions? Rigor, at this level, ultimately allowed me to approach the analysis with a sense of integrity.

Once the data were collected, it seemed important, once again, to create space for both myself and others to "emerge" in both process and product. To this end, I decided to allow each participant's voice to be heard, so as to make clear the connections among the themes of the stories collected. An individual participant "portrait" was created, outlining each person's lived experience and reflections, using, as much as possible, direct quotations from the interview transcripts. I created my own portrait only after completing those of others and chose to present it last in the final document. This clarified the fact that the voice of the other was given its own room to emerge, unhindered by my own thoughts or experiences.

Analyzing the data proved to be the point at which all of the preparation and attention to detail was most needed. Looking at the group as a composite required constant reading and rereading of transcripts and portraits. I was committed to remaining grounded in all the ideas and words of participants, never wanting my personal perspective to predominate or unduly color the group "mural." As such, I found myself in a creative square dance of sorts, moving from partner to partner but always returning to the center, to the place that I had started from, in order to ensure that I was on firm ground.

This process, while rewarding, was not always smooth. Despite all the effort that was taken to ensure rigor and to prevent the personal from overshadowing the collective at the outset, I could not entirely preempt such an occurrence. At one point, I found myself overly focused on the positive aspects of the phenomenon, preferring to look at the victor/gain stance, at the expense of the more negative victim/loss facet. Something within me was intensely uncomfortable with the idea of the great pain, struggle, and suffering that had occurred and continued to be a daily reality for even the most successful students with learning disabilities. I suspect that what caused me to limit my focus was unwillingness, at first, to see the dualistic nature of my own experience. The process of telling my story had forced me to reconnect with painful memories, along with the realization that much stress and frustration remained part of my daily learning and working life. This was a difficult reality to accept.

Try as I might, I simply could not have predicted that such a bias would have emerged, nor could I have completely prevented its occurrence. I now see that the idea of remaining open to the surprise of an emergent research design implies a readiness for all aspects of the unexpected—both positive and negative, wanted and unwanted.

What prevented this bias from interfering with a full and complete telling of the story and presentation of the themes was the rigor put into place by the research design and the life history paradigm. The vigilant way in which "the researcher" approaches the thematic analysis, along with the care and value given to the narratives and research participants, allows for constant internal checkpoints to emerge on the road to analysis. In the end, it was relatively easy to see that such a bias had emerged and that, if left unchecked, it would interfere with the harvest of abundance contained in the data. The difficult part was accepting myself as a learner; flawed and accident-prone, yet safe within the confines of a system that works.

USE OF VISUAL ART IN THE RESEARCH PROCESS

An important element of my research involved the use of visual art. I am an artist who had at one point, for the most part, given up visual creativity in favor of academic pursuits—mostly because of the sheer effort needed to move through school with a learning disability. Now, however, I strongly felt that as part of this endeavor, I should incorporate an artistic component to my work. At first I envisioned this in a somewhat limited manner; I asked all research participants, including myself, to contribute a piece of art that expressed the experience of living as a student with learning disabilities. Later, I found the need to express my feelings and experiences as a researcher through art. Having burst through the barriers between my creative and intellectual selves, I found that both were now needed and valued as part of the research process.

The addition of art proved to be a valuable tool for me in my journey. Though I had not expected to, I began to "draw out" feelings and experiences connected to the research. This served to act as yet another in the internal checkpoints, compelling me to examine and reexamine myself within the duality of my roles as researcher and participant. It was partly because of the art that I was, for example, able to catch my bias toward the positive facets of the narratives (articulated at the expense of painful realities that it also contained). It was certainly the art that allowed me to express my frustration, happiness, and gratefulness for the gift of this intense process. It also allowed me to gain perspective on things, to trust the process and to know that I cycled through moments of negative and positive growth.

In addition to the benefits that the inclusion of artwork offered me personally, it also added to the rigor and quality of the research project itself. First, it offered individuals, whose main roadblocks were in the area of linguistic expression, an opportunity to engage in an alternate form of communication. As such, it became both a vehicle for the elaboration of thoughts and feelings that had elsewhere been expressed, and a mechanism for the discovery of new insights. In this way, it added invaluably to the process of data collection. Second, it offered a means of furthering the relationship between researcher and researched. The process of negotiating, exploring, and explaining the artistic works improved the shared experience and shed new light onto the individual.

Unpredictably, the artistic process also allowed for both the researcher and the researched to view a new facet of the learning-disability experience. For most participants, art was a long-ago practiced magic, something for which most felt they had little facility. Although no one was ever compelled to complete a piece (and in fact one participant declined and others worked collaboratively with me), I did encourage everyone to try to create something. What emerged from this experience, for several participants, was the playing out of an important cycle of self-mistrust, risk-taking, and success. Some of those who attempted an art piece reported that it had been a challenging, even frightening experience but that, in the end, they were pleased to have pushed themselves into new territory. It was interesting to see how this mirrored much of the experiences in the learning sphere. Years of failure had made most participants wary of new "performance" demands, especially in an area where it was assumed no skill or facility existed. Doing the art, then, became a metaphor for so many learning and performance experiences—a sounding board for the internal scripts that play inside the psyche of many individuals with learning disabilities.

This experience sensitized me, in a very crucial way, to the need for constant questioning and vigilance in the delicate area of participant respect. It made me realize that what seems natural to me as an individual, might for others, violate a sense of safety. Speaking with participants about their lives—though emotional and very "big" at times—did not place the same demand on some as the art project did. I had to be extremely cautious, I learned, not to abuse the fragility of participants' self-confidence by asking them to engage in a strange and, in some cases, nerve-racking task. I had to really listen to my fellow participants as they dealt with the anxiety or inconvenience created by the request for artwork. This was another area where the intersection of self and other required great insight.

FINAL REFLECTIONS ON PROCESS

The result of this process, with its systematic attention to detail and high degree of rigor, was handsomely rewarded. What emerged was a work that balanced the individual and the collective, the emotional and the intellectual, the narrative and the thematic. Additionally, I believe that the work—the first to be conducted by an "insider" who has lived the phenomenon—added a fresh perspective to the research on learning disabilities.

Now that I have engaged in inquiry that stems from personal experience, I can see its value with greater clarity. Far from being a liability, it has, in fact, unique benefits. First, it forced me to be clear about my assumptions and biases and to catch them as they emerged, placing them in their proper context. When one is studying a phenomenon, whether or not it relates directly to personal experience, such a deep examination of self is imperative, since it can only benefit the reader to know where the writer is coming from. If my experience is any indication, the more one tries to suppress the self, the more likely one's views and ideas are to intrude upon the information supplied by others, clouding and distorting in counterproductive ways.

Second, as an insider I was able to approach coresearchers in a way that would have otherwise been impossible. The interaction that transpired among us was deeply rooted in our shared experiences and understanding. Even while trying to get at the particulars of their unique narratives, coresearchers and I were able to communicate using a common language and lens. As such, there were nuances, details, and emotions that I was uniquely qualified to detect. While I firmly believe that no one can perfectly replicate a human experience inquiry—since every interaction and understanding is unique—I especially feel that an insider's ability to explore a phenomenon cannot be superseded by an outsider. This does not invalidate an outsider perspective; it simply obviates the fact an outsider's understanding will necessarily differ.

At one point, I was asked by a reviewer of my work to provide a rationale for undertaking research that was so personal. Whereas at the beginning of the project I might have shuddered at such a question—presuming that it essentially invalidated my efforts—in the end I felt secure in explaining my motivation and process. I gladly discussed the reasons for my decision to undertake such a task, the rewards of doing work in this manner, and the safeguards that I put in place in order to ensure that it remained balanced and broad enough to make room for both self and other.

There will always be voices criticizing researchers who look inward and outward, rather than limiting themselves to a unidirectional mode of operation. Whereas I was once part of that chorus that shuns personal involvement in research, I now find the need to change my tune. In fact, I have given up my membership in that group altogether and have joined another choir that allows me to simultaneously function as an individual and as a member of a respected and respectful community. I like being both soloist and accompanist. I think it adds melodic harmony to the music of human experience inquiry.

13

A Life History as Artistic Interpretation

James A. Muchmore

In chapter 3 we discuss the role of serendipity in developing a life history research project. Jim Muchmore's account of his serendipitous encounter with an art exhibit illuminates this notion. For Jim, the unexpected encounter turned out to be an epiphanic moment in his self-identification as a life history researcher.

My first researching epiphany occurred in the unlikely setting of an art gallery. In April 1992, while attending a conference at Wayne State University in Detroit, I wandered into an area where some graduate students in the fine arts program were displaying their work. It was a small room, close to the site of the conference, and a friend and I had entered simply to pass the time while awaiting the start of the next session. The walls were covered with various paintings on canvas—some of them abstract and others more traditional—and several sculptures rested on pedestals that were scattered throughout the room. All seemed very ordinary. I hastily glanced at a few of the pieces and was about to leave the gallery when I noticed a peculiar object mounted on the back wall. It was a wooden box, about the size of a medicine cabinet, and it contained two large porcelain doors that had obviously been hand-molded before being kiln fired. The doors contained an unusual series of symmetrical cells, much like a honeycomb, which gave the entire object a strangely, organic quality. It was as if the box had sprouted from the wall, naturally, rather than being constructed by human hands and deliberately placed there.

Moving closer, I studied its appearance and wondered what this thing was supposed to be. The box's old, weathered wood invited my touch—yet I was reluctant to do so. "Art is for viewing, not for touching," I thought. I paused for a moment and nervously glanced over my shoulder. No one was looking, so I quickly reached out and moved my fingers along the rough wooden surface. Nothing happened. No alarms sounded, and no one shouted at me to stop, so I ventured further and peered behind one of the porcelain doors.

It did not take much effort to open the small, heavy door, as it was perfectly balanced. Someone had obviously crafted it with a great deal of skill. As the porcelain door slowly swung open, I was startled to see a person staring back at me. It was a photograph of a young man. It looked like a high school yearbook picture that had been enlarged and embossed onto a thin, irregular layer of porcelain. I opened the other door to get a better look. The photograph was old, probably from the late 1960s or early 1970s, but the student's expression was timeless. With long, dark hair and the faint beginnings of a mustache, he struck a rather defiant pose. It was a familiar look—a look of student resistance—that I knew well from my own days as a public school teacher. "He's a 'burnout,'" I thought, instantly assigning a meaning to the photograph. Moving closer, I noticed a small crack in the porcelain emanating from one of the student's eyes and gradually thickening as it spread across his face to the edge of the porcelain—a pristine photograph, marred by a jagged crack. "Yes," I thought, "this student must be the archetype of a high school burnout. That must be what the artist is trying to depict." I thought I had figured it out.

While I stood looking at the photograph, I noticed two additional doors beneath it. They were made of glass, and through them I could see what looked like six small drawers. I wondered what, if anything, might be inside them. I wanted to look, but I felt uncomfortable. "But the artist must have intended for viewers to interact with his work," I reasoned. "Otherwise, he would not have put hinges on the doors, and he would not have placed it in such a public location."

Nervously glancing over my shoulder once again, I quickly opened the two glass doors and pulled out one of the drawers. My heart beat faster as I peered inside. I fully expected someone to yell, "Hey, don't touch that!" Again, however, the warning never came—and I was able to look closely at the contents. Inside the drawer were a couple of small, laminated cards. The first one read:

STUDENT IDENTIFICATION CARD
HIGHLAND PARK HIGH SCHOOL, 1968–69
STEVE LENZO, AGE 15, GRADE 10

There was a photograph on the card of the same teenage boy whose picture was embossed on the porcelain. I picked up the card and held it in my hand. Suddenly, this boy was no longer an anonymous "burnout."

The other card was much newer. It showed a grown man with short-cropped hair, a beard, and glasses. He hardly resembled the teenager in the first image, but the name was the same. STEVEN LENZO, it read, SOUTH BRONX HIGH SCHOOL.

"So the boy must have become a teacher," I thought, realizing that my initial interpretation may have been wrong. After all, "burnouts" did not become teachers, did they? I now had two pieces of information, and the young man's life began to take on a new meaning.

In search of additional clues, I reached deeper into the same drawer and found a tattered old report card. It listed the following grades:

ADVANCED BIOLOGY	A
GEOMETRY I	A
SPANISH I	A
PHYSICAL EDUCATION	A
WORLD CULTURE	A
SPEECH	B

These were definitely not the grades of a burnout—all A's and one B. I wondered how my initial impression could have been so wrong.

By now, since no one had challenged me, I was less concerned about interacting with this work of art. I simply wanted to know more about this person, Steven Lenzo. Who was he? Who was the artist? What was the artist's intention in creating this box?

Inside another drawer, I found a silver whistle on an old frayed lanyard, just like the one I still have from my former days as a high school track coach. "Perhaps he was a coach, too," I thought. In posing this question, I was conscious of how subjective my interpretations had been so far. Instead of *uncovering* Steve Lenzo's life, or "pouring it into a container," I realized that I was actually *creating* a version of his life—one that was inextricably linked to my own, for it was through the lens of my own life experiences that I was making sense of these objects. Beneath the whistle was an envelope that contained a note. Pausing before opening it, I once again began to feel uneasy—as if I had broken into someone's house and was rummaging through his private possessions. I felt like an intruder of sorts. First I had opened the porcelain doors. Then I had opened the glass doors and pulled out a drawer. Now I was about to breach yet another barrier by opening this envelope. I wondered if I had gone too far. After all, who was I to poke around this man's personal possessions? But then I remembered where I was. I was in an art gallery—a public place—and this wooden box was a work of art. Nevertheless, I was still very nervous as I opened the envelope and pulled out the slip of paper. It was a memo typed on a half-sheet of stationary from Highland Park High School. Frail and yellow with age, it read:

To: Steve Lenzo

From: All the students of HPHS

Subject: Long Hair

Since school opened, we have tolerated your hair without complaining, but you have let it go too far. We hereby officially ask you to get a haircut. If it is not cut within ten days, we will have to cut it ourselves.

Fair Warning

Sincerely,

Highland Park High School

"Surely this must have been a joke," I thought. "Perhaps he was a burnout after all. Or was he?" I read it again more carefully. "From: All the students of HPHS." Yes, it must have been a joke. Otherwise, it probably would have been signed by a single person—the principal perhaps—not the high school at large. "Steve Lenzo must have had a good sense of humor," I thought, "or at least his classmates did." I carefully refolded the slip of paper, inserted it back in the envelope, and returned it to the drawer.

Opening the next drawer, I found five photographs. The first one was of a smiling adolescent who looked like the teenager in the porcelain yearbook picture, only he was younger and his hair was much shorter. "1964 World's Fair" it read on the back. The second picture revealed a much older version of the same boy, now grown and holding a baby. Could this be Steve's child? Next was a black-and-white photograph of him standing next to a young woman. Perhaps this was his wife, or at least the mother of the child. I hoped the two remaining pictures would provide some definitive answers. One showed a different man—definitely not Steve—holding a different baby. Who was this man? A friend? A brother? I did not know. The final picture revealed a wrecked car—horribly twisted, almost beyond recognition. Perhaps Steve had been killed in this car. Maybe this whole work of art was intended to serve as a memorial to him. I did not know.

Opening another drawer, I found a whole new set of artifacts that further confounded my ongoing interpretations. There was a Washtenaw County Sheriff's Department patch, along with a passport and some foreign money. What did this mean? Had Steve been a law enforcement officer? Had he traveled overseas? Then, I saw a letter written in Spanish and a leather necklace laced with a large blue stone. What did it mean? The drawers were like a row of windows to a large room, and each time I peered into a different one, the view was slightly altered.

Coming to the last drawer, I hoped that I would finally be able to make sense of everything—but instead I encountered only a few more scattered pieces of this man's life: a crumpled draft card, a collection of seeds, and a pocket-sized "Smoky-the-Bear" calendar book for the current year. No answers here, just more questions. Had he dodged the draft? Perhaps he had fled to Mexico during the Vietnam War. And what about the seeds? Could they be drugs? I now envisioned Steve as a burnout again—perhaps evading the draft and hanging out in Central America.

The last item was a stamped envelope with a very recent postmark. Inside, I found a letter that had been handwritten on a single white sheet of stationary. As I read it, the whole story once again began to take on a new meaning. It read:

Dear Peter,

Sorry it has taken me so long to package this. We just got back from a four-day trip to Portland, combined business and pleasure trip. Joe B. was great even during the nine-hour car ride. We saw lots of my old friends, their kids, and spent a couple of nights in a hotel in downtown Portland. Took Joe B. to the zoo too, he liked the monkeys. Here's a brief explanation of the enclosed items.

(1) Cards from South Bronx and Highland Park High School.
(2) Canceled passport from trips to Switzerland and Central America.
(3) The photo Jennifer and I used for our wedding invitation.
(4) Sheriff's patch from my corrections officer uniform.
(5) Draft card from 1972.
(6) Resolution from Honduras Forest Service declaring the town of El Porvenir's watershed to be protected forest zone.
(7) A 50-cordoba note from Nicaragua worth about a penny in 1987.
(8) Whistle I used while lifeguarding at Savyatich, 1972.
(9) Jade necklace of carved foot supposed a Mayan relic given me by an anthropology student in Guatemala.
(10) A coin from Peru (1/2 sol).
(11) Some grass seeds known as "lagrima de san Pedro" in Honduras and worn around baby's necks to ward off evil spirits.
(12) The Smoky calendar is for you.

Love,
Steve

After the conference at Wayne State University ended, I went home to Ann Arbor, but could not stop thinking about my experience with this work of art. I wanted to know more about Steven Lenzo and the artist,

Peter, who had chronicled his life. Early the next morning, I drove back to Detroit and returned to the gallery. When I got there, however, I was surprised to find that the work of art was gone. It had disappeared. In fact, the entire room was empty; nothing remained. It was as if I had dreamed the whole thing. Going into a nearby office, I asked a woman gallery employee what had happened to the exhibit. Before she could reply, I imagined her saying, "I don't know what you're talking about. There hasn't been an art exhibit in this building for years." That would have been too eerie! Instead, she provided a much more plausible explanation. The exhibit was over, and all of the artists had removed their work earlier that morning.

"Was a guy named Peter here?" I asked.

"You must mean Peter Lenzo," she said. "Yes, he was here. In fact, I think he's still in the building."

"What does he look like?"

"He's a tall man in his late thirties with long dark hair pulled back into a ponytail. You can't miss him."

Armed with this information, I raced back out into a hall and immediately spotted a man walking toward me who fit the description.

"Are you Peter Lenzo?" I inquired.

"Yes, I am," he replied with an inquisitive look on his face. "What can I do for you?"

I introduced myself and said, "I saw your work yesterday, and it made a really strong impression on me. I came back for another look."

Peter smiled as I spoke and we then had a long conversation about his work. He told me that he called his wooden box a "reliquary," meaning that it was a receptacle or repository for keeping or storing artifacts. He said that he had made several of these reliquaries—one for each of his siblings in order to repay them for helping to support him while he was in graduate school. This particular exhibit, he told me, had also served as his final project for his master of fine arts degree (Lenzo 1992). He smiled when I told him how I had interacted with it—how I had touched it—and he seemed amused by my reaction. He explained that all of his work was intensely personal yet he had purposely designed it to be as inviting as possible. He wanted people to struggle, as I had, with the tension between wanting to explore it and feeling that it was wrong.

After briefly chatting about his family, Peter invited me to his studio to let me reexplore his brother's reliquary. (Recognizing the very personal nature of Peter's work and the information that it contained, I contacted him again via telephone on April 27, 1995, and received permission to describe it here.) It looked different resting on the studio floor. It seemed smaller and much less mysterious. Yet, as soon as I opened the drawers and started examining the artifacts, I once again found myself trying to piece together Steve's life—this time with the added knowledge gained from my conversation with Peter. With each new encounter, the artifacts took on a slightly different meaning. For instance, Peter told me that Steve was once involved in a serious automobile accident. The entire car had been destroyed yet he had miraculously survived—his only injury being a large circular bruise on his chest caused by the impact of his body against the steering wheel. I thought about this story when I saw the picture of the wrecked car again, and I remembered a similar event in my own life in which my head had shattered the windshield during a head-on auto accident when I was in college. I walked away from that accident completely unscathed—no cuts, no bruises, not even a bump.

In making this reliquary, Peter collaborated with his brother to create a kind of living portfolio. Each object told a different story, and it was my "job" as viewer to piece them together to form a unified whole. The soundness of my interpretations rested not on the items' consistency with an objective truth, but instead on their own internal consistency—the extent to which they made sense within a particular context. I came to this interpretive endeavor with a unique set of personal experiences that informed my initial impressions of his brother—impressions that continually changed and reformulated with the discovery of each new artifact until, eventually, my interpretations could accommodate all of the information at hand. Heavily influenced by my own life history, as well as the time and context of my encounter, my interpretations were highly subjective and idiosyncratic. Another person might have seen things quite differently, or if I had encountered the work of art at a different time or in a different place, I too might have constructed a very different version of Steve's life—for as Denzin states, "No reading or writing of a life is ever complete or final. . . . There can only be multiple versions of a biography or autobiography" (1989a, 46–47).

14

Reflections on "Our Stories": Women in Cardiac Rehabilitation

Lori Ebbesen

Lorri Ebbesen is a practitioner and researcher in the area of cardiac rehabilitation. In the following account, she describes some of the lessons she learned about cardiac rehabilitation and about researching from engaging in life history research with women participants in a cardiac rehabilitation program. For Ebbesen, the explicit connections between research and practice, and the personal and the professional, are central to the overall value of a research project. Ebbesen's account reflects notions about the research process as articulated in chapter 4, the research relationship as discussed in chapter 2, and the issue of audience as discussed in chapter 5.

It was April 4, 1997. I couldn't believe this was happening to me. It couldn't be true. It had to be a mistake. There was no warning. . . . In an expanse of a few minutes—although it felt like hours—my life was turned upside down. I didn't know what I was going to do next. I felt completely out of control . . . shocked, and lonely, and scared. I wanted to know WHY? Why was this happening to me? What had I done to deserve this? Now what?

Countless times, as a cardiac rehabilitation practitioner, I have heard similar accounts of initial reactions to a cardiac event. Countless times I have admired individuals as they adjust to living with heart disease. I have questioned the role that cardiac rehabilitation programs and practitioners play in the process of recovery. I was particularly curious— both personally and professionally—about the experiences of women in

184

cardiac rehabilitation. Personally, my interest stemmed from varied connections with women, including family members, friends, colleagues and cardiac rehabilitation participants. Professionally, I was well aware that the picture of women in cardiac rehabilitation is rather dismal and warrants further exploration.

Given that my practice in cardiac rehabilitation entails listening to people talk about what has been and is significant in their lives, observing them in action, and reviewing their medical and exercise records, it seemed appropriate that my research would do likewise. The purpose of this inquiry project was to describe and to understand the experiences of women participating in cardiac rehabilitation (Ebbesen 1999). I am a strong advocate of the notion that, to be truly comprehensive, cardiac rehabilitation needs to explore with participants what their heart disease means to them and the broader social and familial contexts within which it exists. So, in this inquiry project, I went beyond typical medical and health research practices to consider individual perceptions and expectations, as well as the life context. I set out to explore the personal qualities and life experiences of a few women in a cardiac rehabilitation program; to understand how these qualities and experiences contributed to or influenced their involvement in cardiac rehabilitation; and to understand the meaning these women attached to or derived from their participation in cardiac rehabilitation.

The setting for this inquiry project was the Saskatoon Tri-Hospital Cardiac Rehabilitation Program and its "graduate" component, the Coronary Artery Rehabilitation Group (CARG), both located in Saskatoon, Saskatchewan, Canada. I actively recruited three women with a range of heart conditions to reflect the range of cardiac rehabilitation clientele. They were between the ages of forty and eighty years, had been diagnosed with heart disease, had participated in the Tri-Hospital program and continued as a graduate in CARG, and, perhaps, most important, were willing to participate in my project.

My first "recruit" was Helen, a seventy-four-year-old woman with a nursing background, married, with two children and four grandchildren. Helen had experienced two heart attacks, two angioplasty procedures, and had faced several other health concerns such as arthritis, high blood pressure, back surgery, and hip replacement. She was faithfully accompanied on her treks around the walking track by her "designated walker" and program support person, daughter, Marjorie.

Mary was seventy-six years old at the time of our conversations, a former elementary school teacher, widow, and a mother of two with an uncomplicated medical history. Mary had suffered chest pains and undergone an angioplasty procedure to one coronary artery. Her life story was characterized by an ominous family history of heart disease and a "merry-go-round" lifestyle with an alcoholic husband.

Joan was a fifty-seven-year-old woman with a complex life story. Significant events included a failed first marriage, rebuilding a life for herself and her children, accidental death of her first husband, remarriage, and familial alcoholism. She was a proud grandmother of seven. Her medical challenges were many and included mitral valve stenosis, subsequent valvular surgery, atrial fibrillation, panic attacks, agoraphobia, and claustrophobia.

Each of these women engaged in multiple conversations—five or six— with me in which we shared experiences in cardiac rehabilitation and other life experiences. The time and location for conversations were decided by each woman. We talked about significant events in our lives, feelings and impressions. Each conversation was about one and a half to two hours long, although some were longer. Joan and I once had a "marathon" session of six hours! These conversations were recorded, with each woman's permission, and transcribed, word-for-word as spoken. Following each conversation, each woman was asked to read over a transcript of her conversation and help me derive meaning. Given their central and active role in the process, I viewed each of them as coparticipants, or colearners.

When asked by her daughter what it was that we did when we met, Helen responded, "Mostly talk and laugh and eat." I would like to think that what we were doing was more complex, yet this does, indeed, describe the process in its simplest form. Along with collecting life stories as we talked and laughed and ate, I reviewed cardiac rehabilitation records and personal documents, as available; observed these women within the cardiac rehabilitation setting; had discussions with colleagues; and kept a written, reflexive journal.

Review of cardiac rehabilitation records of each woman allowed insight into program participation, attendance, progress, and medical history. Access to personal documents such as family photographs, cards, letters, and, in Mary's case, a journal, often served as a springboard and helped to enlighten conversations. Observations of these women at the cardiac rehabilitation program complemented written documentation by tapping into such aspects of their participation as instructor and social interactions, energy, enthusiasm, and participation in special events such as coffee parties and costume days. I made use of informal discussions with colleagues to "check out" and confirm some of my ideas and observations. My journal served as both a calendar of events (scheduled conversations and informal connections) and a valuable running commentary of my thoughts, feelings, and impressions throughout the process.

The interpretation of the information gathered was an interactive and collaborative venture. Along with the transcripts of their own conversations, preliminary impressions, comments, and analysis derived from transcripts, documentation and observation insights were discussed or circulated to each coparticipant for her reactions and responses. The analysis involved extensive reviewing of information gathered, extracting significant comments, creating meanings, clustering of ideas or themes common to all stories, and confirming these with coparticipants.

This project was not designed to represent experiences of all women in cardiac rehabilitation; however, insights emerged relevant for other cardiac rehabilitation participants and professionals. The stories of these women provided an understanding of the complexity of life experiences that an individual brings to cardiac rehabilitation. These stories revealed personal qualities (resilience, optimism or a positive outlook, a positive sense of self, and a holistic view of health) and environmental qualities (social support and interactive relationships with health professionals) that appear to facilitate cardiac rehabilitation participation, both initially and on a long-term basis. These stories emphasized desirable features of cardiac rehabilitation programming, the adoption of which may enhance the experience of other women. As well, five themes emerged from these stories regarding the meaning of the cardiac rehabilitation experience: connecting with others, gaining perspective, reaping the benefits, learning with others, and having fun.

As I had wished at the outset, this project provided all of us involved with an exciting and personally meaningful learning adventure in the context of cardiac rehabilitation, something to which each of us is clearly devoted. Together, we integrated life experiences, clarified meaning and purpose, took stock of our lives, and arrived at greater clarity about what has gone well, what could have gone better, and what matters most. Together, we explored what cardiac rehabilitation means to each of us and the role that it plays in our respective lives.

REFLECTIONS ON THIS INQUIRY PATH

Reflecting on my experiences in this inquiry permits a welcome opportunity to articulate "lessons learned" about aspects that seemed to enhance the process and to make visible my struggles and dilemmas.

I was fortunate to have engaged in this project with three women whom I admire and genuinely like. Before this inquiry, I had at least some connection with each of these women. I did not have to struggle with initiating relationships; rather, I had strong foundations on which to build. Relationally, I did not have to deal with closure of relationships. I have the added bonus of continued relationships with these women that greatly enriches my life. The drawback of such familiarity was in the increased sense of accountability I felt toward these women: a profound sense of pressure and responsibility and the burden to "get it right."

When embarking on this journey I considered myself a fledgling life history researcher. I knew Helen better than Mary or Joan and thought it would be advantageous, in terms of comfort, to start the process with someone with whom I was familiar. I now have mixed feelings about this decision. The comfort level was, indeed, enriched, allowing an easy flow to our conversations right from the beginning. There were times in the first two conversations with Helen, however, where I felt I should already know certain details of her story. This feeling hampered my ability to ask "naive" or clarifying questions.

My existing relationships with the other women and their subsequent development was not marred nor threatened by an imbalance of power—real or perceived. As I am primarily a volunteer within the cardiac rehabilitation program and a familiar face on the track and at "cardiac social events," there was no threat to quality of care for Helen, Mary, or Joan. Their regular programming and care at the cardiac rehabilitation program were not jeopardized in any way. There were no hidden or vested interests confounding the process. My multiple roles of volunteer, part-time staff person, and researcher did not appear to muddy the waters or adversely influence this work. From the outset of the project, discussions regarding roles, responsibilities, and expectations were open and direct. This openness carried throughout our conversations and enhanced the quality and richness of experience shared. I was complimented when one of my "editors," Barb, made a special note to this effect:

> Knowing two of these women, I can tell you that reading their stories was like sitting and talking with them personally. Knowing also the high value one of your participants in particular places on her privacy, I congratulate you on having established an atmosphere of trust that allowed her to share so much. . . .

I recognized noteworthy differences between the coparticipants and me. I am younger and have had fewer life experiences, and have not encountered the same kinds of health challenges. Even so, I felt well versed within the context of heart disease and cardiac rehabilitation. Also, I have had my fair share of life experiences and, although they are not personally cardiac specific, they helped me to tune into these women's experiences of loss, change, and challenge. It proved challenging, however, to capture the full context and essence of the time period within which these women matured and lived. I feel I was not as effective as I could have been in portraying the relevance and influence of context, for instance, as related to their pioneer roots and spirit.

My previous observations of, and informal interactions with, these women on the track served as a foundation for sharing and a consistency check of sorts. I had the chance to see the extent to which their stories confirmed what I already knew, or thought I knew, about each woman. Informal connections on the track (and socially) with Helen, Mary, Joan, and, at times, their walking partners were very enlightening and relaxed, adding credibility to information gathered and contributing additional insights into the lives of these women.

I gathered information from various sources, and in a flexible manner, based on the needs and preferences of each coparticipant. Thus, in my contact with each woman, there were variations in terms of number of conversations, location of conversations, specific documents available for review, and my inclusion in social outings. I maintained a valuable closeness to the information gathered and ensured confidentiality by doing such things as transcribing each of the conversations myself. As I wrote in my journal on April 7, 1998: "Transcribing, although extremely time consuming . . . [is] an integral part of my understanding the experiences of these women. It brings me much closer to their life experiences, their manner of speaking . . . them."

I brought to this project a great deal of enthusiasm for the field of cardiac rehabilitation. I appreciate the value of cardiac rehabilitation and the supportive aspects of the group atmosphere. Paradoxically, I probably would not participate in such a program if I had experienced a "cardiac event." This paradox of involvement was an undercurrent driving my attempts to understand the meaning of, and to connect with, the cardiac rehabilitation experience. Through connecting with the coparticipants and other cardiac rehabilitation practitioners as "research buddies," I experienced the community aspect of the cardiac rehabilitation program in a new way.

I struggled with the "I/we" issue throughout the process. Partly, this inquiry was "we"; I firmly believed the other women were coparticipants, and that we were collaborating on a joint project. On the other hand, this inquiry was "I." The analysis and interpretation was largely mine, as was the writing. I was uncomfortable with this reality, perhaps because of the sense of added responsibility I felt. Upon further reflection, I feel the issue of ownership by coparticipants is far more critical than who, ultimately, puts pen to paper. In this inquiry, the women displayed ownership in several ways. First, Helen, Mary, and Joan showed increasing interest in the process by asking such questions as: "When is our next talk?" "Have you got my transcripts yet?" "How is the writing going?" "How is my chapter coming along?" Second, all three women agreed, independently, to use their real names, saying they were proud of their participation and the "product." Third, initial reasons given by Helen, Mary, and Joan for participating were "to help me." When asked in each of their last conversations with me, "What it was like to participate?" the tone of their responses was more personal, reflecting the degree of engagement and connection with the project as well as its transformative potential. For instance, Mary commented: "I think maybe it's been good for me to go through all these things—through all of my life—and realize how it all connected. Being involved in this project made me think about what kind of a life I've had."

Although storytelling—and listening—is a natural part of my cardiac rehabilitation practice, storytelling in written form is not easy for me and is quite a departure from my "learned" and well-ingrained academic writing style. I sometimes wallowed in confusion. I struggled to decipher what was relevant for inclusion in the text. I struggled with writing in a way that honored what the coparticipants had shared. I struggled with writing in a way that would engage readers, allow them to connect closely with the stories, and permit their own interpretations and insights. I also struggled with writing something that would be valued by my peers, themselves researchers but located in a different paradigm.

Uncertainty and ambiguity were inherent in the process. I found myself worrying about the process, the recording equipment, and whether I would be able to come up with "brilliant" questions. I also thought fearfully ahead: "Am I going to be able to 'cut the wheat from the chaff'?" "Will the stories be good enough?" "To what extent will others find this inquiry valuable?" My level of comfort with uncertainty fluctuated in a mysterious ebb and flow.

Engaging in a style of research that involved open and mutual sharing of personal life experiences and feelings was somewhat of a departure for me—I was usually "distant" or absent in the research report. I sat outside my "comfort zone" for most of this project in terms of the degree of transparency required. I was not prepared fully for the challenges and potential opportunities of such an intimate connection and embeddedness between me and the inquiry process. There were times when I felt too close to the issues or situations being disclosed, and needed to stifle my own reactions to parallel events in my life. It was personally challenging and painful to revisit sore spots, as it prompted reliving and rethinking on my part. Ultimately, however, sharing of such intimacies solidified the relationship between the coparticipants and me, and helped me gain clearer perspectives on some of my own life experiences.

Admittedly, the extent to which my "whole story" is portrayed in this project is limited. In conversation I was increasingly comfortable and open in sharing all parts of my life. In writing I presented only elements of my professional self. My reasons were primarily related to issues of personal vulnerability. Certainly the option of anonymity and a pseudonym did not seem viable! Further, I questioned or, perhaps, did not fully understand at the time the relevance of infusing all aspects of my life.

My search for knowledge through this project surpassed my expectations. Participation was transformative for all of us involved. I am no exception, as I noted in my journal on February 14, 1999:

> It has been a deeply moving journey. Trying to understand my professional path to date—and the synergy with my personal path—and to set direction(s) for my subsequent path, has proven challenging, painful at times and comical at others. It proves to be quite a process of reflecting, revisiting, and resolving. At times I have felt the sting of the brambles. At times I have felt I was wandering aimlessly, alone. At times I have felt that I had reached a beautiful and peaceful clearing in the forest, full of flowers, sunshine and warmth.

The experience was a valuable professional development opportunity for me. I discovered how my cardiac rehabilitation practice and my educational background (in kinesthesiology, adult learning, and life history research) are synergistic and complementary, creating a stimulating, dynamic, and personally comfortable mix. I also achieved greater self-knowledge that, in turn, informs my professional practice, and expands my vision of me as cardiac rehabilitation practitioner, researcher, and person.

15

Researching First Nations Educators through Presence, Collaboration, and Advocacy

Jeff Orr

Jeff Orr describes and illustrates the role of life history research in knowledge development, particularly as it reflects "the Aboriginal epistemology of a circular and collective construction of meaning." As such his account connects with chapter 1, which outlines some of the roles and broad purposes of life history research. Orr also provides a glimpse into what a life history account might look like. In so doing, he also demonstrates some of the points about analysis and representation discussed in chapters 5 and 6.

In this account, and the project behind it, I show how a life history researching approach expands understandings about what it means to be a First Nations educator attempting to bring an Aboriginal focus to contemporary First Nations schooling. First Nations education is in a state of transition in Canada. A number of educational jurisdictions have made significant inroads into the development of Aboriginal curriculum and the hiring of Aboriginal staff (Battiste and Barman, 1995). Aboriginal educators who hold an Aboriginal perspective on and commitment to Aboriginal language, culture, knowledge, and governance issues are rarely heard in research or professional literature. Life histories legitimize and solidify Aboriginal perspectives through a documentation of Aboriginal teacher knowledge. They are created in ways that are supportive and respectful of educators who feel silenced by bureaucratic, institutional, political, societal, and community pressures.

I have worked with Mi'kmaq communities (located in the Atlantic provinces of Canada) in an attempt to understand more fully how

Aboriginal teachers' lives are situated in their institutions, communities, and families. My efforts over the past few years have been centered on working with Mi'kmaq educators at the intersection of teaching, program development, and administrative advocacy. This intersection of roles, manifested in my focus on advocacy through presence and collaboration, is the heart of my approach to cross-cultural, life history research.

I present three life history accounts. These life histories represent lives embedded in three very different professional contexts. Susan works in an adult high school run by First Nations educators in a First Nations community; Darlene works in a junior high context in a First Nations community; and Glenda works in a provincial high school serving a predominantly nonnative population. Despite their markedly different roles with very different groups of Mi'kmaq learners, all three educators have strikingly common convictions, and all have been influenced by similar social and historical conditions and contexts. The biographies of all three have been significantly shaped by their families, two especially so by their grandparents, the other by her role as mother. They all place a strong emphasis on influencing student attitudes to protect and nurture Mi'kmaq ways. Together their stories reveal multiple ways the dominant society exerts influence over Mi'kmaq education, and explain how these women are speaking back to this oppressive milieu.

GLENDA: HONORING MY GRANDFATHER'S WISHES

I was born at the tail end of centralization where my people were just removed from their natural habitats and herded into reservations for their "own good." I sure felt lucky and privileged that I wasn't forced to go to the residential school. My grandfather was the one who taught me the ways of his people. My grandfather's greatest fear was that the white man might kill or take control of my spirit. I remember that I often had to reassure him that this would not happen and that I had learned well all that was needed.

When I started school I didn't understand the English language and the ways of the white man. The girl next to me tried to alert me that I was being summoned by the nun, and if I didn't respond I would be punished like the others, but it was too late. My name had been called already and I did not respond. I could instantly see why they were feeling miserable. Their beautiful long braided hair was on the floor. I decided I would free myself from her clutches and make a run for it. I ran all the way home, never stopping for a breath. I arrived home safely in plenty of time and alerted my grandfather to what had occurred.

Only the whites held positions of influence and authority over us in our education system and in our community. Throughout my education I was taught about the accomplishments of the whites but never anything good about the Indians. These attitudes as a young girl made me feel angry and ready to strike out, but I had to remember the teachings of my grandfather.

When I was in grade eight at age fourteen my grandfather returned us back to our home in Nova Scotia. I came back stronger than when I had left. I found that although time had passed, the system still remained the same. I had to attend a junior high school outside of the community. What I was sure about was that I wasn't going to hide my Indian-ness from anyone. Apparently the school had treated the Mi'kmaq students with much disrespect and oppression and I was seen as the villain. The school board and band council met with the elders. The final decision was that we were moved into an inner-city school. This move proved to be more positive; the ideology of racism still lurked in the background but not as aggressively as in the country.

Now that I am a teacher, the rule in my class is that we must not dwell on the negative past and present experiences. Instead we should learn from the past and build on the positives that we have learned and experienced. We as teachers have to start making those cultural bridges or we'll be more distant than ever. The essence of education is based on language and traditional values.

Mi'kmaq children are socialized to act and think in certain ways at home but differently at school. These children suffer culture shock and they need to be gently instructed and guided into the mainstream of the dominant culture. The teacher must realize that we are not here to change the child into something that they are not but to build a bridge between the gaps for a better understanding of both worlds.

A person without a history is like a tree without roots. Students need to be culturally centered and empowered in their learning settings. Our culture is the extended family. One of the principle aspects of empowerment is respect, where information is presented in such a way that students can walk out of the classroom feeling their presence is valued and respected. We struggle against negative experiences of racist or discriminatory attitudes of the dominant culture. Children who are centered in their own cultural background are better students, more disciplined and have greater motivation for the task at hand. Their spirits are intact and they have self-confidence and take pride in what they do.

Through my experiences I try to pass on the positives and learn from the negative forces. I make every attempt to use the medicine wheel as a learning and teaching source. I try to make the atmosphere in my classroom as pleasant and nonthreatening as possible. A team approach is encouraged where people work effectively together to achieve a common goal based on the work decisions of all the participants involved. The purpose of the talking circle is to create a safe environment for students to share their point of view with others without being criticized or judged by others. This process helps people to gain a sense of trust for each other and a strong sense of bonding. Within the circle, sharing, respect, honor, and confidentiality are a priority.

SUSAN: SHOWING STUDENTS THEY "CAN DO IT"

My own children went to high school in the city and they often came home disappointed. I know that their projects were just as good as the other students but I knew they had to try harder to meet the white school system's standards. Most often, they would come home discouraged. I would always tell my children, "You can do it." I don't ever want a student to say, "I can't do it," because they have heard that enough. I was convinced that there was really something in that system that was not right. My children went to school here on the reserve and they struggled to get through to high school. I have three graduates from high school. I went out and got my own education, struggling for my education and beating the system. It wasn't until I went out and taught in a nonnative high school with the nonnative teachers that I realized it was the attitude of the teachers. It wasn't the curriculum. It wasn't the language barrier. It wasn't all this that I heard all of these years. And I said, "For God's sake, no wonder we have such a high percentage of high school failure!"

I think it is important to get students to understand that all First Nations people have social problems and they have to reach out and do something about it. I am there to guide them, to help them, and to believe in them. For instance, the students say they weren't taught how to write an essay in school. I tell them: "There is nobody that can tell you that you can't do it. You can do it. You are not only in charge of your own destiny, you have to follow your destiny. You don't have to accept what is thrown at you."

I praise them and I also introduce them to the use of their own language in schooling. I have noticed that the students are losing their language, but I had to go and ask my elders, "Would you help me if I brought in Mi'kmaq immersion?" I guess that is the greatest goal that I have so far. I want them to go to the elders themselves and to learn from the elders and bring it back to the classroom—speaking to them in Mi'kmaq and helping them realize that their culture is their language.

As Mi'kmaq people you always give respect to the teacher. By appearing timid, as if they do not fully understand things, our students get stepped on. When you are told that your problems are your culture and your language and it is within you, sooner or later you start believing that and you make this little shield around you. I instill in them the strong belief that they can do anything that they want to do and they can do it just like anybody else.

It's all a community thing in my classroom. We all help each other. I'm just guiding them and making them believe that they can do it. We just take it like a family. Students share their knowledge with others and it's not as if their work is private. The objective is being there and helping one another by supporting one another.

DARLENE: LIVING THE VALUES OF HER ELDERS

One of the things that my parents and grandparents stressed to me was my language. My mother always made sure that we spoke Mi'k-maq. Even though we were brought up in a white community because of my father's employment, my summers and holidays were always spent here on the reserve. I'd attend school and live with my grandmother for parts of the year. My father made sure that we knew about our history and the treaties. I guess you could say I was positively brainwashed in childhood by my father to be political, but my grandmother taught us the traditional Mi'kmaq ways. She would tell us a story. She wouldn't come out and say this had to be done, but through telling stories. She was a gentle woman and she was very Mi'kmaq. She taught us through her example that when you kill a moose, whatever is there you always share and it always comes back to you. I think that is the underlying reason why Mi'kmaq people are the way that they are. What goes around comes around. I don't know how it happens but there is always enough for everyone. That is the way my grandmother's house was.

I received a job here as a Mi'kmaq language teacher in K–6 and I had to develop the curriculum from the beginning. The students are learning to read and write in Mi'kmaq. Later, I was the first Mi'kmaq teacher to penetrate the junior high area here. I can remember when we were all called into a room by the administration and she told the teacher off. She told the trainees but she included us in it. She said the language of instruction in this school was English. We were forbidden to speak Mi'kmaq in our teaching. So I got up and I told her, "I'll be damned if I'm going to use English to teach Mi'kmaq." I told her to forget it and I walked out.

The route that I have taken to influence change has been to stand up to the authorities. The last surviving member of the late Grand Chief's immediate family passed away recently. He was a very respected elder in the community. The normal situation is that everything would shut down in the community, including the school, so that everyone could pay their last respects to this person. I went to the administration and asked if I could do this out of respect. I told her that I was in the position of Mi'kmaq language and culture teacher and I feel it is important that I am teaching the children respect in the school. I thought at the time, this would be the best way to show the kids how we should respect elders, by shutting down the school, even for half a day. The administration decided against it.

After the funeral I was asked to go to the board office. They said that I was insubordinate. I thought, "To hell with you." They wanted me to be a hypocrite and I refused. So I sat down that weekend and wrote out my resignation. When I met them I told them, "Well, I felt strongly about the decision I made, and I feel so strongly about it that here is my resignation." They sat there in shock and said, "You can't do this!" and I said, "Yes I can. Just watch me! I am fed up with having administration picking on us for petty things." I thought the worst thing that could happen was that I could be on welfare and I'll be poor. It wouldn't be the first time! People want these kinds of rules because it keeps them in power.

The elders told me that money isn't everything. But they said you have to be there for the children. If you're not there, what is going to happen to the Mi'kmaq language? So I went back with the condition that I attend every funeral and I am going to do it without pay. They told me that I didn't have to do that because the school board passed a decision that gets another person to cover for me. So that way the nonnative staff are obligated to cover for me. I won't compromise. I won't be a hypocrite and teach the importance of respecting the deceased and then not attend their funerals.

On another occasion, we had this workshop here on native spirituality and one teacher saw that the room was packed and this respected member of the Grand Council wanted to attend. This teacher blocked the door so that this Grand Council member couldn't get in the room. He was so insulted and upset. Everyone in the community was so insulted. She said it was because of fire regulations. I told her this is the Mi'kmaq way. You've been here for twenty years, you should know better. You claim to know everything about Mi'kmaq people and you do this? I don't care who you are. You never do that to a Grand Council member. You never do that to an elder. If the fire regulations are so strict, then you get up and you say to the people in the room, "One of the Grand Council members wants to attend the meeting. Would one person give them a seat?" I call it systemic racism because it has subtleties. They are real subtleties.

Although there are a number of children entering the school in kindergarten that are speaking English, their English is a first generation of non-Mi'kmaq speakers. I think the community is losing faith with the Mi'kmaq language and their culture, and the people are frustrated. They feel that, "If my child speaks English, then he will be ahead in the education system when he gets in school because when they start school they have to speak English." But today we have so many Mi'kmaq teachers we're able to have them teach in the Mi'kmaq language.

I know the children that I teach, where they come from and the homes they live in. I practically know what they're going through so I keep my expectations at the level of the kids. I know they are intelligent, but I also know that if they have a project at school that they have to bring in a box or container, that probably half the kids are not going to bring it in so I am going to prepare for that. The teachers in the classroom ask a question and the children are going to sit there and spend the time thinking about it. Basically in the Mi'kmaq culture, before you answer the question you try to think about what you are going to say before you say it. That is a cultural trait, I guess. They also had to translate the sentence in their minds and then try to answer it and they are going to hesitate because people are very shy in the Mi'kmaq culture. The nonnative teacher thinks this child is at a low level of understanding and is not intelligent. The class that is streamed at the bottom often has those kids who don't answer what the teacher wants. They are smart but because they don't understand the teacher—the English-speaking teacher—the teacher assumes that they don't know anything, but it is just that they don't know enough English to know what the teacher is talking about. Then they become a discipline problem because they don't know what the hell is going on up there. Once you put them in with a Mi'kmaq-speaking teacher and the language is Mi'kmaq, it is like a light bulb going on. That lower grade nine class, you can really do a lot with them if you're speaking Mi'kmaq. In the Mi'kmaq language course I try to compensate for what the English teacher has missed in the classroom.

Sometimes when the elders get wind of what's going on in the school, they'll come to me and they'll tell me, "This is the way it should be." I get by on being the middleman because whatever the elders represent to me, I pass on to the children. It is the whole concept that my grandmother taught me about the moose, that it is most important that it goes around. If it goes around, you can be guaranteed that it's going to come back to you.

IMPLICATIONS FOR RESEARCHING LIVES

Researching in First Nations communities has taught me about the promise of life history as both a representational tool and an active methodology. It has taught me to be respectful of its power as a tool for political transformation and the need to not privilege my knowledge and power over the participants in my inquiry work. It reveals that, as in these cases, although these women have remarkably similar educational orientations, the Mi'kmaq community as a whole is riddled with political differences that create deep controversy and paralysis. Life history work has also taught me about the importance of ongoing, trusting relationships in cross-cultural contexts. Gathering these life histories could never have happened in this context if I had not been deeply committed to supporting a broader movement toward self-determination. Life history inquiry processes have helped participants and me to discover, and more fully understand, a way of researching that is in keeping with an Aboriginal way of knowing and being.

These life histories show me—and those like me—why Aboriginal people who are located in both worlds see needs for major structural and political changes in educational institutions. As the articulation of their rich Mi'kmaq linguistic and cultural life histories helps them clarify their values and identities as teachers, they see how their Aboriginal language, values, and worldview clash with the dominant society's notions of schooling. Having their life histories heard by others strengthens their own unfolding stories, which in turn strengthens their political convictions. For instance, since these stories were completed in 1998, all three of these educators have taken further political actions in their institutions to further the causes that they clarified through this research. Darlene sought an administrative position to counter some of the worst features of colonial institution in her community and in the face of these forces, refused to back down, forcing a significant political battle in her community. Susan continues to speak out for language by pushing for further high school programming in Mi'kmaq and supporting some of her less vocal colleagues who are struggling to advocate language programming in other aspects of schooling. Glenda has taken action through the "in-servicing" of white teachers to help educate them about Aboriginal ways of knowing. These Unama'kik Mi'kmaq women represent an example of political hope, yet they continue to work amid contexts that are harsh and unforgiving.

This life history approach has provided me with a compelling entry point into a contextually complex situation, allowing me to explore the intersections and contradictions among personal, social, cultural, and political influences on Mi'kmaq educators' life world (Casey 1993; Cole and Knowles 1995). For instance:

- Darlene was influenced by her mother's and grandmother's worldviews, which she described as "very traditionally Mi'kmaq." She also had grown up largely "off reserve" so was familiar with and conversant in the white society's ways of doing things. This competing tension seemed to draw her back to elders' values, and strengthened her desire to honor their ways, amid the constricting bureaucratic rules of schooling. For many other educators with off-reserve experiences, they see assimilation and institutional ways of the dominant society in a much more positive light.
- Glenda has been strongly influenced by her grandfather's teachings, but she also attended school systems with varying degrees of oppression and assimilation. Through it all, she has maintained a sense of the importance of working to respect and educate her oppressors. She has worked to help them understand and respect Mi'kmaq ways, although her historic anger and humiliation at the hands of oppression is ever present. Many First Nations educators who have experienced similar oppressive situations remain deeply bitter toward their peoples' oppressors.
- Susan too has lived the multiple contradictions of the education system. She has seen her children struggle with the system from her position as a mother who sensed that things were wrong but could not clearly name them. Many educators with similar parenting experiences choose to conform to this white-dominated world.

What remains central for me through this is to continue to work to discern why people believe what they do, and to work toward spaces and processes that will bring these opposing voices into dialogue.

It is critical that the life history researchers cultivate and maintain ongoing, trusting relationships in cross-cultural contexts (Goodson 1992; Clandinin and Connelly 1994). The closer the relationship, the stronger the possibility of deeper insights (Watson and Watson-Franke 1985). St. Denis (1992) has shown that sincerity in Aboriginal research is demonstrated through time and effort but is primarily achieved when communities recognize that researchers' work will benefit the community. My involvement in northern Saskatchewan (Orr and Friesen 1999) and in Una-ma'kik, for example, confirms that trust by Aboriginal people is achieved through sustained work on educational projects that demonstrate support for self-determination. St. Denis, the Royal Commission on Aboriginal Peoples (1992), and Goulet and Aubichon (1997) have urged those wishing to research Aboriginal educational issues to include First Nations people in the process, particularly because of the danger of white researchers misrepresenting Aboriginal knowledge. I expect that Darlene would never have talked to me if I had not come highly recommended by her mother, who I had taught previously, and for whom I "went to the wall" for on a serious issue of conflict between her and another educator when she was virtually powerless. Susan talked to me because I had proven my commitment to her cause by ongoing work in support of Mi'kmaq language programming, and because I stood up in support of her when the principal in her first school practicum placement attempted to punish her for supposed insubordination. Through these women I met Glenda, who opened up to me because of the support I provided these women and others experiencing the clash between institutional and Mi'kmaq values. So I developed trust through advocacy and ongoing commitment to these individuals' lives.

I encourage life history researchers and their participants to play with the method in order to make it fit with ways of knowing and being that are representative of their participants' cultural backgrounds. Life history has proven to be of particular significance for this sort of research program with Aboriginal people, since it can make space for a storytelling process that is in keeping with the Aboriginal epistemology of a circular and collective construction of meaning (Peacock and Holland 1993; Hampton 1995). Grumet (1991) reminds researchers that how we hear and then return the stories told to us greatly influences how well we are able to achieve deeper insight. This narrative way of knowing has helped my research participants and me to develop a collective and collaborative focus that gives greater power and validity to their stories. It has allowed them to discuss issues that are of special importance from their particular identity locations and has enabled them to express why and what it means to be from this location in ways that are clear and believable by others (Hatch and Wiseniewski 1995a). For instance, once when I was sharing some First Nations educators' stories that were constructed using this method with other educators, one person stopped me and said, "That is my story too." This confirmed for me the power of life history to help us understand the issues of importance around us. It also reminded me of the responsibility I have as researcher to do this with care.

16

Compelled to Honor Privacy: Reflections from Researching in a Nursing Home

Elizabeth Oates Schuster

Elizabeth Oates Schuster's account focuses on the ethical principles guiding work with vulnerable populations, specifically nursing home residents. Schuster explores issues associated with the resident's rights of autonomy, privacy, and control, and argues that honoring these rights is contingent on the nature of the relationship between the researcher and the participant. As such, Schuster's account is directly linked to the discussion of guiding principles in chapter 2 and the centrality of relationship as advanced throughout the book.

One afternoon I found Lenora sitting on her bed watching "stories," television stories. As she sat there, absorbed in the daily trials and tribulations of the soap-opera characters, I was struck by the irony that it was *her* stories that I had come to hear, not those of Television City.

Lenora was a ninety-eight-year-old African American woman who began to write stories and poetry at the age of ninety. She had come to the nursing home about two years earlier. Her mind was sharp. Her voice was crisp, her speech distinct and full of nuance. I found Lenora's writing to be like her speech—rich and clear, displaying considerable skill and creativity. I wanted to find out what it was like to become a writer at the age of ninety, especially when living in a nursing home.

She invited me to sit down with her on her bed. I sat down and asked if she minded the interruption of Television City's stories. "Oh," she said, "this is much more important than any old television show. I can watch these anytime. . . . I would much rather spend this time talking with you."

The funny thing about doing research in a nursing home is the imme-diate intimacy—it comes about due to meeting with these elderly people in their rooms, their bedrooms at that. Researching in private spaces? How common is it for research conversations to be had bedside?

I started out by asking Lenora how it happened that a ninety-year-old woman had begun to write, to become a writer, while living in a nursing home. "What is the motivation for writing?" I inquired.

Lenora answered, "[At the other nursing home] the activity coordina-tor . . . always asked me to write something for the monthly paper. I was just searching for something to write. . . . That's all there was to it."

"What does your writing do for you?" I asked. "Living here in the home, is it helpful for you to write?"

Lenora thought for a moment and then replied, "Yes, it gives me some-thing to do to keep my mind off unpleasant things and I just get thinking about things to write, and forget about other things."

When I asked if her life had changed since she'd begun writing, she said, "Well, yes. It seems like something I can contribute."

We talked about the Writing Group, of which she was a member. She told of going to the group because she enjoyed "reading what the others write," adding, "and then it inspires me to go on and write some more."

Many times I'd observed Lenora as she read her work to the group and as she listened intently to her peers' responses to her work. Often, a look of pride, even joy, spread across her face as Allison, the Writing Group fa-cilitator, or one of the residents praised her work.

"Do you like to have your writing read aloud? How does it make you feel?" I asked.

"It makes me feel like I am accomplishing something in my old age," she responded. "It just makes me feel like I have something to live for; to be accepted by others, especially my children, [who] enjoy reading what I write."

I am a gerontologist. I entered the field of gerontology as a result of numerous positive experiences with older adults. These experiences, with many different people in a variety of contexts, motivated me, as an adult in the academy and in my personal life, to look for examples of alterna-tive ways of being old, frail, and dependent, ways that might provide greater opportunity for self-expression and that might enhance one's dig-nity and integrity. I value the wisdom of experience that older adults bring to a relationship. I value the years of life they have lived. I do not believe that, just because the body changes, sags, skin stretched taut yet loose, and appears old and worn, the spirit and life of the being within be-comes valueless, useless, and rejectable. I honor old age and those who live in and with it.

In a much later conversation I asked Lenora to select a few of her writings to read aloud. She included the following poem:

> Snow
> Rain and snow, rain and snow,
> Snow, snow, snow some more.
> I like the snow, I like the way
> The sunshine makes it glow.
> I like to see the sunflakes dancing to and fro.
> I like the way it makes the
> Prism in the sun rays.
> Oh, to watch it is such fun
>
> Lenora, Michigan, 1994

When a resident moves into a nursing home she struggles to maintain an identity. In the process many residents reflect on and interpret past experiences in relation to the new context (Kaufman 1986). For many, a move from one's private home to a nursing home causes an abrupt shift in identity as the individual seeks to find a way to fit into the new environment. A resident still has his or her past experiences and themes to rely on for a sense of inner continuity and with family, but the new institutionalized world, fraught with regimented routine and threat to individuation and privacy, creates discord. The result may be a sense of discontinuity. Add to this the multiple role losses that come from leaving behind life in a community, and the unwelcomed acquisition of a new role as "resident," and it is not difficult to see how one's sense of self is found floating in a nether world. Under these circumstances, any process that might enhance the ability of a resident to regain some control and reestablish identity is valuable. When the writers composed a piece, they were writing about the themes of their lives. When they read and shared their writings with one another, staff, volunteers, family, and friends, they were re-creating identity, grasping, in some cases, onto some semblance of the person they thought they were, as well as exploring the person they had become.

According to Sieber (1993), when conducting sensitive research (as in my case, with people who may not be autonomous due to various mental and physical impairments), the researcher must recognize the vulnerabilities of each person being studied and the ethical issues that might arise. "Some are vulnerable because they lack resources or autonomy (or) . . . they are in a weakened position, and perhaps in an institutional setting" (Sieber 1992, 94). Other central issues to be considered in work such as mine include privacy and respectful communication (Sieber 1993).

In everyday life, the average person gives little thought to the act of getting up, getting dressed, walking, driving, interacting with one's peers. For the resident of a nursing home it is, perhaps, another story. In my experience, if home volunteers or staff did not make the effort to go into residents' rooms and encourage them to get up, get dressed, and come to the Writing Group, for example, few would be able to attend on their own. Almost all were dependent on aides to assist in the morning's rituals—bathing, dressing, eating, or having assistance to get to the dining room. And many do these activities in great pain and discomfort. Many days, a resident simply will not make it to the Writing Group because she is not able to get the assistance she needs. The following statement by Savishinsky (1991, 224–245) reveals a great deal about control and resident autonomy and privacy:

> The degree of control that the elderly could exercise over the setting for visits depended on their power of movement and communication. Mobile residents could more easily agree or decline to go to organized events, and they could spend more time with family members and volunteers in their own rooms, a lounge, or the dining area. While none of these places guaranteed total privacy, some were more protected than others. In the case of bedridden people, as well as patients who preferred to pass the day in hallways and lounges, visitors clearly had to come to them: such residents could accept or refuse their overtures, but they could only choose [among] the people who had decided to approach them.

Gubrium is another researcher who spent a considerable amount of time in a nursing home. These are his reflections on resident privacy (1975, 33):

> Staff believes . . . that patients are less alert (than other more highly functioning adults) to the contingencies of privacy and, "after all, they don't seem to care as much about it." When asked about privacy on the floors, aides typically mention that "most of those up here don't know when they're in their rooms and when they're out of them." Patients cited by aides as not caring about privacy are commonly those whom the staff considers to be senile . . . patients who are concerned about privacy carry a view of it that differs from that of the floor staff. Privacy-oriented patients are constantly vigilant over the boundaries between public and private places.

The above quotations from Savishinsky and Gubrium refer to residents' ability to decide with whom they would like to interact and under what circumstances. These are matters related to privacy.

The ability, or lack thereof, to control one's life is crucial to understanding and developing "the researcher-researched" relationship. The diminished capacity to maintain one's autonomy must be acknowledged in every interaction between the researcher and the researched. The more dependent a person is the more important it becomes to take every step to assure his or her privacy and dignity. This is why a qualitative inquiry process, especially a life history one, is so appealing. It provides a sort of balance to the extremely suppressive context and milieu in which the study of the aged is conducted.

In my experience with the nursing homes where research is conducted, I have not found that research to be controlled by residents. (But I work in a paradigm contrary to much health-related research where researchers enter into a context, collect data, and exit quickly.) On many occasions I have tried unsuccessfully to identify times when it would be good to have conversations with a resident. For example, with a particular person, after agreeing on a time to meet, I showed up only to find her sleeping or engaged in some other private activity such as bathing, taking medication, getting undressed, or using the bathroom. I suppose you could say that in these cases the resident is still in charge of the process, yet when I walk into these situations I feel a tremendous degree of discomfort as I infringe on a private moment. But privacy has different facets, as noted by Sieber (1992, 48):

> Privacy does not simply mean being left alone. Some people have too little opportunity to share life with others, or bask in public attention. When treated respectfully, many are pleased that an investigator is interested in hearing about their personal lives.

This statement reminds me of the many times the Writing Group facilitator requested that I not use pseudonyms in my constructed narratives, as the writers wanted and needed recognition. Privacy also means respectful attention. The statement also brings back the memory of the time I requested an interview with Lenora. My interruption of her "story hour" was something she valued. To have this insight into other ways of perceiving the privacy needs of individuals, who may very well be lonely, is a helpful reminder when I ask for a few moments of their time.

In other instances, residents have been forceful in stating their desires for autonomy and privacy. For example, as I wrote (Schuster 1992, 24) about my interaction with Gwen:

> I interviewed Gwen the week before and she agreed to meet again the following week to read a few of her writings and make comments. That week I approached her after the writing group and she pushed her wheelchair right past me. I asked her if she would like to talk now and she said, "No, I am too tired and I have bowling this afternoon."

This is an example of the power that is still accessible to the resident who is mobile and not cognitively impaired. I am constantly aware of the fragility of independence experienced by nursing home residents and could not justify requesting an interview with anyone I felt would not be comfortable in declining or who would not understand the purpose of the study. These people insisted on a particular kind of privacy. In these instances, it may be likely that a resident would participate because they perceived me as an authority figure, unable to respect their privacy and not able to engage in a reciprocal process, yet holding power over them. Researching lives of nursing home residents requires the balance of a tightrope walker yet the sensitivity of a therapist. Looking into the lives of the elderly is like looking into the mirror of the future, and I know that I want always to be treated with a dignity that preserves my privacy, my identity, and my autonomy.

Nursing homes are institutions. There is no getting around that fact no matter how hard staff, families, and even residents work to emphasize the *home* quality of nursing home, they remain institutional constructs. Persons come to live in a nursing home because they have suffered losses and are not able to function independently. In a world devoid of self-determination and independence for the elderly, those fraught with physical and mental decline, what are the ethical concerns when doing research in a nursing home? I came to the conclusion that of utmost importance are the residents' rights around the issues of autonomy, privacy, and control. The nature of the relationship between the researcher and the participant, then, is key. Of particular importance is how the researcher perceives herself and how she is perceived. These perceptions and beliefs will greatly affect the quality of the interactions and, in turn, the ethical integrity of the work.

Lenora, Gwen, and others taught me some lessons that may help in my professional work and private life. In the case of my research on the Writing Group and its members, the process was truly reciprocal and somewhat weighted in my favor. I received way more than they did, simply by having the opportunity to be in conversation with them and to hear their stories. It is an honor that I cherish.

17

Insights and Inspiration from an Artist's Work, Envisioning and Portraying Lives in Context

J. Gary Knowles and Suzanne Thomas

The account written by Gary Knowles and Suzanne Thomas explicitly connects with chapters 3 and 5. In it they provide an example of how their life history exploration with high school students and their "sense of place" in schools is influenced by the artistic process and representational form of a renowned photographer/artist. They also explain their intention to reach audiences outside of conventional academic venues and how that goal translated into the arts-informed representation of students' experiences.

Having gained inspiration from the artistic enterprise of Marlene Creates (see chapter 3 for an account of Gary's first impressions of her work, its substance, and the place he envisioned for it in scholarship), we began to integrate her artistic processes and forms into our research endeavors. Creates's photography and arrangement of images and artifacts is highly evocative—it is charged with meanings associated with humans in context, of people located in place. It depicts lives in context and provides an artistically creative visual and textual representation analogous to life history research. Creates's model of inquiry consists of assemblages that explore the relationship between human experience and landscape, nature and culture, and sense of place. As she articulates in her artist statement (Creates 1990, 20–21):

> I have been working on the relationship between human experience and the landscape. . . . For the past [ten] years I have worked in remote areas where most of my projects and landworks were related to the "natural" aspects of

sites. Then I became interested in what I would call the "cultural": the people who have lived closest to these places. I began to understand that there
are certain things about their lives that are being left behind—certain things
that matter to them, their experiences of the world that are so different to
mine. From these encounters with elderly country people I developed the
works that are titled: *The Distance between Two Points Is Measured in Memories.*

We began to meld and fuse the artistic processes and perspectives of
Creates's work into our various, separate and collective, life history interests and research projects. Our intention is not to infringe on the creativity and uniqueness of the artist, or appropriate her processes and work,
but, rather, to learn from and be responsive to the discipline of visual art
as a way of informing alternative representational modes of inquiry.
Our venture into more diverse, arts-informed life history information-
gathering processes and representational forms (from our more conventional modes of inquiry) commenced with a single project and has since
expanded into other work.

We see the potential for artists' inquiry processes to greatly enliven and
inform scholarly work by enhancing researchers' conceptualizations of information gathering and the transformation of data and/or artifacts into
representational forms. We envision that arts-informed perspectives,
gleaned and imagined through the perceptive lens of visual artists, may
enrich the complex rendering of personal stories and life histories in ways
that are multitextured, multilayered, and multidimensional. For the moment we outline and provide details of how Creates's work has procedu-
rally or methodologically informed our authentic and innovative engagement in life history explorations. (There are other artists whose inquiry
processes offer much to life history researchers and, in time, we will explore their potential contributions to our more formal yet artful inquiries.)
We are sparked and creatively inspired by the fusion of the artistic into
scholarship; we are enticed by the power of visual art processes and forms
to inform scholarship and know that they, as well as other art forms, can
enrich scholarship within the social sciences more broadly.

In this account we discuss elements of our initial project inspired by
Creates's work and render directions for future explorations. Our inquiry
projects generally are located within the emerging genre of educational
research referred to as arts-informed or arts-based inquiry (for example,
Barone and Eisner 1997; Finley and Knowles 1995). Central to our conception of arts-informed inquiry is the use of an artist's research method
that provides a multidimensional framework for the generation of, at
once, "data" and artifact collection and, in turn, representational forms.
(Other arts-based educational researchers, such as, Barone and Eisner
[1987] and Diamond and Mullen [1999], speak with more emphasis on the

form and quality of the work rather than on processes.) This is a central motivating element for us to push the boundaries of what it means to conduct social science research and to engage in scholarly production. Our goal was to interweave these new insights into our scholarship along with the principles of responsive life history research.

The purpose of our first project was to examine secondary school art students' experiences of "place" in schools (Knowles and Thomas 2000a, 2000b). Our aim was to gain a sense of their contemporary lived experiences of schools as well as those acquired over a lifetime, and to apply our understandings of Creates's artistic processes in our methodological approach.

We define place as an individual and socially constructed reality (Hutchison 1999; Relph 1976)—a notion that interweaves the elements of geographical location, social consciousness, and the meanings derived from experience-in-place. Within the context of this inquiry, we conceived place broadly as a physical location within school (or school property) that, for an individual student, epitomized or characterized specific emotional experiences associated with being a student in school at this point in time. It is a place that represents, in literal or metaphorical terms, a focusing of a student's emotive response to the "sociophysical" context of school (Berleant 1997), working with teachers and interacting and learning with peers. This notion of place was a vague and difficult concept to articulate to students; yet we sense that, from their eventual artistic work and their subsequent conversations with us, they understood the essence of its meaning.

Our intention was to gain insights into students' experiences of school from their vantage perspectives. Students became the prime collectors of research information. They were at once information gatherers, portraiture artists, and interpreters of experience, and assumed full control over their individual inquiry processes. This was important to the project given that little educational research actually engages students in the gathering, arranging, and representing of information gathered about *their* place experiences of school, or any other element of their school experiences related to curriculum or pedagogy, for that matter (Erickson and Schultz 1992).

Our first requests of students were:

- Tell us about your experiences of school (now, and over time).
- Tell us about your place in this school.
- Tell us about a significant or meaningful "place," perhaps within, or immediately outside the school building.
- Convey to us how you see yourself in this place.
- Tell us what you think about school as a place to be.

Above all, we asked the students to create an "authentic portrayal" of their special or significant place within school.

Our second request of students was for them to apply, in their visual and narrative telling of and about "place" in school, a "model" or structure to their inquiry and artistry based on Creates's photographic, life history investigations. We took Creates's work—its "structure" and transparent processes—and reinterpreted and modified it for use in student inquiries. It was intended as a guide, a frame, although the device we created only partially resembles Creates's individual sets of work as installed in art gallery exhibits (see Creates 1990, 1991, 1992). This new, inquiry model framework includes seven linked elements that provided a multi-dimensional representation and format from which the student artists worked. Each of the frames (numbered from left to right in Figure 1), imply a different image: several photographs, a narrative, a sketch, a two- or three-dimensional representation, and found objects.

• The first frame contains a photograph of the student in the foreground—either a self-portrait or a portrait taken by a peer—which identifies the artist/narrator of the "text."

• The second frame is a cognitive "memory map," a line drawing or depiction of the student's emphasized "place" within the school property; it "traces" the lines of the story. We encouraged the students to think of this map as a drawing that would help a newcomer to the school or a friend locate the identified place of significance of the student-artist.

• "Place" as visualized in the memory map/sketch/drawing is photographically represented in the third frame. Here, the visual image shows the student in the "context of place."

• The narrative in the fourth frame represents the student's articulation of experiences of and in "place," and is elicited from the responses to the memory map drawings.

• The fifth frame presents a photograph that depicts a conceptualization of "sense-of-place" that is distinctive to the individual student because it holds personal meaning and significance.

• Through artistic representation, in either a two- or three-dimensional artwork, students render their synthesis of "place explorations," the intention being to authentically represent their lived experience in the context of "place" within school.

• The seventh frame includes artifacts selected by the student as "found objects" that provide a link to the "place."

As mentioned earlier, the students' creations became at once "data" and representations indicative of the inquiry focus. The artworks generated by the students (including associated "artist's statements"), in addition to

Figure 1: Modes of art-making using Marlene Creates's work as inspiration

Photo of Student	Cognitive Memory Map	Photo of Student in "Place"	Narrative	Photo of Context	Artistic Representation	Artifact
student in foreground	pencil sketch of location of "place" in school	student in middle background	statement about experience of "place"	"place" is in foreground	two-/three-dimensional rendering of experience of "place"	"found object" with particular "place" meaning
1	2	3	4	5	6	7

conversations with the students and their teachers, provided a comprehensive synthesis of their "data"/artifact gathering and analyses.

On completion of the students' depictions of experience-in-place, we assumed the task of attempting to uncover the meanings inherent in their work. Conscious of our researcher roles, we viewed the artwork as individuals familiar with schools while, at the same time, as art appreciators who engaged in visual and contextual interpretations of the photographic images and narrative writing (Becker 1998; Harper 1994; Mitchell and Weber 1998). We "interrogated" the works for understandings of the students' individual and collective life history experiences of school. We "asked questions" of the representations themselves, attempting to explore the meanings of the works, much as art viewers may do of a professional artist's exhibition—an example of lives intersecting for mutual meaning-making (Denzin 1994). With sensitivity, rather than a spirit of artistic connoisseurship, we wanted to bring to bear on these student images the full range of our own experiences with art and artifacts of social and cultural communities.

Through conversations students revealed an awareness of the connection between interior and exterior landscapes, self and place. The assemblages of artwork rendered student understandings of the interconnections between people and place, and their developing insights into the links between sense-of-belonging and finding a "sense of community." Students expressed a commonality of emotions that encompass "feelings of isolation," a "sense of vulnerability," and a need for a "sense of belonging" at school, and conveyed that they view schools as large monolithic structures that constrain freedom—impersonal institutions that no longer promote "community spirit" or provide them with a "sense of community." These were also themes recognized by viewers of the students' artwork as it was exhibited at a contemporary art gallery in Toronto.

The exhibit provides a forum for communication, as the multiple representations become a complex language and visual dialogue that empowers students by giving voice to their experience. We reached beyond the academic, institutional setting to inform the community at large of the social conditions of schools, and of students' experiences within institutional, educative contexts. It is our intent that this work will inform conventional knowledge about students' experiences of school, will challenge assumptions about sense of place and/or placelessness, and will pose insightful questions about schools as primary sites of adolescents' educational learning.

We envision that life history perspectives seen through the lens of visual artists may enrich the complex rendering of stories and personal life histories in ways that are multitextural, multilayered, and multidimensional. We apply the constructs derived from Creates's work with the intent to infuse more organic processes into our research endeavors, to embed our work in processes that honor our own unique perspectives of the world, and to extend the potential for scholarship to communicate with community beyond the academy.

We have invited, and some students have agreed, to participate in this exploratory life history research project in subsequent years in order to represent a continuum of a life lived at school and in institutions of learning. We also envision future expansion of this inquiry by engaging within educational communities, including preservice, beginning, and experienced teachers, in a similar exploration of "sense of place" within their professional and educational contexts. We also see the value of extending this approach or some form of it into the work that Gary (with Ardra Cole) has done with teacher education professors within universities (see Cole, Elijah, and Knowles 1998; Knowles, Cole, and Sumsion 2000). Contributions of the arts to processes and forms of representing seem particularly promising for sifting out understandings of the complex interaction between individual lives lived within organizational and institutional contexts. We see this, especially, as useful for socialization studies where life histories are central.

The potential for visual documentations of lives and contexts that Harper (1994), Becker (1998) and others advocate for researching sociological constructs is appealing but limited by its historical and intellectual heritage. Our intention is to infuse more organic processes into our research endeavors. And, while the structure of the seven-element frame may at first seem limiting, it enables a multidimensional window into lives and contexts not possible with more constrained approaches. Our intention in using constructs derived from Creates's work is to extend the potential for scholarship to communicate with community beyond the academy and to embed our work in processes that honor our own unique perspectives on the world. As "researcher-artists" we need to establish relationships and work with people in the organic ways that reflect who we are as researchers and people. We must forge the heart of our work ourselves. We invite researchers to enter into this or a similar artistically inspired process of life history research so as to explore many other elements of lived experience in a diversity of contexts.

18

Rereading "Anne": Using Images in an Artful Inquiry

Maura McIntyre

Maura McIntyre draws on her arts-informed life history inquiry into horticultural therapy practices to invite readers to engage in an experiential investigation of researcher subjectivity. McIntyre's focus on the role of interpretation throughout the research process links her account to chapters 5 and 6. She explores the role of imagination and emotion in research interpretation and the intersections of researcher, participant, and audience in the intersubjective interpretation of another's experience.

In the study *Garden as Phenomenon, Method, and Metaphor: An Arts-informed Life History View* (2000), I explored the practical knowledge of two counseling practitioners (one being myself), who developed the new practice of horticultural therapy while working in an agency or hospital setting. Using life history methodology and arts-informed processes of researching and representation, I investigated how innovative practice is influenced by and develops out of the personal and professional history of each individual practitioner. In my focus on the practitioner over time I considered the new practice in the context of personal and professional development. Implications in the area of practitioner health and renewal are explored. By situating each professional in context, the process through which the new therapeutic practice developed into programming in the agency or hospital setting is also examined.

In this account I invite you to engage in an experiential investigation of researcher subjectivity in this artful life history inquiry. Using my clinical skills as a therapist in working with countertransference, I operationalize a mental image that I formed during an interview with a research participant. You are invited to participate in the image in order to explore how nonverbal subtexts can be used artfully as "data." In the discussion, I explore and explain how the countertransference process works for me in therapy and in research in order to foreground issues of "researcher neutrality" and "research objectivity." I encourage other life history researchers to postpone transcribing field impressions and interview tapes into words. Suggestions are made about how to utilize silence and nondiscursive expressive modalities as sense making tools in research relationships.

> She reminds me so much of Anne.
>
> Once the image has formed itself (in my mind, with my senses, in my body) the sense of Anne in the room is so full and immediate, it is so, so complete, her spirit is so powerful, that I almost laugh out loud in recognition.
>
> Anne.
>
> And when I tell you this—that the room is filled with my sense of Anne—what are you imaging? What images are coming forward?
>
> (Pause)
>
> Are you able to get past me—past my face, my body, my voice, to conjure up Anne?
>
> (Pause)
>
> Do you have an Anne that you are thinking of? Your mother, your sister, your teacher, your girlfriend from high school? Is your name Anne?
>
> (Pause)
>
> But maybe you don't know an Anne. Maybe you grew up in a place, in a language without Anne.
>
> What if I tell you about the Anne I'm imagining? If I tell you about her then you will know more about me. If you recognize her I will know more about you. We can compare notes about Anne and use your/my image of her as a starting place in talking about my research.

"A child of about eleven, garbed in a very short, very tight, very ugly dress of yellowish gray wincey. She wore a faded brown sailor hat and beneath the hat, extending down her back, were braids of very thick, decidedly red hair. Her face was small, white and thin, also much freckled; her mouth was large and so were her eyes, that looked green in some lights and moods and gray in others."

But I still won't know if you would have imagined Anne when I did. Would you have said: "AHA! Anne?"

(Pause)

"So far the ordinary observer; the extraordinary observer might have seen that the chin was very pointed and pronounced; that the big eyes were full of spirit and vivacity; that the mouth was sweet lipped and expressive; that the forehead was broad and full; in short our discerning extraordinary observer might have concluded that no common place soul inhabited the body of this stray woman-child. . . ."

My image is of an Anne who has an incredible intellect and an imagination to match.

Who has a big heart.

Who challenges authority.

Who makes mistakes and has a temper.

My image of Anne is distinctly Canadian.

(Pause)

She is not a singer.

She is a fictional character.

She "should" have been a boy.

My image is of an Anne who definitely (defiantly) spells her name with an "e."

My image is of Lucy Maude Montgomery's "Anne," specifically from her first book, *Anne of Green Gables* (1908), which I read at age nine from a paperback volume given to me and inscribed in the front cover by my grandfather. The image of Anne that I formed then was later fleshed out by reading other books in the series and by rereading the original as I grew older. Then when I was in my twenties I saw the movie and another image of Anne was cast in my mind's eye.

But when I finally meet Anne, when I feel her presence in the room so palpably I almost laugh out loud in recognition, I am a researcher engaged in an in-depth life history interview. In connecting my image of Anne to the context in which it has formed (with my research participant in a long-term geriatric care facility), I begin to tease out what the image of Anne has to do with me, with my research participant, and with the inquiry as a whole.

Reflecting on my action, first, I understand more fully what has occurred to me previously only as irony and coincidence. This is the facility where my grandfather died twenty-five years ago. It is the facility where I now bring my mother to see the physician who is treating her for Alzheimer's disease. It is where my dear friend Ruth works, whom I call when I need help figuring out the next steps in caring for my mother. It is "The Institution"; the end point of my capacity to creatively give care, where my mother's name sits on the waiting list. It is through my image of Anne that I can begin to understand this interconnectedness, that is, how my inquiry (which, originally, had specifically not targeted individuals working in geriatric chronic care facilities), into the life and work of therapists developing innovative practice (specifically horticultural therapy) has landed me right here right now. So far (and I know there is more to come!), the image of Anne has served as a powerful elicitor device that has caused me to reconsider what to bring to the foreground in the self-study section of my inquiry.

When I shift my attention back to my research participant I consider the same image and why it is so illuminated in her presence. In working with my image of Anne, by following the associations it evokes and allowing it to take shape, I not only acknowledge my place as coresearcher, I use my subjective responses in the research relationship as an ally to generate understanding of the research phenomenon. In psychotherapy, this practice is called countertransference. Broadly defined, countertransference refers to the "feelings and thoughts that are stirred up in the psychotherapist by the patient's verbal and nonverbal communications" (Richards 1990, 234). Originally, countertransference was conceptualized by Freud as a hindrance and an "obstacle to the psychoanalytic work" to be overcome because it muddies the waters of the psychotherapist's neutrality (Richards).

Countertransference reframed can be used as a valuable tool in psychotherapy. Underpinning a postmodern understanding of countertransference is the assumption that my responses to the client may be used as a valid tool in the intersubjective sense-making process in which we are engaged. As Bollas suggests (1987, 209), "By cultivating a freely roused emotional sensibility, the analyst welcomes news from within himself [sic] that is reported through his own intuitions, feelings, passing images, fantasies, and imagined interpretive interventions." Even if I don't grasp what my responses mean, I "have a sense of a meaning that is present and which requires support in order to find its way toward articulation" (Bollas, 209).

In a countertransference reaction, I may be responding to aspects of the client that are nonverbal or preverbal, to parts of himself or herself that were previously lost, but that may need to be externalized, shared, and legitimized, and possibly integrated into the client's current state of being (Bollas 1987). The therapist who works with countertransference believes in a nonessentialized self; that is, she does not regard herself or her client as possessing a formed and fixed identity. The fluidity of both the client's and therapist's subjectivity is precisely what can give rise to insight and positive change in each individual.

When I pay attention to my countertransference I acknowledge my subjective responses; when I operationalize these responses I find a way to make them available, and potentially useful, to both myself and to the client (Bollas 1987). In sharing my countertransference, I must be "judicious and clinically responsible," that is, I must be clear that what I am bringing forward is in the service of the client (Bollas, 210). Further, in order to remain faithful to the emergent nature of my own intuitions, feelings, and images, I need to remain creative. As a result, I might not express my countertransference verbally to the client; instead I might sketch out an image, rearrange figurines in the sandbox, or play a fragment of music on the tape deck. Together with the client I can then test the usefulness of my responses: as "subjective objects" they can be brought forward and put on the coffee table between us as "interpretations . . . meant to be played with—kicked around, mulled over, torn to pieces—rather than regarded as the official version of the truth" (Bollas, 206).

In my role as researcher, I believe that I am equally prone to subjective responses. When I employ my clinical skills in working with countertransference as a therapist to better fulfill my research agenda, I adhere to similar processes, while keeping in mind the different purpose of my work. As Kvale is careful to point out in his comparison between the therapeutic and research interview, "in therapy the main goal is the change of the patient, in research it is the obtaining of knowledge" (1999, 105). When I open myself and embrace my varied responses to my research participant as a source of potentially useful material, I am engaging with the complexity of a full range of knowledge-producing processes. I allow the image of Anne to materialize.

To facilitate this process, I resist the temptation to translate my research participants' experience into words. In order to move our research projects along, we often transcribe interviews and record field impressions as near to the interview or observation situation as possible. In our rush to capture these experiences in words, motivated in part by the high currency of written text in academe, I believe we often prematurely transform data and compromise our capacity to explore nondiscursive modalities in interpreting and representing research material. That is not to say that alternative forms of text-based representation that use interview transcripts and field notes as a starting point lack creativity; to the contrary, the work of Glesne (1997), Lawrence-Lightfoot (1994), and Richardson (1992), to name just a few, is evidence of the outstanding work that can be done within text-based structures.

As Kvale suggests, however, "current interview research is often subject to the tyranny of verbatim transcripts and formalized methods of analysis" (1999, 105). In the therapeutic interview, on the other hand, "body language," facial expressions and other nonverbal indicators are expected to be considered in interpretive process. To highlight the lessons that current social science researchers might learn from the therapeutic interview, Kvale speculates:

> That if the tape recorders had been available in Vienna at Freud's time, there might not have existed any powerful psychoanalytic theory or practice today; a small sect of psychoanalytic researchers might still be reading and categorizing their transcripts, and discussing their reliability rather than emphatically listening to the many layers of meaning revealed in the embodied therapeutic interrelations.

As Poland and Pederson suggest, "what transcription and qualitative research based on transcripts cannot adequately capture are a broad range of methods of expression that are primarily nonverbal or that do not rely on written text (academic or popular prose or poetry)" (1998, 7). If we are to explore the multifaceted value of our research images, I believe that we need to do more with our images *before* we put them into words. When we regard "texts generated through the transcription of interview recordings, even so-called verbatim transcripts [as] only partial accounts of the original interactions, then our job as researchers includes attending to the imagistic subtext" (Poland and Pederson 1998, 6).

I am conscious of what I see as my obligation *not* to fill in the blanks with words from the beginning stages of the research process. In my horticultural therapy project, this resistance began in the very first in-depth interview, where I allowed and even encouraged silence. In keeping with the spirit of the work of Poland and Pederson (1998), I believe that to access new ontological and epistemological frontiers in research, we need to reconceptualize our relationship to silence. In looking for meaning in silence, in allowing ourselves to conjure up images in periods of silence rather than filling them with words, we regard silence as a friend rather than an enemy in research. Once the relational field of the research relationship has been broadened to include nuanced silence as a significant "data" collection site, I need to actively listen to the silence and my own feelings during these moments, as potential data about the phenomenon under investigation. If I see my subjectivity as a "doing rather than a being," then what might initially appear to be a passive state of contemplation, is in fact a very active process of internal "production and transformation" (Robinson 1991, quoted in Bloom 1996, 2). In viewing my subjectivity as "nonunitary," I have the freedom not only to respond, but also to be transformed by my clients and research participants alike (Bloom).

After leaving the interview situation, metaphorically, I attempt to maintain the silence. Carefully tucking my interview tapes away, I do not rush to transcribe them. Instead of transcribing and recording my field impressions in words, I try to alternatively represent my impressions. In my experience the words will not go away (after all, they are on tape!); precisely for that reason the images become my priority to work with immediately. I look to a variety of media and materials to draw out my images and capture my associations, including color, fabric and clothing, landscape, fiction, and poetry. In keeping with the work of Poland and Pederson, I believe that "self expression through nondiscursive modalities, such as music, dance, photography, and visual art . . . require different approaches to capturing meaning and communication that, although often silent in a verbal sense, are nonetheless pregnant with meaning" (1998, 7).

Once the images are formed, I may or may not share them with the research participant. The image, or images that emerge, are not "The Truth" about the research participant any more than they are "The Truth" about me; instead they can be used as a touchstone in the ongoing meaning-making process. Paralleling the process of sharing a countertransference response with a client, when negotiating the meaning of such images with a research participant, I am clear that the images are mine, as are the feelings and associations that triggered them.

I "feed back" my images to the research participant in a variety of indirect or direct ways. I might position a copy of *Anne of Green Gables* (Montgomery 1908) on top of my pile of papers at our next interview, and then wait to see if it is noticed. Or I might tell my participant directly how much I admire Anne, and how much she reminds me of her and why. The research participant may or may not resonate with the image or how I have associated it with her. She may or may not have an "Aha, Anne!" reaction. That is, Anne may or may not serve us as a point of connection. Either way, however, our mutual understanding will be increased through sharing the image. When an "interview is literally an *inter-view*, an interchange of views between two persons conversing about a theme of mutual interest," then I have the freedom to share my image while not becoming overly invested in a particular interpretation (Kvale 1999, 101). When knowledge is "interrelational and structural," how the image "makes sense" in the relationship is its potential in the production of knowledge (Kvale, 105). My image of Anne gives me new clues about the focus of the inquiry. In exploring these clues alone (What does the image of Anne mean to me?), and with my research participant (Does she resonate with the image of Anne?), I have found a new point of entry into the inquiry.

I have invited you to engage with my image of Anne in an attempt to lend an experiential quality to the way in which we form images in research relationships. While you are imagining me imagining Anne imagining my research context, we are exploring a variety of activities not usually associated with more conventional life history research. We are acknowledging the role of emotion and imagination in research. We are acknowledging that communication occurs in silence and in images, that in these wordless spaces I have responses to you and you have responses to me. We might even have shared a laugh or a tear (which I hope you will tell me about sometime). When these nuanced activities are made explicit and are incorporated into research as legitimate processes, when we choose to work together to find ways to operationalize silence and integrate our image repertoires into our work, then we are making our inquiry artful. In approaching life history research as artful inquiry we need to reconsider both our research processes and products. As new representational forms in research gain epistemological value, so too must alternative research processes. As researchers we need to make ourselves available to these new possibilities. We need to be willing to work with Anne.

19

Moments in Time

Ilze Arielle Matiss

Ilze Matiss explicitly addresses the notion, set out in chapter 5, that any interpretation of human experience is, by its very nature, partial and limited by the inadequacy of all descriptive systems. She explores the transient nature of lives lived and the importance of research texts reflecting this quality. Her research is about the lives of Latvian-Canadian women as lived in the dramatically changing context of a newly independent "home" country.

Moments in time allow ideas to unfold,
to be noticed, explored, understood.
Something is noticed and sparkles,
it is its "moment in time."
I have feelings, experiences, challenges . . .
that demand my attention at this moment in time.
Yesterday's ideas change in meaning when viewed
in today's moment in time.
And tomorrow—another moment, another time—
will again bring new meanings,
reinterpretations of moments in time.

In my experience, life history research (Plummer 1983) allows the researcher to honor "moments in time." Research and, indeed, life itself is comprised of layer upon layer of interconnected moments in time. In this account I explore two examples of my relationship with moments in time in my life history study titled *Lives in Changing Contexts: A Life History*

Analysis of Latvian-Canadian Women's Stories about Being Latvian (1998). I explore moments in time in terms of its relationship to emerging research questions and their importance in contextualizing meaning, as well as its relationship to the notion of "voice" in the research process itself.

I begin this account with a moment in time in 1992 that was pivotal to the beginning of my research journey that unfolded into the life history study of which I speak. It reflects a moment in time in the unfolding of my research question. It represents the moment in time when my research process really began, since this was the first entry of my own life history journal. It, in this moment in time, gives an insight into the writer of this account, me, and transforms itself into your introduction to me and my work.

BEGINNING THE JOURNEY

1992 Winter Olympics

I watched the Olympic opening ceremonies on Saturday morning. This was the first Olympics since World War II that the Baltic states of Estonia, Latvia, and Lithuania had been able to compete as independent countries under their own flags. This was going to be an exciting and meaningful moment; I knew that before hand. As I watched the first athletes march into the stadium—carrying their flags, representing their countries—for a moment, I felt only the excitement of what we, usually, all feel at the beginning of these games. This is an important worldwide event. Part of me also realized, oh yeah, Estonia, Latvia, and Lithuania (really *Igaunija, Latvija,* and *Lietuva*) should also be coming on soon!

The burst of emotion, my eyes swelling and gushing with tears of both joy and pain, as the Estonian Olympic team was seen coming into the stadium, took me by surprise. This was an incredible moment. I have a hard time pulling together everything that it represented for me. The joy, of course, was that they were all there. That they were able to be there.

The pain was larger—I'm not sure if it was larger than the joy or what I expected. I think, no, I feel that the pain was larger than I had expected. Thoughts intruded. First, the hardship that these countries were now enduring. Wow, it probably took a lot for them to get their uniforms together. My own experiences, observations, and images of Latvia came to mind. I wondered about the quality of their nutrition during this winter. The Soviet regime valued their athletes and artists. I wondered how much the current governments could now support and help them. In the pain is also the anger of what the Soviet regime has done to our fatherlands.

For me the experience had a number of, no many, contexts. It grabbed feelings and thoughts from many inner and outer levels and layers. There is this incredible pride I feel. This country that once most, then many, and now few people had never heard of was now once again holding its rightful place in the Olympics, in the world. I think that last sentence already refers to my feelings about Latvia more than Estonia. It's close to the heart. At some level I felt a real connection, a sense of belonging. At another level I felt a disconnection, and a powerful, desperate sense of being different. Hmm, part of the pain! I also felt sorry for the athletes, but really for the people they represent. Why? Because of the hardship I project onto them. Then I think that they would be appalled at my thoughts and feelings. They must feel incredible pride and sense of accomplishment. What a feat. As I wrote this, I was mostly thinking about Latvia.

Guilt—my life and theirs—I'm not sure.

I dried my eyes, blew my nose, and regained my composure. We had already flipped between the French and English CBC stations to by-pass the commercials. I was watching the opening ceremonies again when on to the screen came our little Latvia (*musu maza Latvija*). Well here we go again, closer to home now. I felt all of the above. But now I think I really feel this pride. I think that at some level this is still all so unbelievable. Germany is reunited and competing together. These fragments still continue to burst within me unpredictably.

In contrast, it almost feels like the announcers have numbed out. They don't grasp this. They say it, but it doesn't sound like they feel it. It doesn't resonate for them in the same way. My tears pouring again, I choke them back with a laugh. Loosen the tension. Breathe. Sigh. I exchange some thoughts about this with my husband. The opening ceremonies continue. I think to myself—Geez, here I go again, getting overemotional again!

The historical events, which began with Gorbachev's policy of glasnost and perestroika and that led up to Latvia's declaration of in-dependence in August 1991 and the disintegration of the Soviet Union, are raising questions about the meaning of the community in exile and, ultimately, where we belong. Many thoughts, feelings, and fragments still need weaving, connecting, and understanding. "That's my job" are the words that came to mind as I wrote that. I think about my [research work]. I suspect I'm not the only one. That's why I need to explore, elicit, and pull together—to find a part of this collective, yet individual experience of lives in a changing context. To realign that with our changing world. . . .

This was how my research journey began. Did I engage you in my narrative? This begins to pull together in a raw form the complexity of the underlying issues, emotions, questions, ideas, conflicts, and challenges that I was drawn to explore eventually through the stories of six second-generation Latvian-Canadian women.

Did you guess that I am a second-generation Latvian-Canadian woman? I was born in Canada in 1964 and raised in a thriving, Latvian-Canadian community-in-exile in Toronto, Ontario.

The writing of my own life story was inspired by the power of narrative as a means of expressing stories about living in two cultures, experiences of exile, and feelings of marginalization in literary works. My exposure to these ideas and works allowed me to honor my experience, and summoned up the courage to write about it so that my voice would begin to be heard. My introduction to narrative research further validated for me the gathering of stories of Latvian-Canadian young people who had just moved or were about to move to Latvia in the late 1980s and early 1990s, as the republic was testing the possibilities for independence from the Soviet Union. This became the pilot work for my research, which in a later moment in time led to the life history study of six Latvian-Canadian women's stories about being Latvian and their lives in changing contexts. This brings me back to the first notion of moments in time in life history research that I mentioned at the beginning of this chapter—emerging research questions and the importance of contextualizing meaning.

Some time ago I wrote:

> There is a story here that needed to be told. This story was waiting to be written long before the method appeared. I collected stories. The collection of stories felt meaningful yet elusive, but the life history method gave it power and voice and allowed the focus to emerge. I am a second-generation Latvian-Canadian woman. The research journey that I embarked on with my coparticipants allowed our voices to be heard regarding our experiences of growing up in an exile community in Canada, our gifts and struggles with growing up in more than one culture and language, and how our lives have changed over moments in time, particularly in relation to Latvia's regained independence and the end of the exile period in the West.

This paragraph begins to illustrate this first idea about moments in time, that the context is crucial to making meaning of people's stories and understanding their experiences. The life history approach explores interesting stories in a social, political, cultural, historical, and psychological context. In the case of my study, layers of contextual information emerged throughout the work, and a representation of the context preceded the participants' stories to assist the reader in understanding the stories.

This exploration of Latvian-Canadian women's lives in changing contexts occurred at a unique moment in time, just as Latvia was regaining its independence after fifty years of Soviet occupation, and young Latvian-Canadians born-in-exile in Canada and other Western countries were considering moving to Latvia. The context-sensitive nature of life history work honored the very essence of what felt important to explore in this research, that is, what impact this changing context has on people. What did it mean to grow up in-exile? What does it mean that Latvia is independent? What does no-longer-in-exile mean? What impact has this had on the lives of individual Latvian-Canadian women? What are their experiences? What are their dilemmas? Where is home? Where do we/they belong? These were among the questions that emerged in the stories and in their contextual analysis.

The second idea in this account is about "voice" and moments in time in the research process. Life history work allows the researcher to honor stories, the gathering of stories, the voices of the storytellers, the collaboration between researcher and participants (in my case coparticipants, since mine was one of the six stories being told), and allows the researcher and participants to acknowledge and capture the ever-changing, ever-unfolding moments, the emerging nature of life, of their lives, of their stories.

The ever-changing moments in time seemed especially relevant in this study because it felt like everything was changing so rapidly from one moment to the next, both in Latvia and in the exile communities. Changes occurred in all spheres imaginable—political, social, financial, cultural, psychological, interpersonal, intergenerational, East versus West. Thoughts, interpretations, feelings, relationships appeared to be understood at one moment, only to take on a new meaning in another.

Our stories are ever changing and evolving, a flow of moments in time. Life history work allows for this, acknowledges this. Questions are continually generated and explored; the spirit of life history embraces growth and change and craves to explore, question, and understand new ideas and viewpoints. I found that underlying beliefs were extremely important in my study. I interviewed participants over such a flow of moments in time. In "real time" the interviewing spanned over several years, but in moments in time it felt much more dramatic in terms of changes in Latvia, political, economic, interpersonal, and personal challenges, changes in our diminishing, yet still surviving, community-in-exile, and ever-changing issues and challenges in East-West relations. In view of all of this, the notion of voice emerged and blossomed in importance.

As a collaborative process, the research became a collective process of telling and retelling the stories of our lives, the stories of our communities. In telling stories, we thought out loud. Sometimes when we read

those words in transcripts at a later time, they did not sound right anymore. In respecting "voice" in the flow of our stories, there was always
the opportunity to change, elaborate, and correct what we had said. There
were also times when what we had to say did not seem to fit in a new
moment in time, and so the process also captured changing voices.

When I began the study, my intention was to explore the renegotiation
of ethnic identification that I, based on my own experiences and observations, guessed was occurring at both individual and community levels as
a result of Latvia's independence and the end of the community-in-exile
era in the West. During the course of the study, however, I became aware
that renegotiation of identity emerged as one of my personal issues. In the
process of telling our stories over time, we each explored the meaning and
direction of our lives beyond the ethnic experiences. The reevaluation of
our lives in changing contexts was colored not only by the exhilaration of
regaining our dream of independent Latvia, but also the pain of disillu-
sionment in discovering the difference between the idealized and the real
Latvia after fifty years of separation. At this same moment in time we are
also facing the imminent loss of our community-in-exile due to assimilation and attrition.

Looking back on this work, I see from another moment in time that
large pieces of the stories focus on the losses, margins, challenges, conflicts, displacements, dislocations, and disappointments. This reflects a
part of the collective story at that moment in time. If I were to rewrite my
story, or indeed any part of the study anew, many things would be different, because this is a different moment in time and I find myself in a different place in relation to some of the experiences that I wrote about.
Today I might wonder more about other layers of those stories and what
they say about us, our parents, our grandparents: about our grandparents' courage to start over; about our parents becoming part of the educated mainstream while also being actively involved in the "margins" of
Canadian society in the 1950s, '60s, '70s, and beyond; about how our differences allowed us to excel and to fit in, not only to our Canadian society, but also to our Latvian communities. How can we, in all the various
combinations imaginable, collaborate in spite of our differences? What
would bringing East and West closer together look like? What will future
moments in time bring?

Transparency in life history research allows the possibility for these
changing views and voices, for future reinterpretations in new moments
in time. The life history approach allows the researcher to explore and acknowledge each new piece, each new idea in the context of a moment in
time that is still emerging, transforming, evolving—such is the nature of
stories, such is the reality of our lives.

We can learn from the story of where we have been, even if it no longer seems to hold true for us. Just because the story has changed, moved on, and perhaps does not seem to fit anymore, does not mean that telling it is not valuable. It captures the "truth" at that moment in time. The life history approach encourages the researcher to give voice to how things were by exploring their meaning in context, give voice to how things are now, and allow that voice to change in the future, in another moment in time.

Endings

Writing
the Professor: Thomas

J. Gary Knowles

In these, the concluding pages of the book, we return to Gary's story of Thomas, the environmental studies professor. Whereas we began with an excerpt—the chapter "Beginnings: Researching the Professor: Thomas"—from the final section of the draft manuscript, we conclude with an excerpt from the beginning of that manuscript—because, as with all good life history research, the end should take us back to the beginning.

The life story told . . . is a true story with lies—lots of lies. The life story is true in that it represents many elements of Thomas Albert's biography. The truth is in the essence of his experience as a university professor of environmental studies. But the truth is also that Thomas Albert is not his real name; it is a pseudonym.

I first met Thomas in the summer of 1995 when he visited the small community in which I was living over the summer. At that point we decided to collaborate, although that collaboration was ill defined and embryonic in scope. Over the subsequent years we have talked a great deal and I have gleaned his story—although not always with ease or comfort. Much was painful for him—and myself, if I am honest—but, in the end, he agreed that the representation I have crafted of him . . . honors the

---

This passage is drawn from an unpublished manuscript that represents a life history study of Thomas, an environmental studies professor. It is edited for the purposes of this book. The passage presented here is the beginning of the manuscript, where I frame the work and the story.

spirit of his life experiences. Both of us have made meaning in the process of preparing [the manuscript].

The story has lies, too—many of them, at that—designed to protect the innocent and the guilty, as it were, those whose lives may be hurt or elevated in the process of revelation. Some of the lies—if I can call them such—are a result of me taking seriously the notions of artistic and literary license. These are lies of embellishment. . . . There are other lies as well and these are the figments of my imagination. They are the lies born out of the necessity to fill in some of the "blank spots" of a life retold. They are lies intended to embrace the literary qualities of Thomas's experience, and to complete the written account. All of these lies are the lies of a storyteller.

In the complexity of the lies told within [the pages of the manuscript] is the essence and simplicity of truth.

Thomas's story, at least the university part of it, is not unusual but, because these kinds of stories are seldom told in public, I convinced him to reveal much of his life to me. This was tremendously laborious work for both of us. Given my interest in life history as inquiry method, it is only natural that the account of Thomas's life takes a life span approach to understanding elements of his professional experience. Part of my reward is seeing the story in print. . . . I found other rewards quite surprising, especially the synergy of two intersecting professors' lives—his and mine—given my belief that researchers research what it is that we need to know, both personally and professionally. But, more important, Thomas's story may have great value for other readers whose lives intersect with his in the similarity of experiences, contexts, or circumstances. For Thomas, the benefit may well have been in the telling.

Throughout the process of bringing this story to print I have endeavored to maintain the integrity, the wholeness, and the spirit of Thomas's early life, his later university experiences, and his connections with people, places, and communities. It is these matters, after all, that mean most to Thomas as he lives out his fifth decade and life beyond the time frame and scope of this book.

I've tried to honor Thomas's experience by moving the camera lens of my penship from and between the minute-by-minute experiences to the big-picture, year-by-year experiences and events of his life. Much of the story hinges on turning points or critical incidents in his life. As one who honors the lives of others in his researching and teaching, he'd call these life events "epiphanies." I've tried to convey the very personal, and the intimate, as well as the professional. I have endeavored to honor his feelings about the academy and work within its walls and spheres of influence by focusing on issues or experiences or aspirations or dreams that occupied his mind. Even the forms of my writing have varied, with some sections more literal and some more metaphorical. All told, I've tried to paint the canvas of his life in big brushstrokes as well as in fine lines. I've tried to paint in ways that are harmonious with Thomas's life—his life directions and processes.

Finally, throughout the process of reconstructing elements of Thomas's experience—a researching process with which he, as a university professor, was very familiar—he read and clarified my interpretations and representations of his life. This process was, in reality, an extended conversation about finding common ground. Usually we came to mutually satisfying resolutions about points of difference. He felt that there were occasions in the final text where he wished to clarify or emphasize my representations of his life. In the spirit of contemporary life history inquiry we sought, together, a vehicle through which he could articulate his perspective.

Each chapter of the book begins and ends with Thomas's words. His quotes at the beginning of each were gleaned from several sources; they were either spoken in conversation with me, written in personal correspondence, or written in a journal, all over the last almost five years. Imbedded in the main text are Thomas's words (quoted from the same narrative sources), which I've strung together, sometimes as a jeweler threads beads on a string to create a beautiful necklace. (His ideas, too, I've often strung together, although not in direct quotes.) The lowly footnote is another mode through which Thomas's words augment my telling of his story. Intermittently throughout the account (which I crafted) he offers explanations and clarifications that allow readers access to another layer of understanding of his life lived in and around the margins of the academy. (I would have preferred that these brief commentaries by Thomas appeared in the margins as they were written but the technical aspects of achieving this in the production process were not able to be resolved satisfactorily.) At both the end of each chapter and as footnotes, then, are brief responses from Thomas to the next-to-final draft that he read in its entirety and in one sitting. I asked him to respond as he felt fit. Mostly he made brief comments, in handwriting, at the end of each manuscript chapter and they appear largely unedited. On other pages of the draft he made comments directly on the paper, between the lines, and these are the footnotes. Thomas has marked the work as he now marks the scholarly work of his students.

References

Achenbaum, W. A. 1999. "Recovering Our Roots through Gero-Biography." *Contemporary Gerontology: A Journal of Reviews and Critical Discourse, 5*(3): 76–78.

Acker, J., K. Barry, and J. Esseveld. 1996. "Objectivity and Truth: Problems in Doing Feminist Research," in *Feminism and Social Change: Bridging Theory and Practice*, ed. H. Gottfried (pp. 60–87). Chicago: University of Illinois Press.

Allport, G. W. 1942. *The Use of Personal Documents in Psychological Science*. New York: Holt, Rinehart & Winston.

Anderson, B. G. 1990. *First Field Work: The Misadventures of an Anthropologist*. Prospect Heights, IL: Waveland Press.

Anderson, E. 1990. *Street Wise: Race, Class and Change in an Urban Community*. Chicago: University of Chicago Press.

Angrosino, M. V. 1998. *Opportunity House: Ethnographic Stories of Mental Retardation*. Walnut Creek, CA: AltaMira Press.

Ashton-Warner, S. 1963. *Teacher*. New York: Simon & Schuster.

———. 1979. *I Passed This Way*. Auckland, New Zealand: Reed Methuen.

Aston, J. 2000. "Shaping Their Lives: Accommodating Career and Motherhood." Ph.D. thesis, University of Toronto, Ontario, Canada.

Bakhtin, M. 1981. *The Dialogic Imagination*. Austin: University of Texas Press.

———. 1989. "Discourse in the Novel," in *The Critical Tradition: Classic Texts and Contemporary Trends*, ed. D. H. Richter (pp. 781–791). New York: St. Martin's Press.

Ball, S. J., and I. F. Goodson. 1985. "Understanding Teachers: Concepts and Contexts," in *Teachers' Lives and Careers*, ed. S. J. Ball and I. F. Goodson (pp. 1–25). London: Falmer Press.

Banks, A., and S. Banks, eds. 1998. *Fiction & Social Research: By Ice or Fire*. Walnut Creek, CA: AltaMira Press.

Banks, M. 1998. "Visual Anthropology: Image, Object and Interpretation," in *Image-Based Research: A Sourcebook for Qualitative Researchers*, ed. J. Prosser (pp. 9–23). London: Falmer Press.

Banks, M., and H. Morphy, eds. 1997. *Rethinking Visual Anthropology*. New Haven, CT: Yale University Press.

Barone, T., and E. Eisner. 1997. "Arts-Based Educational Research," in *Complementary Methods for Research in Education*, 2d ed., ed. M. Jaeger (pp. 73–116). Washington, DC: American Educational Research Association.

Barry, D. 1996. "Artful Inquiry: A Symbolic Constructivist Approach to Social Science Research." *Qualitative Inquiry*, 2(4): 411–438.

Battiste, M., and J. Barman. 1995. *First Nations Education in Canada: The Circle Unfolds*. Vancouver: University of British Columbia Press.

Becker, H. 1966. "Introduction," in *The Jack-Roller*, ed. C. R. Shaw (pp. v–xvii). Chicago: University of Chicago Press.

Becker, S. 1998. "Visual Sociology, Documentary Photography and Photojournalism: It's (Almost) All a Matter of Context," in *Image-Based Research: A Sourcebook for Qualitative Researchers*, ed. J. Prosser (pp. 84–96). London: Falmer Press.

Behar, R. 1993. *Translated Woman: Crossing the Border with Esperanza's Story*. Boston: Beacon Press.

———. 1996. *The Vulnerable Observer: Anthropology That Breaks Your Heart*. Boston: Beacon Press.

Berleant, A. 1997. *Living in the Landscape*. Kansas City: University Press of Kansas.

Bertaux, D. 1981. "From the Life-History Approach to the Transformation of Sociological Practice," in *Biography and Society*, ed. D. Bertaux (pp. 29–45). Beverly Hills, CA: Sage Publications.

Bloom, L. R. 1996. "Stories of One's Own: Nonunitary Subjectivity in Narrative Representation." *Qualitative Inquiry*, 2(2): 176–188.

Blumenfeld-Jones, D. 1995. "Fidelity As a Criterion for Practicing and Evaluating Narrative Inquiry," in *Life History and Narrative*, ed. J. A. Hatch and R. Wisniewski (pp. 25–35). London: Falmer Press.

Blumer, H. 1969. *Symbolic Interactionism: Perspective and Method*. Englewood Cliffs, NJ: Prentice-Hall.

Bogdan, R. C., and S. K Biklen. 1998. *Qualitative Research in Education: An Introduction to Theory and Methods*, 3d ed. Needham Heights, MA: Allyn & Bacon.

Bollas, C. 1987. *The Shadow of the Object*. New York: Columbia University Press.

Bowman, J. 1991. *Report to the College of Teachers on Teacher Education in British Columbia*. Vancouver: British Columbia College of Teachers.

Bramwell, L. 1984. "Use of the Life History in Pattern Identification and Health Promotion." *Advances in Nursing Science*, 7(1): 37–44.

brown, b. 1999. "Lost Bodies and Wild Imaginations: Expressing the Forbidden Tales of Childhood Sexual Abuse through Artful Inquiry." Ph.D. thesis, University of Toronto, Ontario, Canada.

Brown, K. M. 1991. *Mama Lola: A Vodou Priestess in Brooklyn*. Berkeley: University of California Press.

Burke, J., and S. Kern. 1996. "Is the Use of Life History and Narrative in Clinical Practice Reimbursable? Is It Occupational Therapy?" *The American Journal of Occupational Therapy*, 50(5): 389–392.

Busier, H-L., K. A. Clark, R. A. Esch, C. Glesne, Y. Pigeon, and J. M. Tarule. 1997. "Intimacy in Research." *Qualitative Studies in Education,* 10(2): 165–170.

Campbell, A. 1984. *The Girls in the Gang.* Cambridge, MA: Blackwell.

Carnegie Forum on Education and the Economy. 1986. *A Nation Prepared: Teachers for the 21st Century.* New York: Carnegie Foundation.

Carter, K. 1993. "The Place of Story in the Study of Teaching and Teacher Education." *Educational Researcher,* 22(1): 5–12, 18.

Carter, K., and W. Doyle. 1996. "Personal Narrative and Life History in Learning to Teach," in *Handbook of Research on Teacher Education,* 2d ed., ed. J. Sikula, T. J. Buttery, and E. Guyton (pp. 120–143). New York: Macmillan.

Casey, K. 1993. *I Answer with My Life: Life Histories of Women Teachers Working for Social Change.* New York: Routledge.

Cayley, D. 1995. *George Grant: In Conversation.* Concord, Ontario: Anansi.

Chaplin, E. 1994. *Sociology and Visual Representation.* London: Routledge.

Church, K. 1995. "Forbidden Narratives: Critical Autobiography As Social Science," in *Theory and Practice in Medical Anthropology and International Health,* S. M. DiGiacomo, series editor, vol. 2 (pp.1–160). Amsterdam: Gordon and Breach Science Publishers.

Clandinin, D. J., and F. M. Connelly. 1994. "Personal Experience Methods," in *Handbook of Qualitative Research,* ed. N. Denzin and Y. Lincoln (pp. 413–427). Thousand Oaks, CA: Sage Publications.

———. 2000. *Narrative Inquiry: Experience and Story in Qualitative Research.* San Francisco: Jossey-Bass.

Cole, A. L. 1989. "Researcher and Teacher: Partners in Theory Building." *Journal of Education for Teaching,* 15(3): 225–237.

———. 1991. "Interviewing for Life History: A Process of Ongoing Negotiation," in *Qualitative Educational Research Studies: Methodologies in Transition,* ed. I. F. Goodson and J. M. Mangan, vol. 1 (pp. 185–208). London, Ontario: RUCCUS.

———. 1998. Personal communication to K. Gates, October 1.

———. 2000a. "Academic Freedom and the Publish or Perish Paradox in Schools of Education." *Teacher Education Quarterly,* 27(2): 33–48.

———. 2000b. "Teacher Educators and Teacher Education Reform: Individual Commitments, Institutional Realities." *Canadian Journal of Education,* 24(3): 281–295.

Cole, A. L., and J. G. Knowles. 1993. "Teacher Development Partnership Research: A Focus on Methods and Issues." *American Educational Research Journal,* 30(3): 473–496.

———. 1995. "Methods and Issues in a Life History Approach to Self-Study," in *Teachers Who Teach Teachers: Reflections on Teacher Education,* ed. T. Russell and F. Korthagen (pp. 130–151). London: Falmer Press.

———. 1996. "Beginning Professors and the Reform Agenda: Reform or Response?" *Teacher Education Quarterly,* 23(3): 5–22.

———. 1998. "Reforming Teacher Education through Self-Study," in *The Heart of the Matter: Teacher Educators and Teacher Education Reform,* ed. A. L. Cole, R. Elijah, and J. G. Knowles (pp. 41–54). San Francisco: Caddo Gap Press.

———. 2000. *Researching Teaching: Exploring Teacher Development through Reflexive Inquiry.* New York: Allyn & Bacon.

Cole, A. L., R. Elijah, and J. G. Knowles, eds. 1998. *The Heart of the Matter: Teacher Educators and Teacher Education Reform*. San Francisco: Caddo Gap Press.

Cole, A. L., J. G. Knowles, b. brown, and M. Buttignol. 1999a. *Academic Altarcations* (first installation in "Living in Paradox," a multimedia representation of teacher educators' lives in context), presented at the annual meeting of the American Educational Research Association (April), Montreal, Quebec, Canada.

———. 1999b. *A Perfect Imbalance* (third installation in "Living in Paradox," a multimedia representation of teacher educators' lives in context), presented at the annual meeting of the American Educational Research Association (April), Montreal, Quebec, Canada.

———. 1999c. *Wrestling Differences* (second installation in "Living in Paradox," a multimedia representation of teacher educators' lives in context), presented at the annual meeting of the American Educational Research Association (April), Montreal, Quebec, Canada.

Cole, A. L., and M. McIntyre. 2001. "Dance Me to an Understanding of Teaching: A Performative Text." *Journal of Curriculum Theorizing* (summer) n.p.

Collier, J., Jr., and M. Collier. 1986. *Visual Anthropology: Photographs As Research Method*. Albuquerque: University of New Mexico Press.

Connelly, F. M., and D. J. Clandinin. 1990. "Stories of Experience and Narrative Inquiry." *Educational Researcher, 19*(4): 2–14.

Conway, J. K. 1989. *The Road from Coorain*. New York: Vintage Books.

———, ed. 1992. *Written by Herself, Autobiographies of American Women: An Anthology*. New York: Random House.

Cornbleth, C. 1986. "Ritual and Rationality in Teacher Education Reform." *Educational Researcher, 15*(4): 5–14.

Creates, M. 1990. *The Distance between Two Points Is Measured in Memories, Labrador 1988*. North Vancouver, British Columbia: Presentation House Gallery.

———. 1991. *Places of Presence: Newfoundland Kkin and Ancestral Land, Newfoundland 1989–1991*. St. John's, Newfoundland: Killick Press.

———. 1992. *Marlene Creates: Land Works 1979–1991*. S. G. Garvey, ed. and curator. St. John's, Newfoundland: Memorial University of Newfoundland.

Denzin, N. 1984. "Interpreting the Biography and Society Life Project." *Biography and Society Newsletter, 2*: 5–10.

———. 1989a. *Interpretive Biography*. Newbury Park, CA: Sage Publications.

———. 1989b. *Interpretive Interactionism* (Sage University Paper Series on Applied Social Research Methods, vol. 16). Newbury Park, CA: Sage.

———. 1994. "The Art and Politics of Inquiry," in *Handbook of Qualitative Research*, ed. N. K. Denzin and Y. Lincoln (pp. 500–515). Thousand Oaks, CA: Sage Publications.

Detzner, D. F. 1992. "Life Histories in Southeast Asian Families," in *Qualitative Methods in Family Research*, ed. J. F. Gilgun and G. Handel (pp. 85–102). Newbury Park, CA: Sage.

Dews, C. L. B., and C. L. Law, eds. 1995. *This Fine Place So Far from Home: Voices of Academics from the Working Class*. Philadelphia: Temple University Press.

Diamond, C. T. P., and C. A. Mullen. 1999. *The Postmodern Educator: Arts-Based Inquiries and Teacher Development*. New York: Peter Lang Publishing.

Dilthey, Z. W. 1987. *Introduction to the Human Sciences*. Toronto, Ontario: Scholarly Book Services.

Dollard, J. 1935. *Criteria for the Life History.* New Haven, CT: Yale University Press.

Ducharme, E. R. 1993. *The Lives of Teacher Educators.* New York: Teachers College Press.

Dunlop, M. J. 1986. "Is a Science of Caring Possible?" *Journal of Advanced Nursing,* 11(6): 661–670.

Dunlop, R. 1999. "Boundary Bay: A Novel As Educational Research." Ph.D. thesis, University of British Columbia, Vancouver, Canada.

Ebbesen, L. S. 1999. "Women in Cardiac Rehabilitation: Our Stories." Ph.D. thesis, University of Toronto, Ontario, Canada.

Eckhert, P. 1989. *Jocks and Burnouts: Social Categories and Identity in the High School.* New York: Teachers College Press.

Edel, L. 1984. *Writing Lives: Principia Biographica.* New York: N. W. Norton.

Eiblmayr, S. 1998. "Martha Rosler's Characters," in *Martha Rosler: Positions in the Lifeworld,* ed. C. de Zegher (pp. 153–172). Cambridge, MA: MIT Press.

Eisner, E. 1991. *The Enlightened Eye: Qualitative Inquiry and the Enhancement of Educational Practice.* New York: Macmillan.

———. 1993. "Forms of Understanding and the Future of Educational Research." *Educational Researcher,* 22(7): 5–11.

Ellis, C., and A. P. Bochner, eds. 1996. *Composing Ethnography: Alternative Forms of Qualitative Writing.* Walnut Creek, CA: AltaMira Press.

Erickson, F., and J. Shultz. 1992. "Students' Experience of the Curriculum," in *Handbook of Research on Curriculum,* ed. P. W. Jackson (pp. 465–487). New York: Macmillian/American Educational Research Association.

Etter-Lewis, G. 1993. *My Soul Is My Own: Oral Narratives of African American Women in the Professions.* New York: Routledge.

Finley, S., and J. G. Knowles. 1995. "Researcher As Artist/Artist As Researcher." *Qualitative Inquiry,* 1(1): 110–142.

Fleisher, D., and D. M. Freedman. 1983. *Death of an American: The Killing of John Singer.* New York: Continuum.

Franzosa, S. D., ed. 1999. *Ordinary Lessons: Girlhoods of the 1950s.* New York: Peter Lang.

Freud, S. 1909. "Analysis of a Phobia in a Five-Year-Old Boy," in *Standard Edition of the Complete Psychological Works,* trans. J. Strachey, vol. 10 (pp. 5–149). London: Hogarth Press, 1958.

———. 1911. "Psycho-Analytic Notes on an Autobiographical Account of Paranoia," in *Standard Edition of the Complete Psychological Works,* trans. J. Strachey, vol. 12 (pp. 9–82). London: Hogarth Press, 1958.

Fullan, M., and F. M. Connelly. 1987. *Teacher Education in Ontario: Current Practices and Options for the Future. A Position Paper Written for the Ontario Education Review.* Toronto: Ontario Ministry of Education and Ministry of Colleges and Universities.

Fullan, M., F. M. Connelly, and N. Watson. 1990. *Teacher Education in Ontario: Current Practices and Options for the Future.* Toronto: Ontario Ministry of Education and Ministry of Colleges and Universities.

Garvey, S. G., ed. and curator. 1993. *Marlene Creates: Land Works 1979–1991.* St. John's, Newfoundland: Memorial University of Newfoundland.

Gates, K. M. 2000a. "Challenging Conventional Order to Promote Equality: A Life History Study." Ph.D. thesis, University of Toronto, Ontario, Canada.

————. 2000b. "The Experience of Caring for a Loved One: A Phenomenological Study." *Nursing Science Quarterly, 13*(1): 54–59.

Gilgun, J. 1999. "Mapping Resilience As Process among Adults with Childhood Adversities," in *The Dynamics of Resilient Families. Resiliency in Families,* ed. H. McCubbin, vol. 4 (pp. 41–70). Thousand Oaks, CA: Sage Publications.

Glaser, B. G., and A. L. Strauss. 1967. *The Discovery of Grounded Theory: Strategies for Qualitative Research.* New York: Aldine de Gruyter.

Glesne, C. 1997. "That Rare Feeling: Re-Presenting Research through Poetic Transcription." *Qualitative Inquiry, 3*(2): 202–221.

————. 1999. *Becoming Qualitative Researchers: An Introduction,* 2d ed. White Plains, NY: Longman.

Glesne, C., and A. Peshkin. 1992. *Becoming Qualitative Researchers: An Introduction.* White Plains, NY: Longman.

Goetz, J., and M. D. LeCompte. 1984. *Ethnography and Qualitative Design in Educational Research.* New York: Academic Press.

Goodman, P. 1964. *Compulsory Mis-Education.* New York: Horizon.

Goodson, I. F. 1981. "Life Histories and the Study of Schooling." *Interchange, 11*(4): 62–76.

————. 1983. "The Use of Life Histories in the Study of Teaching," in *The Ethnography of Schooling,* ed. M. Hammersly (pp. 27–53). Driffield, UK: Nafferton.

————. 1988. "History, Context, and Qualitative Methods," in *The Making of Curriculum,* ed. I. F. Goodson (pp. 93–116). London: Falmer Press.

————. 1991. "Teachers' Lives in Educational Research," in *Biography, Identity and Schooling: Episodes in Educational Research,* ed. I. F. Goodson and R. Walker (pp. 137–140). London: Falmer Press.

————. 1992. *Studying Teachers' Lives.* London: Routledge.

————. 1995. "The Story So Far: Personal Knowledge and the Political," in *Life History and Narrative,* ed. J. A. Hatch and R. Wisniewski (pp. 89–98). London: Falmer Press.

Goodson, I. F., and A. L. Cole. 1994. "Exploring Teachers' Professional Knowledge: Constructing Identity and Community." *Teacher Education Quarterly, 21*(1): 85–105.

Goodson, I. F., and C. Fliesser. 1994. "Exchanging Gifts: Collaborative Research and Theories of Context." *Analytic Teaching, 15:* 47–52.

Gorelick, S. 1996. "Contradictions of Feminist Methodology," in *Feminism and Social Change: Bridging Theory and Practice,* ed. H. Gottfried (pp. 23–45). Chicago: University of Illinois Press.

Goulet, L., and B. Aubichon. 1997. "Learning Collaboration: Research in a First Nations Teacher Education Program," in *Recreating Relationships: Collaboration and Educational Reform,* ed. H. Christiansen, L. Goulet, C. Krentz, and M. Maeers (pp. 115–127). Albany: State University of New York Press.

Grumet, M. 1991. "The Politics of Personal Knowledge," in *Stories Lives Tell: Narrative and Dialogue in Education,* ed. C. Witherall and N. Noddings (pp. 67–77). New York: Teachers College Press.

Gubrium, J. 1975. *Living and Dying in Murray Manor.* New York: St. Martin's Press.

Gustavsen, G. A. 1981. "Selected Characteristics of Home Schools and Parents Who Operate Them." Ph.D. dissertation, Andrews University, Berrien Springs, Michigan.

Hall, C. 1998. *Heroic Self: Sociological Dimensions of Clinical Practice.* Springfield, IL: Charles C. Thomas Publisher.

Hammersley, M. 1979. *Research Methods in Education and the Social Sciences.* Milton Keynes, UK: Open University Press.

Hampl, P. 1996. "Memory and Imagination," in *The Anatomy of Memory: An Anthology,* ed. J. McConkey (pp. 201–211). Oxford: Oxford University Press.

Hampton, E. 1995. "Towards a Redefinition of Indian Education," in *First Nations Education in Canada: The Circle Unfolds,* ed. M. Battiste and J. Barman (pp. 5–46). Vancouver: University of British Columbia Press.

Harper, D. 1982. *Good Company.* Chicago: University of Chicago Press.

———. 1987. *Working Knowledge: Skill and Community in a Small Shop.* Chicago: University of Chicago Press.

———. 1994. "On the Authority of the Image: Visual Methods at the Crossroads," in *Handbook of Qualitative Research,* ed. N. K. Denzin and Y. Lincoln (pp. 413–412). Thousand Oaks, CA: Sage Publications.

———. 1997. "An Argument for Visual Sociology," in *Image-Based Research: A Sourcebook for Qualitative Researchers,* ed. J. Prosser (pp. 24–41). London: Falmer Press.

Hatch, J. A., and R. Wisniewski, eds. 1995a. *Life History and Narrative.* London: Falmer Press.

———. 1995b. "Life History and Narrative: Questions, Issues, and Exemplary Works," in *Life History and Narrative,* ed. J. A. Hatch and R. Wisniewski (pp. 113–135). London: Falmer Press.

Heidegger, M. 1962. *Being and Time,* 7th ed. New York: Harper-Collins.

Herz, R., ed. 1997. *Reflexivity & Voice.* Thousand Oaks, CA: Sage Publications.

Heshusius, L., and K. Ballard, eds. 1996. *From Positivism to Interpretivism and Beyond.* New York: Teachers College Press.

Holmes Group. 1986. *Tomorrow's Teachers.* East Lansing, MI: Holmes Group.

———. 1990. *Tomorrow's Schools: Principles for Design of Professional Development Schools.* East Lansing, MI: Holmes Group.

Holt, J. 1969. *The Underachieving School.* New York: Dell Publishing.

———. 1976. *Instead of Education: Ways to Help People Do Things Better.* New York: E. P. Dutton & Co.

Hones, D., and C. Cha. 1999. *Educating New Americans: Immigrant Lives and Learning.* Mahwah, NJ: Lawrence Erlbaum Associates.

Hood, L. 1988. *Sylvia: The Biography of Sylvia Ashton-Warner.* Auckland, New Zealand: Penguin Books.

———. 1990. *Who Is Sylvia?: The Diary of a Biographer.* Dunedin, New Zealand: John McIndoe.

hooks, b. 1996. *Bone Black: Memories of Girlhood.* New York: Henry Holt & Co.

Howarth, W. L. 1980. "Some Principles of Autobiography," in *Autobiography: Essays Theoretical and Critical,* ed. J. Olney (pp. 84–114). Princeton, NJ: Princeton University Press.

Hutchison, D. 1999. "Perspectives on Place in Education." Ph.D. thesis, University of Toronto, Ontario, Canada.

Illich, I. 1970. *Deschooling Society.* New York: Harper Colophon Books.

Jackson, M. 1995. *At Home in the World.* Durham, NC: Duke University.

Jipson, J., and N. Paley, eds. 1997. *Daredevil Research: Re-Creating Analytic Practice.* New York: Peter Lang Publishing.

Johnson, M. 1993. *Moral Imagination: Implications of Cognitive Science for Ethics.* Chicago: University of Chicago Press.

Jones, S. H. 1998. *Kaleidoscope Notes: Writing Women's Music and Organizational Culture.* Walnut Creek, CA: AltaMira Press.

Josselson, R., ed. 1996. *Ethics and Process in the Narrative Study of Lives,* vol. 4. Thousand Oaks, CA: Sage.

Josselson, R., and A. Lieblich, eds. 1993. *The Narrative Study of Lives,* vol. 1. Thousand Oaks, CA: Sage.

———. 1995. *Interpreting Experience: The Narrative Study of Lives,* vol. 3. Thousand Oaks, CA: Sage.

———. 1999. *Making Meaning of Narratives: The Narrative Study of Lives,* vol. 6. Thousand Oaks, CA: Sage.

Kaplan, A. 1993. *French Lessons: A Memoir.* Chicago: University of Chicago Press.

Kaseman, M. L., and S. D. Kaseman. 1990. *Taking Charge through Home Schooling: Personal and Political Empowerment.* Stoughton, WI: Koshkonong Press.

Kaufman, S. 1986. *The Ageless Self: Sources of Meaning in Late Life.* Madison: University of Wisconsin Press.

Kilbourn, B. 1998. *For the Love of Teaching.* London, Ontario: Althouse Press.

———. 1999. "Fictional Theses." *Educational Researcher, 28*(9): 27–32.

King, P. 1989. "A Woman of the Land." *Image: Journal of Nursing Scholarship, 21*(1): 19–22.

Kluckhohn, C., H. Murray, and D. Schneider. 1955. *Personality in Nature, Society and Culture.* New York: Knopf.

Knowles, J. G. 1989. "Cooperating with Home School Parents: A New Agenda for Public Schools?" *Urban Education, 23*(4): 392–411.

———. 1991a. "Fox in the Chicken Coop or Goose in the Nest Laying a Golden Egg? Reflections on Researching Home Schools. *Home Education Magazine, 8*(1): 15–17, 39–41, 49.

———. 1991b. "Parents' Rationales for Operating Home Schools." *Journal of Contemporary Ethnography, 20*(2): 203–230.

———. 1992. "Models for Understanding Preservice and Beginning Teachers' Biographies: Illustrations from Case Studies," in *Studying Teachers' Lives,* ed. I. F. Goodson (pp. 99–152). London: Routledge.

———. 1993. "Life-History Accounts As Mirrors: A Practical Avenue for the Conceptualization of Reflection in Teacher Education," in *Conceptualizing Reflection in Teacher Development,* ed. J. Calderhead and P. Gates (pp. 70–92). London: Falmer Press.

———. 1994. "Metaphors As Windows on a Personal History: A Beginning Teacher's Experience." (Special Issue) *Teacher Education Quarterly, 21*(1): 37–66.

———. 1998. "Home Education: Personal Histories," in *Home-School Relations,* ed. M. L. Fuller and G. Olsen (pp. 302–330). New York: Allyn & Bacon.

Knowles, J. G., and A. L. Cole, eds. 1996. "Beginning Professors and Educational Reform." (Special Issue) *Teacher Education Quarterly, 23*(3).

Knowles, J. G., A. L. Cole, and J. Sumsion, eds. 2000. "'Publish or Perish': The Role and Meaning of 'Research' in Teacher Education Institutions." (Special Issue) *Teacher Education Quarterly, 27*(2).

Knowles, J. G., and A. L. Cole, with C. S. Presswood. 1994. *Through Preservice Teachers' Eyes: Exploring Field Experiences through Narrative and Inquiry.* New York: Merrill.

Knowles, J. G., and D. Holt-Reynolds. 1991. "Shaping Pedagogies against Personal Histories in Preservice Teacher Education." *Teachers College Record, 93*(1): 87–113.

———, eds. 1994a. "Using Personal Histories in Teacher Education." (Special Issue) *Teacher Education Quarterly, 21*(1).

———. 1994b. "Personal Histories As Medium, Method, and Milieu for Gaining Insights into Teacher Development: An Introduction." *Teacher Education Quarterly, 21*(1): 5–12.

Knowles, J. G., and J. A. Muchmore. 1995. "'Yep! We're Grown Up Home-Schooled Kids—and We're Doing Just Fine, Thank You Very Much.'" *Journal of Research on Christian Education, 4*(1): 35–56.

Knowles, J. G., and S. Thomas. 2000a. *Experiencing School: Lived Experience Portrayed in Context* (version 1). Multimedia exhibit at the annual meeting of the American Educational Research Association (April), New Orleans.

———. 2000b. "Experiencing School: Lived Experience Portrayed in Context" (version 1). Paper presentation made at the annual meeting of the American Educational Research Association (April), New Orleans.

Knowles, J. G., S. E. Marlow, and J. A. Muchmore. 1992. "From Pedagogy to Ideology: Origins and Phases of Home Education in the United States, 1970–1990." *American Journal of Education, 100*(1): 195–235.

Kohli, M. 1981. "Biography: Account, Text, Method," in *Biography and Society,* ed. D. Bertaux (pp. 61–76). Beverly Hills, CA: Sage Publications.

Kvale, S. 1995. "The Social Construction of Validity." *Qualitative Inquiry, 1*(1): 19–40.

———. 1996. *InterViews: An Introduction to Qualitative Research Interviewing.* Thousand Oaks, CA: Sage Publications.

———. 1999. "The Psychoanalytic Interview As Qualitative Research." *Qualitative Inquiry, 5*(1): 87–113.

Lakoff, G., and M. Johnson. 1980. *Metaphors We Live By.* Chicago: University of Chicago Press.

Langness, L. L. 1965. *The Life History in Anthropological Science.* London: Holt, Rinehart & Winston.

Langness, L. L., and G. Frank. 1981. *Lives: An Anthropological Approach to Biography.* Novato, CA: Chandler & Sharp Publishers.

Larson, E., and S. C. Fanchiang. 1996. "Life History and Narrative Research: Generating a Humanistic Knowledge Base for Occupational Therapy." *The American Journal of Occupational Therapy, 50*(4): 247–250.

Lau, E. 1989. *Runaway: Diary of a Street Kid.* Toronto, Ontario: Harper Collins.

Lawrence-Lightfoot, S. 1994. *I've Known Rivers: Lives of Loss and Liberation.* New York: Addison-Wesley Publishing.

———. 1999. *Respect: An Exploration.* Reading, MA: Persus Books.

Lawrence-Lightfoot, S., and J. Hoffmann-Davis. 1997. *The Art and Science of Portraiture.* San Francisco: Jossey-Bass.

Leininger, M. M. 1985. "Life Health-Care History: Purposes, Methods and Techniques," in *Qualitative Research Methods in Nursing,* ed. M. M. Leininger (pp. 119–132). Orlando, FL: Grune & Stratton.

Lenzo, P. 1992. Master of Fine Arts thesis exhibit. (April) Art Gallery, Wayne State University, Detroit, Michigan.

Lewis, R. 1998. "Impact of the Marital Relationship on the Experience of Caring for an Elderly Spouse with Dementia." *Aging and Society, 18*(2): 209–231.

Lieblich, A., and R. Josselson, eds. 1994. *Exploring Identity and Gender: The Narrative Study of Lives,* vol. 2. Thousand Oaks, CA: Sage.

———. 1997. *The Narrative Study of Lives,* vol. 5. Thousand Oaks, CA: Sage.

Lincoln, Y., and E. G. Guba. 1985. *Naturalistic Inquiry.* Beverly Hills, CA: Sage Publications.

Loizos, P. 1993. *Innovation in Ethnographic Film: From Innocence to Self-Consciousness, 1955–85.* Manchester, UK: Manchester University Press.

Marshall, C., and G. B. Rossman. 1989. *Designing Qualitative Research.* Newbury Park, CA: Sage Publications.

Mathews, J. 1988. *Escalante: The Best Teacher in America.* New York: Henry Holt.

Matiss, I. A. 1998. "Lives in Changing Contexts: A Life History Analysis of Latvian-Canadian Women's Stories about Being Latvian." Ph.D. thesis, University of Toronto, Ontario, Canada.

Mayberry, M., J. G. Knowles, B. D. Ray, and S. E. Marlow. 1995. *Home Schooling: Parents As Educators.* Beverly Hills, CA: Corwin Press/Sage Publications.

Maykut, P., and R. Morehouse. 1994. *Beginning Qualitative Research: A Philosophical and Practical Guide.* London: Falmer Press.

McAuley, W. J., S. S. Travis, and M. P. Safewright. 1997. "Personal Accounts of the Nursing Home Search and Selection Process." *Qualitative Health Research, 7*(2): 236–254.

McIntyre, M. 2000. "Garden As Phenomenon, Method, and Metaphor: An Arts-Informed Life History View." Ph.D. thesis, University of Toronto, Ontario, Canada.

McIntyre, M., and A. L. Cole. 2001. "Conversations in Relation: The Research Relationship in/as Artful Self-Study. *Journal of Reflective Practice, 2*(1): 5–25

McLaren, P. 1986. *Schooling As a Ritual Performance.* London: Routledge & Kegan Paul.

Measor, L. 1985. "Critical Incidents in the Classroom: Identities, Choices and Careers," in *Teachers Lives and Careers,* ed. S. J. Ball and I. F. Goodson (pp. 61–77). Lewes, UK: Falmer Press.

Measor, L., and P. Sikes. 1992. "Visiting Lives: Ethics and Methodology in Life History," in *Studying Teachers' Lives,* ed. I. F. Goodson (pp. 209–233). London: Routledge.

Merriam, S. 1988. *Case Study Research in Education: A Qualitative Approach.* San Francisco: Jossey-Bass.

Middleton, S. 1992. "Developing a Radical Pedagogy: Autobiography of a New Zealand Sociologist of Women's Education," in *Studying Teachers' Lives,* ed. I. F. Goodson (pp. 18–50). London: Routledge.

———. 1993. *Educating Feminists: Life Histories and Pedagogy.* New York: Teachers College Press.

———. 1998. "Schools at War: A Life-History Analysis of Learning and Teaching in New Zealand, 1939–1949." *Discourse: Studies in the Cultural Politics of Education, 19*(1): 53–74.

Miles, M. B., and A. M. Huberman. 1994. *Qualitative Data Analysis: An Expanded Sourcebook*, 2d ed. Thousand Oaks, CA: Sage Publications.

Miller, S. G. 1994. "Borderline Personality Disorder from the Patient's Perspective." *Hospital and Community Psychiatry*, 45(12): 1215–1219.

Mitchell, C., and S. Weber. 1998. "Picture This! Class Line-Ups, Vernacular Portraits and Lasting Impressions of School," in *Image-Based Research: A Sourcebook for Qualitative Researchers*, ed. J. Prosser (pp. 197–213). London: Falmer Press.

Moffatt, M. 1989. *Coming of Age in New Jersey: College and American Culture*. New Brunswick, NJ: Rutgers University Press.

Montgomery, L. M. 1908. *Anne of Green Gables*. Toronto, Ontario: Ryerson Press.

Morales, A. L. 1998. *Medicine Stories: History, Culture and the Politics of Integrity*. Cambridge, MA: South End Press.

Muchmore, J. A. 1999. "Knowing Anna, Knowing Me: A Teacher's Story of Professional Development." Ph.D. dissertation, University of Michigan, Ann Arbor.

Murray, H. A. 1938. *Explorations in Personality*. New York: Oxford University Press.

Myerhoff, B. 1974. *Peyote Hunt: The Sacred Journey of the Huichol Indians*. New York: Cornell University Press.

———. 1979. *Number Our Days*. New York: Dutton.

———. 1982. "Life History among the Elderly: Performance, Visibility, and Remembering," in *A Crack in the Mirror: Reflexive Perspectives in Anthropology*, ed. J. Ruby (pp. 99–120). Philadelphia: University of Pennsylvania Press.

Neill, A. S. 1972. *Neill! Neill! Orange Peel*. New York: Hart Publishing Co.

Neilsen, L. 1998. *Knowing Her Place: Research Literacies and Feminist Occasions*. San Francisco and Great Tancook Island, Nova Scotia: Caddo Gap Press and Backalong Books.

Nielsen, J. M. 1990. "Introduction," in *Feminist Research Methods: Exemplary Readings in the Social Sciences*, ed. J. M. Nielsen (pp. 1–37). Boulder, CO: Westview Press.

Oakley, A. 1981. "Interviewing Women: A Contradiction in Terms," in *Doing Feminist Research*, ed. H. Roberts (pp. 30–61). London: Routledge & Kegan Paul.

Olesen, V. 1994. "Feminisms and Models of Qualitative Research," in *Handbook of Qualitative Research*, ed. N. K. Denzin and Y. S. Lincoln (pp. 158–174). Thousand Oaks, CA: Sage Publications.

———. 2000. "Feminisms and Qualitative Research at and into the Millennium," in *Handbook of Qualitative Research*, 2d ed., ed. N. K. Denzin and Y. S. Lincoln (pp. 215–256). Thousand Oaks, CA: Sage.

Orr, J., and D. Friesen. 1999. "'I Think That What's Happening in Aboriginal Education Is That We're Taking Control': Aboriginal Teachers' Stories of Self-Determination." *Teachers and Teaching: Theory and Practice. A Journal of the International Study Association of Teacher Thinking*, 5(2): 219–241.

Patai, D. 1994. "Sick and Tired of Scholars' Nouveau Solipsism." *The Chronicle of Higher Education*, 23 (February): 52.

Patton, M. Q. 1990. *Qualitative Evaluation and Research Methods*, 2d ed. Newbury Park, CA: Sage Publications.

Peacock, J., and D. Holland. 1993. "The Narrated Self: Life Stories in Process." *Ethos*, 21(4): 367–383.

Personal Narratives Group, eds. 1989. *Interpreting Women's Lives: Feminist Theory and Personal Narratives*. Bloomington: Indiana University Press.

Peshkin, A. 1991. *The Color of Strangers, the Color of Friends: The Play of Ethnicity in School and Community.* Chicago: University of Chicago Press.

Philip, M. 1998. "UN Committee Lambastes Canada on Human Rights." *The Globe and Mail* (December 5), p. A7.

Plummer, K. 1983. *Documents of Life: An Introduction to the Problems and Literature of a Humanistic Method.* London: George Allen & Unwin.

Polakow, V. 1993. *Lives on the Edge: Single Mothers and Their Children in the Other America.* Chicago: University of Chicago Press.

Poland, B., and A. Pederson. 1998. "Reading Between the Lines: Interpreting Silences in Qualitative Research." *Qualitative Inquiry,* 4(2): 293–312.

Polanyi, M. 1958. *Personal Knowledge: Toward a Post-Critical Philosophy.* Chicago: University of Chicago Press.

Polkinghorne, D. E. 1995. "Narrative Configuration in Qualitative Analysis," in *Life History and Narrative,* ed. J. A. Hatch and R. Wisniewski (pp. 5–23). London: Falmer Press.

Prosser, J., ed. 1998. *Image-Based Research: A Sourcebook for Qualitative Researchers.* London: Falmer Press.

Radford, J. L. 1996. "Children's Social Power in Their Relationships with Adults: Implications for Child Sexual Abuse Primary Prevention Programs." Ph.D. thesis, University of Toronto, Ontario, Canada.

Raskin, M. 1996. "Ed Kienholz and the Burden of Being an American," in *Kienholz: A Retrospective: Edward and Nancy Reddin Kienholz,* ed. W. Hopps (pp. 38–43). New York: Whitney Museum of American Art/Distributed Art Publishers.

Rawls, J. 1989. "The Justification of Civil Disobedience," in *The Right Thing to Do: Basic Reading in Moral Philosophy,* ed. J. Rachels (pp. 254–270). New York: Random House.

Ray, R. 1998. "Feminist Readings of Older Women's Life Stories." *Journal of Aging Studies,* 12(2): 117–127.

Reinharz, S. 1992. *Feminist Methods in Social Research.* New York: Oxford University Press.

Relph, E. 1976. *Place and Placelessness.* London: Pion.

Renehan, E. J., Jr. 1992. *John Burroughs: An American Naturalist.* Post Mills, VT: Chelsea Green Publishing.

Richards, J. 1990. "Countertransference As a Complex Tool for Understanding the Patient in Psychotherapy." *Psychoanalytic Psychotherapy,* 4(3): 233–244.

Richards, T. J., and L. Richards. 1994. "Using Computers in Qualitative Research," in *Handbook of Qualitative Research,* ed. N. K. Denzin and Y. S. Lincoln (pp. 445–463). Thousand Oaks, CA: Sage Publications.

Richardson, L. 1990. *Writing Strategies: Reaching Diverse Audiences.* Qualitative Research Methods Series, vol. 21. Newbury Park, CA: Sage Publications.

———. 1992. "The Consequences of Poetic Representation: Writing the Other, Rewriting the Self," in *Investigating Subjectivity: Research on Lived Experience,* ed. C. Ellis and M. Flaherty (pp. 125–137). Newbury Park, CA: Sage Publishers.

———. 1994. "Writing: A Method of Inquiry," in *Handbook of Qualitative Research,* ed. N. K. Denzin and Y. S. Lincoln (pp. 516–529). Thousand Oaks, CA: Sage Publications.

Ricoeur, P. 1984. *Time and Narrative,* vol. 1, trans. K. McLaughlin and D. Pellauer. Chicago: University of Chicago Press.

———. 1991. *From Text to Action: Essays in Hermeneutics II,* trans. K. Blamey and J. B. Thompson. Evanston, IL: Northwestern University Press.

Rose, A. 1999. "Graduate Students with Learning Disabilities: A Life History of Learners and Their Learning." Ph.D. thesis, University of Toronto, Ontario, Canada.

Rose, S. 1988. *Keeping Them Out of the Hands of Satan: Evangelical Schooling in America.* New York: Routledge.

Rosenwald, G. C., and R. L. Ochberg, eds. 1992. *Storied Lives: The Cultural Politics of Self-Understanding.* New Haven, CT: Yale University Press.

Royal Commission on Aboriginal Peoples. 1993. *Ethical Guidelines for Research.* Ottawa, Ontario: Supply and Services Canada.

Rudderman, E. B. 1986. "Gender Related Themes of Women Psychotherapists in Their Treatment of Women Patients: The Creative and Reparative Use of Countertransference As a Mutual Growth Experience." *Clinical Social Work Journal,* 14(2): 103–126.

Saillant, F. 1990. "Discourse, Knowledge and Experience of Cancer: A Life Story." *Culture, Medicine and Psychiatry,* 14(1): 81–104.

Saldaña, J. 1998. "Ethical Issues in an Ethnographic Performance Text: The 'Dramatic Impact' of 'Juicy Stuff'." *Research in Drama Education,* 3(2): 181–196.

Sarason, S. 1990. *The Predictable Failure of Educational Reform.* San Francisco: Jossey-Bass.

Saul, J. R. 1995. *The Unconscious Civilization.* Concord, Ontario: Anansi.

Savishinsky, J. 1991. *The Ends of Times: Life and Work in a Nursing Home.* New York: Bergin & Garvey.

Schmidt, M. 1994. "Learning from Experience: Influences on Music Teachers' Perceptions and Practices." Ph.D. dissertation, University of Michigan, Ann Arbor.

Schmidt, M., and J. G. Knowles. 1994. "'Why Don't They Listen to Me?': Cooperating Teachers' and Supervisors' Advice to Music Student Teachers." Paper presented at the annual meeting of the Association of Teacher Educators (February), Atlanta, Georgia.

———. 1995. "Four Women's Stories of Failure As Beginning Teachers." *Teaching & Teacher Education,* 11(5): 429–444.

Schoem, D., ed. 1991. *Inside Separate Worlds: Life Stories of Young Blacks, Jews, and Latinos.* Ann Arbor: University of Michigan Press.

Scholes, R. 1981. "Language, Narrative, and Anti-Narrative," in *On Narrative,* ed. W. J. T. Mitchell (pp. 200–208). Chicago: University of Chicago Press.

Schön, D. A. 1987. *Educating the Reflective Practitioner.* San Francisco: Jossey-Bass.

Schuster, E. 1992. "Tension in the Field: Personal Reflections and Interpretations on Researching in a Nursing Home." Paper presented at the eleventh annual Human Science Research Conference (June), Rochester, Michigan.

Schwalbe. M. 1995. "The Work of Professing (A Letter to Home)," in *This Fine Place So Far from Home: Voices Of Academics from the Working Class,* ed. C. L. Barney Dews and C. Leste Law (pp. 209–331). Philadelphia: Temple University Press.

Seidman, I. E. 1991. *Interviewing As Qualitative Research: A Guide for Researchers in Education and the Social Sciences.* New York: Teachers College Press.

Shaw, C., ed. 1930. *The Jack-Roller.* Chicago: University of Chicago Press.

Shostak, M. 1983. *Nisa: The Life and Words of a !Kung Woman.* New York: Vintage.

Sieber, J. 1993. "The Ethics and Politics of Sensitive Research," in *Researching Sensitive Topics,* ed. C. Renzetti and R. Lee (pp. 14–26). Newbury Park, CA: Sage Publications.

———. 1992. *Planning Ethically Responsible Research: A Guide for Students and Internal Review Boards.* Newbury Park, CA: Sage Publications.

Sikes, P. 1985. "The Life Cycle of the Teacher," in *Teachers Lives and Careers,* ed. S. J. Ball and I. F. Goodson (pp. 27–60). Lewes, UK: Falmer Press.

Smith, L. M., D. C. Dwyer, J. J. Prunty, and P. F. Kleine. 1988. *Innovation and Change in Schooling: History, Politics, and Agency.* London: Falmer Press.

SmithBattle, L., and V. Leonard. 1998. "Adolescent Mothers Four Years Later: Narratives of the Self and Visions of the Future." *Advances in Nursing Science, 20*(3): 36–49.

Spark, M. 1993. *Curriculum Vitae: Autobiography.* Boston: Houghton Mifflin.

Spradley, J. P. 1979. *The Ethnographic Interview.* Forth Worth, TX: Holt, Rinehart & Winston.

St. Denis, V. 1992. "Community-Based Participatory Research: Aspects of the Concept Relevant for Practice." *Native Studies Review, 8*(2): 51–74.

Steir, C., ed. 1978. *Blue Jolts: The Stories from the Cuckoo's Nest.* Washington, DC: New Republic Books.

Strauss, A. L., and L. Rainwater. 1962. *The Professional Scientist.* Chicago: Aldine Press.

Tesch, R. 1990. *Qualitative Research. Analysis Types and Software Tools.* New York: Falmer Press.

Thomas, W. I., and F. Znaniecki. 1927. *The Polish Peasant in Europe and America.* Chicago: University of Chicago Press.

Tierney, W. G. 1998. "Life History's History: Subjects Foretold." *Qualitative Inquiry, 4*(1): 49–70.

Tompkins, J. 1996. *A Life in School: What the Teacher Learned.* Reading, MA: Addison-Wesley.

Toronto Disaster Relief Committee. 1998. *Homelessness in Toronto: State of Emergency Declaration.* Toronto, Ontario: Toronto Disaster Relief Committee.

Trapedo-Dworsky, M., and A. L. Cole. 1999. "Teaching As Autobiography: Connecting the Personal and the Professional in the Academy." *Teaching Education, 10*(2): 131–138.

Vozzola, E. 1998. "We Dream, You Do: 'Great' Grandmothers Teach a Lesson in Women's Changing Roles." *Teaching of Psychology, 25*(4): 289–291.

Wagner-Martin, L. 1994. *Telling Women's Lives: The New Biography.* Newark, NJ: Rutgers University Press.

Walsh, A., and E. Crepeau. 1998. "'My Secret Life': The Emergence of One Gay Man's Authentic Identity." *The American Journal of Occupational Therapy, 52*(7): 563–569.

Watson, L., and M. Watson-Franke. 1985. *Interpreting Life Histories: An Autobiographical Inquiry.* New Brunswick, NJ: Rutgers University Press.

Weitzman, E. A. 2000. "Software and Qualitative Research," in *Handbook Of Qualitative Research*, 2d. ed., ed. N. K. Denzin and Y. S. Lincoln (pp. 803–820). Thousand Oaks, CA: Sage Publications.

Werner, O., and G. M. Schoepfle. 1987. *Systematic Fieldwork: Ethnographic Analysis and Data Management*, vol. 2. Newbury Park, CA: Sage Publications.

White, R. W. 1952. *Lives in Progress: A Study of the Natural Growth of Personality*. New York: Holt.

———, ed. 1963. *The Study of Lives*. New York: Atherton Press.

Will, R., and V. Fast Braun. 1997. "Nurses' Professional Values." Unpublished manuscript.

Williams, M. D. 1993. *An Academic Village: The Ethnography of an Anthropology Department, 1959–1979* (n.p.).

———. 1973. *The Man in the Principal's Office: An Ethnography*. New York: Holt, Rinehart & Winston.

———. 1994. *Transforming Qualitative Data: Description, Analysis, and Interpretation*. Thousand Oaks, CA: Sage Publications.

Woods, P. 1987. *Inside Schools*. London: Routledge.

Wrye, H., and J. Churilla. 1979. "Looking Inward, Looking Backward: Reminiscence and the Life Review." *Frontiers: A Journal of Women's Studies*, 11(2): 77–84.

Yow, V. 1994. *Recording Oral History: A Practical Guide for Social Scientists*. Thousand Oaks, CA: Sage Publications.

Author Index

Subject Index

meaning in people's stories, 226; observations of Thomas, 4; of professorial life, 3; of personal development, 215; of place, 210; questions to elicit contextual information, 30; as reference point, 79; role of, 22–24, 81; of school, 210; stories of action within theories of context, 13; stories placed in, 22, 23

conversations, 72–79; agenda as focus of inquiry, 72; as building blocks, 77–78; clarifying purposes with participants, 74; connections through, 147; creating a conducive atmosphere, 75; developing questions, 73–74; direction, *vii*; intentional life history conversations, 2; interview as interview, 222; mock conversation session, 74; open-ended questions, 35, 73, 81; questioning accepted facts about family, 80; questions used in life history research, 30; questions based on guiding principals, 73; questions after each conversation, 77; venues, 75

Creates, Marlene, 57–60, 208–14

criteria: for judging life history work, 159; of rigor in life history research, 122–27 critical incidents, 2, 42; *See also* epiphanies

documentation of site visits, 82–84

"doing" life history research, 70–92

empathy through reflexivity, 29–31

epiphanies, 2, 119–20, 158, 231–32

epistemology, orientation of life history, *vii*, 35

fidelity and ethical ideals, 152–63; autonomy (self-determination) in relationship, 155–56; beneficence (to do good) in relationship, 158–61; contesting conventional order to promote equality, 153–54; ethical principals as ideals, 154–55; justice (fairness) in relationship, 161–63;

nonmaleficence (to do no harm) in relationship, 156–58; in process and research findings, 153

home education: autobiographical accounts, 141; home educators' negative experience with researchers, 46, 56, 142; media coverage, 46, 53–54, 62, 139, 144; my life inducing research text, 138–40; reasons for, 54–56, 140; receptiveness to researching, 140–42; relationality and mutuality as natural processes 143; research lives of home educators, 53–56; responsibilities to home education community, 143–44

insights and inspiration, in artists' work, 208–14; arts-based educational researchers, 209, 214; arts-informed life history, 209; Creates, Marlene, 208–12, 214; memory map, 211; narrative, 211; photographic life history investigations, 211, 213; portraits, 211; researcher-artists, 214; sense of place, 211, 214; socialization studies, 214

intersecting self as researcher and researched, 170–76; examining lived experience, 171; incorporating into data collection and thematic analysis, 171–73; insider in research process, 175; reflections on process, 175–76; use of visual artwork in research process, 173–75

interview guidelines and schedules, 73

introductions, crucial to life history, *vii*

life history: analysis processes and issues, 98–101, 162; as artistic interpretation, 177–83; co-creating meaning, 150–51; defining elements of life history research, 125–27; developing a life history project, 57–61; as double autobiography,

reflexivity, 90, 141–42; Ardra's
reflexive account, 31–43; being
reflexive in research, 42–43;
developing empathy through,
29–31; in research, 30; ongoing
reflexivity and responsiveness,
89–92; reflexive inquiry, *ix*;
reflexively shaping profiles, 159;
reflexivity journal, 90–91, 186
relationality, 26–28, 113, 138, 141;
aspect of research, 145; authors'
perspectives on, 27; elements of
relationality, 113; humanistic
standpoint, 27; intimacy in
research, 27; and mutuality as
natural processes, 143; practical and
relational elements, 43; principles
and conditions of doing life history
research, 26
representation: alternative, 107, 209;
artful representation in life history
socialization, 214; arts-informed
perspectives within research, 58;
arts-informed professes of
researching and, 215; descriptive
accounts, 117–118; fictional,
118–119; forms of, 10; form and
structure of stories told, 117;
imagining possibilities for
representational forms, 102–7;
issues to consider, 104; life history
as artistic interpretation, 177–83;
lenses of analysis and, 2; modes of,
2, 212; participants' and
researchers' roles, 113–15;
preparation for analysis and, 94;
premise of memory is selective, 119;
realizing possibilities for
representational forms, 121–22;
research and art only partial, 103;
telling as interpretation, 119; use of
visual artwork in research process,
173–75
research subjectivity, 90; incorporating
self in data collection and thematic
analysis, 171–73; insider in research
process, 175; acknowledging one's

own research biases, 46–49;
participants' and researchers' roles
in interpretation/ representation,
113–15; research process as human
interaction, 45–48; two
subjectivities, 149–50; understand
self as research, 48–57; we research
who we are, 89
research relationship, *vii*, 1–5, 68–69,
145–51; authentic research behavior,
26; author's perspectives at odds
with conventional views of, 27;
autonomy (self-determination) in,
155–56; beneficence (to do good) in
relationship, 158–61; care,
sensitivity and respect, 43–44;
challenging hierarchical practices,
26–27; challenging notions of
hierarchy and power, 71; children's
power relationships with adults,
91–92; developing empathy
through reflexivity, 29–31; ethical
relationships, binding matrix of,
152; example of traumatic
experience as a research "subject,"
157; finding language of
negotiation, 28; healthy
relationship, 72; implicit
expressions of hierarchies, 28;
intimacy in research, 27; intrusions
into daily life, 31–43; justice
(fairness) in, 161–163; language as
metaphor in, 28–29; mutuality,
28–29, 156; nonmaleficence (to do
no harm) in research, 155, 156–58;
partnership research as opposed to
negotiation, 28–29; relationality,
26–28; between researcher and
participant, 26–28, 59, 145–47;
researcher as observer, 143;
researching an area of mutual
interest, 29; resonating through
shared gender, 147–48; roles, 28;
sensitivity to source communities,
143; using ethical principles as
ideals, 153, 154–63; vulnerability of
being researched, 204

About the Contributors

Jacquie Aston is in private practice as a psychotherapist in Toronto, Ontario, Canada. She has a particular interest in helping people discover their potential and follow their own life path. As the mother of three adult children, she is familiar with the challenge of accommodating career and family life.

Ardra L. Cole is a professor of education within the Program of Adult Education and codirector (with J. Gary Knowles) of the Centre for Arts-Informed Research at the Ontario Institute for Studies in Education, University of Toronto, in Ontario, Canada. Her career has focused on teacher learning, teacher education, and ways of researching. With Maura McIntyre, she is currently involved in a community-centered, arts-informed project on Alzheimer's disease.

Kathryn Church is a Toronto-based independent researcher who works primarily in the areas of community mental health and economic development. She is an experienced ally of the psychiatric survivor movement, and is author of *Forbidden Narratives: Critical Autobiography as Social Science*. Dr. Church is also the curator of *Fabrications: Stitching Ourselves Together*, an intimate ethnography of work, women, and wedding dresses in central Alberta. The exhibit, which features twenty-three dresses handmade by her mother, toured across Canada in 2000 and 2001.

Cathy Crowe is a "street nurse" in downtown Toronto, Ontario, Canada, engaged in the field of "street health." She has a long-standing interest in the politics of health care and sees her role—as a nurse—as a witness in the struggle for social justice. She cofounded the Toronto Disaster Relief Committee, which led the national campaign to have homelessness declared a national disaster.

Lori Ebbesen is an exercise specialist with an academic background in physical education and cardiac rehabilitation. She is interested in health promotion and health issues, and is especially interested in translating health and wellness theory into patient well-being. She is an institution-based researcher for the Healthy Heart Program at the University of Saskatoon, Saskatchewan, Canada.

Kathleen Gates is a professor of nursing at Ryerson Polytechnic University, Toronto, Ontario, Canada. She is a practice-oriented nurse-educator who works in mutual relationships with students of nursing and new nurses to promote the health of people from culturally diverse communities. She has a particular interest in promoting the well-being of families who have elderly members with dementia.

J. Gary Knowles is a professor of education within the Learning and Teaching Specialization and codirector (with Ardra L. Cole) of the Centre for Arts-Informed Research within the Department of Adult Education, Community Development, and Counseling Psychology, the Ontario Institute for Studies in Education, University of Toronto, in Ontario, Canada. He has made numerous alternative-format, scholarly presentations grounded in the visual arts. He is an exhibiting artist, and his recent work documents elements of the East Coast fishing community where he lives.

Ilze Arielle Matiss is raising two children. She recently completed a doctoral degree at the University of Toronto in Ontario, Canada, and has been working in the field of school psychology with the Toronto Board of Education for the past decade. She is currently expanding her passion for life history research into the area of narrative therapy.

Maura McIntyre is a counseling practitioner who uses the vehicle of horticulture in her work. She recently completed a doctoral degree in counseling psychology from the University of Toronto, having studied at the Ontario Institute for Studies in Education, Toronto, Ontario, Canada. She is an exhibiting arts-informed researcher and, with Ardra Cole, is exploring issues and experiences associated with those who suffer Alzheimer's disease.

James A. Muchmore is a professor of teacher education within the Department of Teaching and Professional Development, College of Education, Western Michigan University, Kalamazoo, Michigan. His research focuses on literacy, autobiography, and teacher development—with a particular emphasis on understanding the lives and careers of teachers. He is formerly an English, social studies, and special education teacher in public schools. He has recently worked extensively in professional development school classrooms and with secondary school teachers to bring about improved practice.

Jeff Orr is a professor of education at St. Francis Xavier University in Antigonish, Nova Scotia, Canada. He has been involved with First Nations education in Saskatchewan and Nova Scotia as a teacher, teacher educator, researcher, and teacher union leader since 1984. He researches and publishes works related to First Nations and Mi'kmaq teacher education and classroom citizenship education, using narrative-life history methods.

Avi Rose is a counseling psychologist at the Counselling and Development Centre, York University, Toronto, Ontario, Canada. As an educator, writer, artist, and researcher, he is also a faculty member at Kolel, a liberal adult education institute in Toronto. He is particularly interested in the experiences and development of adults with learning challenges.

Suzanne Thomas is an arts-informed inquirer who is passionate about exceeding the edges and boundaries of traditional academic discourse. Her work focuses on life history explorations of place and "sense of place" within natural and cultural contexts. A former language and visual arts teacher, she is currently pursuing a doctoral degree at the University of Toronto in Ontario, Canada. Her thesis challenges conventional thesis/dissertation forms and expresses her belief that "art as inquiry" has the power to evoke, inspire, awaken visions and imaginings, and to transport readers/viewers to "new worlds."

Elizabeth Oates Schuster is a professor of gerontology and Director of the Gerontology Program in the Department of Social Work at Eastern Michigan University, Ypsilanti, Michigan. She is interested in literacy and the elderly, has explored the function and processes of a nursing home writing group, and is currently about to embark on a study of journaling with elderly nursing home residents. She is the cofounder of two award-winning community programs: Traveling Young at Art Program (intergenerational), and Elderwise, an Institute for Learning and Retirement (lifelong learning).

Renee Sarchuk Will is a professor of nursing and psychiatric nursing in the School of Health Studies, Brandon University, in Manitoba, Canada. She has worked extensively with nurse educators, exploring their practice-based knowledge, and is preparing to embark on a major study of experiences of living and dying.